ASIDE FROM TEACHING ENGLISH

Acknowledgments

This book stems in part from questions asked by
my students during my thirteen years of teaching college English. "If I major in English,
what can I do with it after I graduate?" many
of them wondered. My search for answers was
intensified during the year 1974-75, when, as
a counselor in the Placement Center of the University of Washington, I tried hard to help
qualified candidates find either college teaching positions or alternative ones. One of the
typical questions I heard was "I have these advanced degrees, but how do I find anyone to
hire me?" Partly because so many candidates who
were well prepared to teach English came in with
such questions, and partly because my own teaching experience had been in English, I began to
put together a bibliography and a few suggestions about finding alternatives to teaching
English.

When Prof. Robert Heilman of the English
Department at the University of Washington
urged that I write to publishing and business
firms to ask how people with backgrounds in
English could be useful to them, I was glad to
do so. But I had no sooner begun to look into
these fields than other areas, such as government agencies, university nonacademic staffs,
continuing education programs, and the media,

v

seemed to demand investigation as well. The
flood of questions from job candidates coming to
my office led to provisional answers, and these
in turn to still more questions. The further
anyone goes in exploring ways to enter these
fields, the more one sees the impossibility of
definitive answers. The present handbook is the
second edition of a shorter one which was focused more sharply upon the Pacific Northwest.
Both editions aim simply to offer guidelines for
(and *not* a directory of) some of the many possible alternatives to those teaching positions
that students of English language and literature
have traditionally held.

Nobody could write a book that attempts to
touch as many bases as this one does without depending heavily upon the kindness as well as the
knowledge of many people--friends, former students, colleagues, and strangers across the
country who obligingly answered my inquiries.
Among many people who were helpful with both
information and encouragement I particularly
want to thank William Bliss, director of the
Yale Alumni Placement Service; Prof. Benjamin
Boyce of the English Department, Duke University; Dean Mary Frances Cram of Linfield College, Oregon; Linda Daniel of the *Seattle Times;*
Rep. Jeff Douthwaite of the Washington State
Legislature; Kenneth Haas of Korvette, Inc.,
New York City; Randolph Hollis of Seattle; Barbara Huston of the *Seattle Post-Intelligencer;*
Fred Pneuman of the Weyerhaeuser Corporation;
and Prof. Myron White, chairman, Department of
Humanistic-Social Studies, University of Washington. I am grateful to the several hundred
interviewees whose experiences provide the core
of this book. I thank not only the large group
who have specifically authorized quotation from
their oral or written comments, but the even
larger number whose questionnaire responses I

have paraphrased and summarized in making
various points.

Anyone incautious enough to write about the
current job situation must be concerned about
several pitfalls. There is the constant chance
of making inaccurate statements about a particular field, and there is the very real danger of
sounding either devastatingly gloomy or irresponsibly optimistic about a situation that
affects thousands of people's lives and liveli-
hoods. In an effort to guard against both error
and glibness, I have shown various portions of
the manuscript to people knowledgeable in the
corresponding areas. Thus the book has benefited greatly from the various insights and
comments of the following persons: Pauline
Christiansen, director of composition, Bellevue
Community College, Washington; Barbara Gill,
director of public relations, Seattle YWCA;
Prof. William Irmscher, director of composition,
Department of English, University of Washington;
Emily Johnson, former director, Office of Schol-
arly Journals, University of Washington; Prof.
William Johnston, Department of Communications,
University of Washington; Barbara Kidder of
Seattle; Donna Martyn, director, Office of
Placement Services, Harvard University; Assist-
ant Dean Russell Mauch, Columbia-Greene Commun-
ity College, Hudson, N.Y.; Ellen Messer-Davidow,
special assistant to the president, University
of Cincinnati; Anne Monger, Office of Placement
Services, Harvard; Constance Remo, Office of
Placement Services, Harvard; Prof. John Schacht,
School of Communications, University of Illi-
nois; Prof. James Souther, Department of Humanistic-Social Studies, University of Washington;
Constance Wells, director of noncredit studies,
University of Washington; and Prof. Neal Woodruff, Department of English, Coe College, Iowa.

In addition, I frequently tapped the knowl-

edge and experience of former colleagues from
the Placement Center of the University of Washington, notably Lucille Borrow, Deryl Lusty,
and Phyllis Needy, all of whom read the manuscript and helped me update my observations
about the complicated and fluid issues involved
in pointing out alternatives to teaching positions.

It would have been harder to start this
project than it was had I not initially had the
help of Carol Elaine Dooley, now assistant professor of English at the University of New Mexico, who did some of the early interviewing and
correspondence. And I feel that the revision
might never have been finished had I not been
able to call upon Gloria Campbell, instructor
in the Department of English, Shoreline Community College, to help me tie up loose ends and
upon Angela Hollis of Editorial Consultants,
Inc., to share with me the job of making the
index.

My most heartfelt thanks, however, go to
five people. Prof. Robert Heilman was not only
responsible for my undertaking this book but
read and made wonderfully detailed suggestions
upon much of it. Mary Coney, lecturer in the
Department of Humanistic-Social Studies, University of Washington, read and talked over with
me all the chapters as they evolved. Prof.
Rosemary VanArsdel, Department of English, University of Puget Sound, Tacoma, Washington, by
using the preliminary edition of this book as
a text in her Writing Institute, stimulated
student comments that provided useful guidelines
for revision. Prof. Ivan Settles, acting director of the Placement Center, University of Washington, believed in this project enough to cut
through incredible bureaucratic red tape in
order for the first edition to be published in
1976. Above all, my gratitude goes to my hus-

band, Arthur Bestor. He endured much while I
was writing this volume; and, though he believes
above everything else in "pure research," he
provided numerous insights into the practical
problems explored here.

Despite the efforts of these friendly critics and commentators, I have probably left out
important points and have let inaccuracies creep
into my treatment of others. I shall be glad to
have these matters called to my attention so
that they can be corrected in possible revisions. I hope, however, that whatever errors
appear will not distract the reader from the
book's main point, that is, that the world is
wide, and that there are many uses to which one
can put a degree in English other than by following in the footsteps of one's college instructors and trying eventually to replace them
in the classroom.

Contents

To the Reader

Today there are so many books on how to look
for and find a job that it could take weeks
to read and digest just the ones that have
appeared since 1970. There are books telling
how to find your first summer job, books for
those about to graduate from college, books
for the under-forty group, books for those over
forty, books for career switchers, and books
telling women how to go to work even if "your
husband objects, your children are too young,
and there's nothing you can do anyway."
. Why then still another book on the job
search?

The particular reason for this one is the
need that became apparent to me during the time
I was a counselor in the University of Washington Placement Center. As the field of teaching
began to offer fewer and fewer openings, people
of varying backgrounds, among them that of English, looked for other options. The last group
included college students considering majoring
in English, recent B.A.'s in English wondering
what kinds of positions they were fitted for,
graduate students in English looking ahead,
persons with M.A.'s or Ph.D.'s in English
searching for their first job, and Ph.D.'s in
English from other years trying to change jobs
or start new careers. Finally, other counse-

lors pooled their information with mine as we
tried to decide how to help these job-seekers.
It is mainly for these six groups, all with a
background in English language and literature,
and for their many counterparts throughout the
country, that I am writing now. (A seventh,
consisting of people in other branches of humanities than English—such fields as classics,
comparative literature, speech, history—will
probably be able to use much of the information
here offered to specialists in English; but in
the interest of keeping my topic manageable, I
am concentrating upon the needs of the first
six groups.)

Let me point out first certain things that
this book does *not* undertake to do and then
indicate what you can expect to find in it. It
does not purport to give lists of specific job
vacancies: openings come and go too rapidly.
It does not offer statistics and projections
showing exactly how many hundred editors, reporters, information specialists, technical
writers, and public relations persons will be
needed in this country in the next ten years:
this is the function of the latest volume of
the *Occupational Outlook Handbook*, published
by the U. S. Department of Labor.

Nor does this volume attempt to be a comprehensive state-by-state guidebook, with good,
better, and best places to apply in each region.
The original form in which my findings appeared
was that of a 105-page pamphlet published in
1976 by the ASUW Lecture Notes Office for the
University of Washington Placement Center.
When the University of Washington Press asked
me to prepare the present much revised and ex-
panded edition, I widened the geographical base
of the information gathered. The examples,
particularly from the Midwest, the South, and
the East Coast, are illustrative rather than

exhaustive. While continuing to draw a good deal of the material from the University of Washington and surrounding areas in the Pacific Northwest, I have balanced it whenever possible with examples from elsewhere, not striving for even distribution of evidence.

I am using as my starting point the city of Seattle and its educational, business, and governmental institutions *not* because Seattle is such a cultural paradise that everyone with a background in English should rush out here to find a job. Far from it. Instead I am starting with this area somewhat in the spirit of the anthropologists who, in reporting on one Mexican village or one Portuguese town, consider each of these as prototypes of many other towns and villages--or in the spirit of the sociologists Robert and Helen Lynd, who in singling out Muncie, Indiana, as "Middletown" investigated this one city with the hope that they would thereby illumine ways of life across the nation.

I hope, therefore, that all readers using this book will freely translate, apply, extrapolate. If a government agency or a group of editors or a handbook of vocational information is mentioned as originating in Washington or Oregon, I hope that you will automatically ask yourself, wherever you are as you read, "Do we have anything like that here? If not, why not? What's the nearest thing to it? If we do have something like it, what use can I make of it in my own job search?"

What readers can expect to find in this book, then, is not so much a compendium of "hard information," as suggestions and guidelines based on interviews with or questionnaire responses from more than 350 employers and successful job-seekers in fields where people with backgrounds in English can fill a need.

The umbrella phrase, "backgrounds in English," may surprise or trouble some readers. "Aren't there vast differences," they may ask, "between the preparation of someone who has a B.A. in English, who will have studied it in his four-year undergraduate course along with many nonrelated subjects, and the person with a Ph.D., who will have spent two or three years exclusively in courses and seminars in literature, passed a comprehensive examination, and completed, for the dissertation, a piece of original research usually involving a single author, topic, or literary work?"

There certainly *are* differences, and nobody is more keenly aware of them than a jobless Ph.D. who sees an editorial or writing position for which he feels qualified go to someone who has not carried his academic work beyond the B.A. It is surprising but true that occasionally, however, in these days of upsets in employment patterns, B.A.'s, M.A.'s and Ph.D.'s do compete for the same jobs. Each group has its own particular strong points, and wherever you are, you may have to learn to turn them to your advantage.

The points in favor of job candidates with B.A.'s are that they are usually not considered "overqualified": they do not have years of academic habits built up through teaching or independent research to unlearn; and, moreover, employers feel comfortable in offering them entry-level salaries. Job-seekers with M.A.'s can be glad that they have an added qualification, without having made such a great investment of time and money in an academic career that a nonacademic employer hesitates to hire them. Candidates with Ph.D.'s have something of a negative image to overcome in the minds of employers who may consider them overspecialized. As later chapters will show, however, Ph.D.'s

have learned much that is valuable outside of
academia; sometimes, too, by backtracking and
picking up certain skills that they did not
have time to learn along the way, they may make
more rapid progress in business, publishing, or
government employment than they otherwise would.

The first half of Chapter 2 is particularly
intended for those of you wondering what kind
of position you can find after graduating with
a B.A. in English. The second half of Chapter
2 and all of Chapters 4 and 5 are designed to
speak to the concerns of those with M.A.'s or
Ph.D.'s. All the other chapters offer information potentially useful to both groups.

Although this handbook focuses mainly upon
how and where to look for jobs, I have occasionally discussed not only the strategies of
the job search but something of what certain
relatively unpublicized jobs involve. I have
done this deliberately. Many of you with degrees in English have only a generalized notion
that somewhere out in the world people *do* edit,
work on university and hospital publications,
make indexes, design and teach courses for
adults, or do research and writing for government agencies. Since there are few hard-and-
fast job descriptions for some of these posts,
you tend to approach job counselors with the
knowledge that such work exists but with no
sense of what it involves or whether you may
be already qualified to do it. I have tried
therefore to give just enough of a picture of
what people do in these and other jobs so that
those interested will follow up by reading the
fuller treatments of them listed in the
Bibliography.

As you read this book, please bear in mind
that while some of the persons I quoted have
made a successful transition from being an
English graduate student or teacher to becoming

a continuing education specialist, administrative assistant, free-lance editor, university
information specialist or editor, city editor
of a daily paper, editor of a publishing house,
director of a management training program for a
chain of stores, or government analyst, other
people whom I consulted went directly to their
present fields as their first choice. I can
hardly emphasize enough the fact that many of
these people, although they have advice for
you who may want to get into these fields from
the now over-crowded one of English, did not
themselves seek out their jobs as "alternative
careers." Teachers and students of English,
book publishers, writers, reporters, technical
editors, columnists, critics--all of them members of professions dealing in words and ideas
in an attempt to influence people--tend to
operate on different hypotheses as to what is
central and what is alternative. It is easy
to forget how closely a job-seeker's notion of
"alternatives" depends on where his or her job
search first led.

   Yet wherever your particular starting place,
I hope that these comments from interviewees,
and especially these suggestions from other job-
seekers, will be a stimulus to your self-
assessment and then to your own imaginative
plan of action.

ASIDE FROM TEACHING ENGLISH

CHAPTER 1

"But There Are No Jobs"— Or Are There?

> We're in trouble. We have all these
> reports to get out, and the people on
> our staff can find the material but
> somehow don't seem able to write it
> up. Do you know anyone who can help
> us?--Query from director of a state
> social and health services agency to
> a university editor

> The applicant must be able to write in
> a logical and effective style, without
> jargon, and should be prepared to sub-
> mit samples of previous work which
> demonstrate this quality.--Advertise-
> ment for policy analyst, educational
> policy research center

As students of English language and literature
in the mid-1970s, many of you find your professional future unclear. You may feel that
society is sending you double and conflicting
messages: if you have an undergraduate major
in English, you may be passed over as "a generalist"; yet if you have an advanced degree,
employers may call you "too specialized" or
"overqualified." Who then *is* employable?

3

   Writers in the popular media and in academic
journals keep reflecting (and adding to) your
worries. Undergraduates with leanings toward a
major in English or in other humanities fields
hardly need the *Time* and *Newsweek* articles of
the spring of 1976 to remind you that unemployment among new humanities graduates is high,
that as one senior put it, "after college, there
is no free lunch."[1]
   Graduate students, too, have been feeling
for several years the effects of being in a saturated market. As economists Dael Wolfle and
Charles Kidd pointed out in an *AAUP Bulletin*
article in the spring of 1972, "from 1861 . . .
through 1970, American universities awarded
340,000 doctor's degrees. Half of these degrees
were awarded in the last nine years of the
period. If current projections are borne out,
another 340,000 will be awarded in the 1971–80
decade."[2] Since according to certain projections there will by 1985 be three times as many
new Ph.D.'s as will be needed in the arts and
the humanities,[3] some of you have concluded that
the job situation is hopeless. So, on the
assumption that there is no need in American
society today for people with your kind of education, you look for any port in a storm, any
paying job at all, whether as taxi driver, hospital orderly, waitress, or welder.
   Some of you, having happened upon blue-
collar jobs that you enjoy and find lucrative,
may plan to keep them for a long time. One person I know with a degree in medieval English
literature is earning so much money working for
a builder, and a former English teacher seems so
well situated as a butler and house man, that
neither one feels he can afford to stop. Both
say that they are glad to have had the education
they did because it makes their lives more
interesting, even though they do not plan to

depend directly upon it for a living.

Other well-educated job-seekers realize that by temporarily taking jobs for which they are theoretically overqualified they can learn much about people and about American life that helps them in a long-range plan. Many social workers, vocational counselors, writers, reporters, and teachers have benefited in their later careers from their experience in a wide variety of occupations. Some who have not taken such jobs wish now that they had done so. When asked what she would do if she were graduating from college today, Gloria Steinem said recently that she probably would start by taking a job with a law enforcement agency, as one of the best ways to learn about people and their deepest needs.[4]

But, unless you find that holding an alternative job which gives little or no scope for your background in English is rewarding in terms of money, satisfaction, or widened experience gathered for later use, perhaps you should reconsider. Presumably you would be glad to avoid the trap pointed out by Donna Martyn, director of Harvard's Office of Placement Services. She finds that many who have looked in vain for academic jobs seize upon manual or clerical ones "because they believe that by so doing they have put off making a real choice or a permanent commitment."[5] They think they can always quit the vacuum cleaner sales business or the construction company and start over, any time they decide to.

This chapter is intended to show that such a complete turn-around as some of you have been making may not be necessary. Before you decide to abandon or postpone all thought of entering a field where you can use much of your background in English, you should take a fresh look.

By way of just one example, there is a paradox that you overlook when you decide to turn

your back upon your undergraduate or graduate
work in English and start all over in a more
"practical" field. At the very time when vacancies in English teaching positions--the traditional goals of the majority of English majors
and of nearly all graduate students in English--
have diminished, the need for people who can
write clearly, dig out information, and organize
what they find is becoming more and more urgent.
     As Edwin Newman, Reed Whittemore, Gene
Lyons, James Degnan, Jean Stafford, Ralph H.
Lewis, A. B. Giametti, and many other recent
observers have pointed out, today there is widespread complaint among business executives and
government officials that job applicants can't
write, that their own employees can't write,
that the consulting firms with whom they deal
don't send back reports written in understandable English.[6] One article after another, in
the popular media and in educational journals
alike, makes the point that there is an urgent
need on all levels for people who can communicate clearly. "Errors we once found commonly
in applications from high-school graduates are
now cropping up in forms from people with four-
year college degrees," reports a personnel
official of the Bank of America.[7] "It used to
be that if you hired a college graduate, you
could expect to get someone who was literate.
. . . Now there are no longer any guarantees.
. . . He or she may be competent in engineering, but illiterate. . . ."[8]
     This is hardly the time, then, to give up,
to decide that those of you who have studied,
practiced, and perhaps taught the art and craft
of writing are no longer needed. It *is* the time
to take a fresh approach to job hunting. You
must make your skills visible; you must show
employers that you can help meet their needs.
As many who have tried it have found, this is

not a bad time for would-be teachers of English
to think of other careers than those inside the
traditional classroom and instead to contem-
plate going out "into the world" and instructing
men and women in business and the professions
how to write. It can be exhilarating to discover that the world at large has need of you.
In offices, banks, hospitals, schools of nursing
and social work, as well as in various businesses, there are definite opportunities for
showing adults how to deal with writing problems that arise in their businesses or professions, and how to communicate clearly and suc-
cinctly what needs to be communicated.

I am not talking about mere "remedial English." Most of the jobs touched upon in this
handbook involve far more than showing someone
else what is incorrect about his or her writing.
If you do land such an alternative job, you can
expect to be writing, editing, or teaching in
areas extending far beyond textbook rules. How,
for instance, would you as an editor help
rewrite a government report on criteria and
standards for nursing homes so that one of its
main points, the priority of patients' rights,
would have maximum impact? How would you sum-
marize in twenty pages a 700-page report of a
nursing research project? What kinds of
articles would you include in a museum newsletter or an alumni quarterly to ensure their
being read instead of thrown into the waste-
basket? How would you design a writing course
for a group of urban planners with advanced
degrees and professional experience, whose
reports are so wordy and abstract their their
clients either don't read or don't understand
them? How would you help a psychologist draw
the line in his articles between needless jargon and necessary technical terms?

If you can draw upon and build your experience in doing research, in organizing, writing, rewriting, and editing your college or graduate school papers, if you can keep your audience in mind, and if you aren't overawed by new subject-matter, you may find yourself doing all kinds of work that is not only needed but valued. What is more, it is far from routine; it represents an intellectual challenge as you adapt to new situations many of the techniques you have learned as a student of English.

Such a shift in the kind of work you are looking for may not at first come easily. "People may resist alternative jobs out of ignorance," points out William Bliss, director of the Yale Alumni Placement Service. "They do not know what the editor of a house organ does."[9] There are other reasons for resistance, too. Some candidates have focused for so long upon what Donna Martyn of Harvard calls "the personal and social expectations of an academic position,"[10] that they drop in to a placement center, ask perfunctorily about alternatives to teaching jobs, and then play what Eric Berne calls "the game of 'Yes, but. . . .'"[11] Objections and excuses abound: "But I'm too inexperienced; nobody would hire me." "But I'm too *old* to change." "I can't seem to find business or government agencies advertising for people with my background." "I didn't major in science, so how could I ever do technical writing?" "The money you get for teaching adult education courses just isn't worth my time--not after all I've invested in getting my degrees." "I wouldn't want to be stuck in an office from eight to five."

Although asking for advice and then objecting in turn to each piece of counsel received is a common human reaction, it is an extremely self-defeating one for the job hunter. It can lure you into complete apathy, or it can lead

those of you who want to teach to comb once
again the Modern Language Association lists of
teaching vacancies, to mail out yet another hundred inquiries, and to do little or nothing
while you wait to hear from them all. Those who
fall into this trap are not unlike the compulsive people mentioned in a recent book on
problem-solving by James L. Adams of Stanford
University. Some people, he points out (quoting
Edward deBono), when faced with a problem, tend
to keep working on and on at the same solution,
like post-hole diggers who try

> to dig holes deeper and bigger, to make
> them altogether better holes. But if
> the hole is in the wrong place, then no
> amount of improvement is going to put
> it in the right place. No matter how
> obvious this may seem to every digger,
> it is still easier to go on digging in
> the same place than to start all over
> again in a new place. Vertical think-
> ing is digging the same hole deeper;
> lateral thinking is trying again
> elsewhere. [12]

A half-dozen brief case histories may give
you some idea of how to look freshly at your
degree in English as an entry to satisfying and
well-paid work. Perhaps they will help you to
choose another place to dig instead of digging
the same hole deeper. Some of the examples
illustrate ways in which you may be able to get
new teaching posts created in untraditional
settings; others show a few of the many ways
you may be able to apply what you know in other
ways than by formal teaching.
      A woman with a Ph.D. in English found in
the Sunday papers an advertisement directed *toward students, not toward teachers,* in which

a nearby four-year institution urged adults
with unfinished B.A.'s in economics, political
science, and business to complete their requirements at a new branch of the school. It
occurred to her that although many of the
courses listed would presumably involve writing
papers, no English offerings were listed. The
next day she visited the administrators of the
program, showed them syllabi of writing courses
for adults that she had given elsewhere, and
offered to adapt them for the new clientele.
Subsequently she was hired, and for the past
year she has given both writing and literature
courses to varied and lively groups of adults.

An English Ph.D. candidate who could not
find work closely related to her special interests decided to see what kind of job with the
city government most appealed to her, and to
train herself for it. Starting in as a secretary, she set her sights upon the position of
program analyst for one of the departments,
took three courses on her own time to help
qualify herself for it, passed the examinations,
and three years after starting back to work was
hired for the job she really wanted. She says
that in this job she makes use of her writing
and research abilities every day.[13]

A young man who made an unusually thorough
and imaginative survey of the English teaching
job market, the alternative job market, and the
whole placement process found that he was valued
by the small college hiring him because of this
extra knowledge. In fact, he received a joint
appointment whereby he was to spend half of his
time teaching English and the other half setting
up and administering a placement center for the
college. His feeling that he was in a good
position to advance into either a teaching or
an administrative career has recently been vali-
dated, since he has now been offered the post of

assistant academic dean at his institution.

Two women, one a university staff editor with a B.A., additional graduate work, and years of editing experience, the other a college English teacher with a Ph.D., both of whom had done considerable free-lance editing, decided to combine forces. Inviting a few other editors to join them, they formed a ten-person corporation. Now, after two years, the group has completed more than fifty projects, ranging from copy-editing short articles to revising, copy-editing, and indexing scholarly volumes. Since most of the members do this work as moonlighters from other commitments, more associates are being brought in to handle the continued requests for editorial help.[14]

Two recent university graduates who had majored in English and creative writing wanted to get some teaching experience after their mid-year graduation, even though neither one had planned to make teaching her career. Having designed a writing course for adults, they volunteered to give it on a trial basis through a local school system's adult education program. Their first venture was successful; they have been asked to give other courses for pay; and moreover, they can now add teaching experience to their other qualifications.

A Ph.D. candidate in comparative literature discovered through a chance conversation that several faculty members in one of her university's programs were discouraged with the writing done by undergraduates in their courses. Although these faculty members were thinking of looking for someone to teach writing, they had not yet made any specific plans. Upon hearing of the possibility, the student offered to work out a course using subject matter from the sponsoring department. She was immediately appointed to a teaching assistantship for the

purpose, and will probably continue next year
as lecturer.

As these examples show, there may be path-
ways that only you yourself can open up and explore. It is up to you to invent, promote, or
create your job. Read ads imaginatively. Pick
out and prepare yourself for the kind of position that you would consider ideal. Have more
than one specialty. Consider starting your own
group or corporation to perform services which
you find are needed. Volunteer a brief sample
of what you can do (but don't let yourself get
stuck in a volunteer spot beyond an agreed-upon
time). Finally, don't overlook the possibility
of demonstrating to an agency or institution
that you are the person to fill a need that they
were only beginning to perceive.

Above all, the successful job-seekers quoted
in this book urge you not to be discouraged.
Those of you who have a B.A. in English should
test for yourself rather than swallow whole the
generalizations made in the media and elsewhere
about the current uselessness of humanistic
training. You may find that the prophets of
doom have overstated the case. Those of you
who have or are working toward advanced degrees
should read--with a sense of the promise, and
not merely the warning contained in it--the conclusion reached by Wolfle and Kidd: "Many new
doctorates will enter non-traditional jobs and
will do work that has not attracted many of
their predecessors. . . . Few of them will be
unemployed, but few will be employed in college
and university teaching and research."[15]

In a broadened horizon there is always hope.
Somewhere--perhaps in a place you little ex-
pect--there awaits you an interesting career
that can engage your writing ability, your experience in collecting and organizing information, and even your pleasure in the interplay of

ideas. Keep in mind a comment on careers made
recently in a talk by Gloria Steinem: "Progress
lies in the direction in which you haven't
been."[16]

CHAPTER 2

Taking Inventory

Pick out your strongest skills--the
things you have done best, and enjoyed the most.--Richard Nelson Bolles,
What Color Is Your Parachute?

One of the problems in looking for
alternatives to teaching jobs is that
most jobseekers don't believe that
studying English helps them to do anything else. Most English faculty
members themselves don't believe that
what they teach has any application
beyond the classroom.--Kenneth Haas,
Ph.D., English, now in charge of
management development training at
Korvette, Inc., New York City

It has become conventional for people with
B.A.'s in English to sound as apologetic about
their qualifications as most housewives do.
Probably the two statements most often made in
counselors' offices are: "I'm majoring in English, but I don't know why, I certainly won't
be able to *do* anything with it," and "I graduated with a major in English five years ago, so

of course I realize that I have no marketable
skills."[1]

People with graduate degrees in English tend
less toward apology than to a sense of outrage.
"I've spent six years, and more money than I
could afford, getting my M.A. and Ph.D. in English," a vigorous young man with an excellent
academic record once exploded to me in the University of Washington Placement Center, "and now
I find that I have a commodity that no employer
seems to want."

Whether you have an undergraduate or a graduate degree, the better your academic record,
the more convinced some of you become, as you
look seriously around the job market for the
first time, that you are good for nothing else
than to continue the academic study of English.
In fact, there is a tendency to look back at
your accomplishments in much the same disillu-
sioned way in which, in the first part of *The
Bell Jar*, Esther Greenwood looked at hers:

> The one thing I was good at was
> winning scholarships and prizes, and
> that era was coming to an end.
> I felt like a racehorse in a world
> without racetracks or a champion col-
> lege footballer suddenly confronted
> by Wall Street and a business suit,
> his days of glory shrunk to a little
> gold cup on his mantel with a date
> engraved on it like the date on a
> tombstone.[2]

Natural though these reactions are in the
present state of the job market, you should try
to get past them as soon as possible so that you
can get on with the business of seeing just what
it is that you *do* have to offer, and to whom.

Richard Bolles' recent book, *What Color Is Your Parachute?*, may be a good catalyst for your analysis of your assets; in fact, taking a few hours to sit down with Bolles' fifth chapter and write out his assignments in self-assessment may be the best investment of time you make in your whole job search. Another stimulating book, and one that complements *Parachute*, is Richard K. Irish's *Go Hire Yourself an Employer*.[3] Both Bolles and Irish have two salutary effects upon most readers. These books can open your mind to a wider variety of career possibilities than people have ordinarily considered; at the same time, by insisting that you list and inventory your specific areas of experience and strength, these authors help you identify a *range* of related jobs on which you can concentrate your application efforts rather than simply using the "scattered shot" method.

After reading Bolles and Irish, those of you with B.A.'s in English should take out any papers or reports you wrote as undergraduates and look at them objectively. What capabilities do they reveal that could be of use to an employer? Perhaps they show that you can read and digest large masses of material, summarizing it in manageable form. Perhaps they offer evidence that you don't get swamped by your material, that you can narrow down a topic and within that topic find a point to make or a thesis to prove. Let's hope that there's also evidence of organizational skill, of the ability to lead the reader through your argument from one point to another while keeping in mind the kind of audience you're writing for. The chances are that your papers will show, too, that you know how to use libraries and to keep digging until you find what you're looking for; that you can compare and contrast and weigh your evidence; that you can pay attention to words, both to their precise definitions and their nuances; that perhaps you have learned something about bringing information from other fields—history, psychology, philosophy, or the history of science, for example—to bear on the work of literature or the author about whom you were writing.[4] Finally, as important as any other single thing which you may have learned, your group of finished papers should be tangible evidence that you can finish what you start writing, working against a deadline, whether in the classroom or under the conditions in which most jobs are performed in the "real world."

I am far from suggesting that you shower your undergraduate papers upon a prospective employer; what I am recommending is that you look at them closely yourself, to analyze what it is that you do best, to convince *yourself* that you as an English major have something to offer. Next, you must picture yourself using these accomplishments in dealing with other fields than literary or academic ones. Make a list of the techniques about which you feel confident and of others that you think you could learn, and keep them in mind later when you talk with people who are getting out newsletters, writing environmental impact statements, doing public relations, working on political campaigns, producing advertising copy, editing technical articles, writing or evaluating social work case histories, analyzing job candidates' recommendations, or fulfilling other business or professional demands.

Your biggest immediate job is to change your thinking about yourself, to move from seeing yourself as just another dutiful student who "was always good in English" to seeing yourself as a professional. You must feel that you know how to plunge in and take hold of a subject, how to diagnose what it is that you need to know,

how to follow it up, and how to interpret your
subject in writing--or in talks, multimedia presentations, and other forms--so that you can
make it clear and important to your audience.
In order to do this, of course, you should have
had as much practice as you could get as an
undergraduate in writing papers and making various kinds of presentations. Prof. Robert
Stevick of the University of Washington advises:
"Choose courses in which the professor makes you
write a lot of papers and will tear them apart
if necessary. Try to find a professor who's a
bearcat on the subject of style." If you've
already graduated and have somehow slid by without doing a lot of writing, it's still not too
late: either take evening courses or commit
yourself to a project, such as doing publicity
for a political candidate or a school board,
where you absolutely have to produce results
under pressure.

In case you are dubious about the practicality of turning yourself from a good student
of English who does well on assigned papers into
a professional who has something to offer to
employers, consider the following comments from
Angela Hollis. After finishing her sophomore
year at the University of Oregon, she took
several years out to do secretarial and other
work for an advertising agency. Upon entering
the University of Washington as a junior, she
considered her major carefully, choosing English because of her interest in writing and her
sense that there were career possibilities in
this major. As she says,

> I intended to get a degree that would
> be "practical," in the sense that
> doors would be opened toward a career,
> but not so practical that it was of no
> more interest to me than the form

letters I had typed as a secretary.
My decision: English, where I would
learn to research, organize, analyze,
and write with facility about a broad
base of material--in short, to communicate. And not just about Fielding
and Fitzgerald, either. I determined
to take at least one course in as
many major fields as I could, then to
translate them into relevancy for today's world, which I would be re-
entering in two short years: psychology, sociology, ecology/engineering,
history, philosophy, geology, and so
on.

Upon receiving my degree, I analyzed
my position, giving no thought to the
chance of failure. From previous work
experience I brought to the job market
determination, a knowledge of how things
work "out there" and of what the criteria of success were. From school I
brought enthusiasm, a whetted intellectual and creative appetite; I had become a lateral thinker; I had a good
base of knowledge. My studies ranged
from Dostoevsky to how the sewer system
in Seattle works, and I had the ability
to write, to communicate, about either.

My first job after graduation was
as editor and production supervisor
for an operations/curriculum manual
for a medical program on a local campus. I really went to the interview
just for practice in being interviewed.
I came out of that interview with a
job offer and a large black notebook
that held the outline that my new
colleagues and I would transform into
a book over the next year. They hired

me on the basis that I could write and
that I would learn the technical steps
as I went along--and that was something
I *did* know how to do--to *learn*. I
found my familiarity with ways of finding and using resource material invaluable. I rewrote and reorganized the
book by the same methods I had used in
papers in school, then made its style
consistent and put it through production only one step ahead the whole way--
my bible (the *Chicago Manual of Style*)
in one hand, and the telephone receiver
in the other, talking with the university director of publications, whom I
quoted often in my meetings with the
medical faculty.

Following that project, I copy-
edited another book in the medical
field, this time a technical research
volume. It was a smooth job, and my
familiarity with the *Chicago Manual*
served me well. The next project was
a joint venture with a colleague; we
indexed a literary volume for a university professor. First, we taught
ourselves the indexing process, then
applied it; and we now have another
marketable skill as well as a little
more sense of organization.

The following project also came
about because of my experience with
the medical program. A local bank
wanted their policy manual reorganized and rewritten; the editor would
report directly to the president of
the bank. The format was similar to
the medical program's, and when the
bank executives read of my experience
in production, they added production

supervision to their contract. Banking
jargon was a cinch compared to medical;
I read a basic bank operations text and
used it as a resource book. They hired
me on the basis that I could communicate, and asked me to prepare some style
sheets for their staff as a whole.

Currently, I am copyediting a book
sponsored by a local plant magazine publisher. I had begun growing plants and
doing copious reading on the subject
two years ago; now my interests and my
work have intersected.

A year and a half out of school, I
have editing and some writing experience in medical, academic, business/
financial, and botanical fields. And
I can still learn.[5]

With her graduation only eighteen months
behind her, Hollis has made a good start, at a
time when many of her classmates have been
wringing their hands over the impossibility of
"doing anything with their English majors."

Some of you, however, taking notice of the
fact that four of the five jobs Hollis found
consisted largely of editing or writing, may
protest that your aptitudes don't lie in those
directions. "Isn't there anything an English
B.A. can do besides write--or teach?" you may
ask.

Indeed there is.

Returning to the question of what you must
have learned in the process of getting your B.A.
in English, when you think over your courses and
what you did in them you will almost certainly
find that you learned to read closely, discri-
minating among the meanings and interpretations
of words; to dig out information; to read (and
retain, for as long as necessary) large quanti-

tities of material; to compare and weigh conflicting pieces of evidence; and especially to
read empathetically, entering into the lives
and backgrounds of characters in fiction and
drama very different from your own.

All these skills are valuable components of
many different kinds of work. As several English majors with minors in psychology or in education have found lately, there are jobs in
devising and pre-testing questionnaires, both for
educational psychology projects and for marketing surveys. There is also, as Kenneth Haas of
Korvette, Inc., in New York City reports, a
growing subfield in which people skilled in the
precise use of English can serve as "interface"
between computer programmers and the businesses
hiring them. (This is *not* computer programming,
which of course requires a mathematical background, says Haas; the people of whom he is
speaking are intermediaries, who may not even
know the difference between COBAL and FORTRAN.)[6]

If your special talents lie in digging out
information or in evaluating ideas, an appropriate channel would be as a research aide to a
legislator or other government official, doing
background research on issues for officeholders
and their speech writers.[7] Other possibilities
are grant proposal writing[8] or administrative
work on nonprofit foundations such as one of the
state councils on the humanities, your state's
council on higher education, or the Council for
Basic Education. Several relatively new fields
in planning, whether urban or health, are also
worth investigating.

If you can assimilate quantities of material
easily, there are possible spots in government[9]
and also in publishing. One of the common mis-
conceptions about publishing is that most people
in it are either potential writers or frustrated
ones. Actually there are several dozen special-

ties within publishing for which other abilities
are more important than writing talent.[10] One
type of position involves reading and screening
unsolicited manuscripts; after such a beginning,
you might eventually become one of your firm's
acquisitions editors. (Although you would usually set down on paper your evaluation of a new
manuscript, your main tasks would be to read
masses of material quickly, yet perceptively
enough to compare a manuscript with its possible
competitors. After making a decision in concert
with others on the staff, you would also deal
with the author.)

If your main strengths seem to lie in your
ability to weigh and compare, to balance conflicting evidence, there are specialties such
as being a claims representative, a paralegal
assistant, or, eventually, with added work experience, possibly a company ombudsman or labor
mediator.

Finally, if you felt most at home in your
reading when you were entering imaginatively
into the lives and milieux of people you read
about, there is a series of fields for which
you have an important qualification. If you
can empathize, if you can really listen to other
people, if you can see what they are trying to
do and either help them do it or explain to them
what their available alternatives are, you have
an important ingredient for a career in social
case work, in sales management training, various
kinds of nonclinical counseling (student services, geriatric, adoption, drug rehabilitation,
minority, abortion). You could be a consumer
advocate, a customer service representative, a
fund raiser for a nonprofit institution. You
could be a coordinator of volunteers for a hospital or a city school system; you could be a
"patient services coordinator" at a hospital or
a "patient advocate" for nursing homes; you

could be an interviewer for the personnel department of a business, or for new customers of
a bank; you could be one of the admitting personnel in a hospital office. Again, you could
work full time with the alumni association of
your college or university, or do public relations for any of the kinds of institutions just
mentioned.

But, once you see some of these positions
as ones where you could use your skills and
talents, how do you make your qualifications
as clear to an employer as they are to you?
You must certainly not say that you "want to
work with people." Every employer has heard
that phrase far too often. Nor should you just
present him or her with your transcript, with
its revelation that you are at home in English
and American literature from Beowulf to Barth,
and expect to be immediately seen as the ideal
person to deal with patients, customers, or
clients.

Specific approaches toward various kinds of
jobs will come up in the following chapters. To
generalize briefly here, you can make the connection between the job you want and your valuable (though as yet untested) background in
one or more of the following ways:

Inform yourself. Learn all you can about
several jobs in these client-centered fields
through talking with people who hold them, reading in the *Dictionary of Occupational Titles* and
other material in your public library or placement center, watching the newspapers for open
meetings and seminars you can go to (for example, the annual one-day workshops sponsored by
the Public Relations Society of America). Consider taking continuing education or community
college courses in your chosen field, or returning to college on an "unclassified fifth year"
status.[11]

Get first-hand experience. If you're still
an undergraduate, summer jobs or part-time or
volunteer work during the school year will count
heavily in your favor. If you already have your
B.A., it's often still possible to get internships or short-term jobs that offer direct contact with your chosen field. If you can afford
it, you may find, as many other job-seekers
have, that a period of part-time volunteer experience helps you get the "feel" of a job area
and weighs in your favor at an interview.

Document the results of this experience so
as to help you yourself as well as a potential
employer discover what you got out of it. In
other words, get down on paper (in outline or
list form if the idea of writing a report causes
you too many mental blocks) what kind of
clients, patients, or customers you listened
to, what their recurrent problems or questions
were, what kind of program you would like to
see to deal with their situation if you could
do anything you wanted to, how it might be
funded (or how the employer would be the gainer
in time, money, or good will), what problems
need further investigation, what interconnec-
tions you see between what you took part in and
the work of other agencies or offices. Not all
these categories will apply to what you've done;
but the point is that you should take the initiative in designing any kind of report you wish
so as to show what you did, how it fits into a
larger picture, and where you see that your experience, however brief, could lead.

Be inventive. If there aren't any such
openings as the one you hope for, see whether
you could demonstrate that there is a need to
be filled, as one medical receptionist, Mary
Sartor, is doing at this very moment.

During my work as secretary/

receptionist for two surgeons I noticed
that so many of the patients came from
out of town, and if their surgery was
critical and a member of their family
came to stay during the hospitaliza-
tion, he or she would be pretty much
at sea. I did a lot of listening and
began to realize that most of these
patients' relatives didn't know where
to stay, what the resources of the city
were that they could utilize when they
weren't actually with the patient, or
whom they could ventilate their worries
to. The doctors were too busy; the
nurses had all they could do to deal
with the patients; even the hospital
social workers were merely "patient-
oriented," letting the patients' relatives exist in a frightening vacuum.[12]

After several months of becoming more and more
concerned with the patients' relatives' problems, Sartor began to design a service which
will soon start on a trial basis in one of the
large Seattle hospitals. If she gets funding
for a trial period, at first she will staff the
service herself, eight hours a day, taking a
leave of absence from her regular job to do so.
Eventually she hopes, and with reason, that the
hospital where it starts will incorporate a
"patients' families' services coordinator" into
their regular staff and that other hospitals
across the country will follow the lead.
        Those of you with graduate degrees, however,
may feel that your problems are different from
those of Hollis or Sartor. First, you probably
intended to teach; and second, for the past few
years you probably haven't felt yourself free
either to volunteer or to diversify, to take at
least one basic course in each field that

appeals to you. Having concentrated upon English or American literature, and upon one
period or author or literary type within one
or the other of these, you feel all too ready
to be told that you are "overspecialized and
overqualified."

You, probably even more than the new B.A.,
need to sit down and read Bolles' book, *What
Color Is Your Parachute?*, and then to write out
the self-assessment exercises in his Chapter 5.
You also should look back over your papers,
both undergraduate and graduate, to see what
research and writing techniques you have mas-
tered that you could transfer to other situations. You will presumably have learned still
more than a B.A. about how to dig deeply for
information, how to sift through vast amounts
of material to find small relevant nuggets, how
to put together a bibliography on your topic,
and how to work independently and effectively.
These capabilities are valuable to employers,
provided that you yourself have confidence in
your ability to use them in other situations
than the seminars in which you first learned
them.

In case these comments on the wide applica-
bility of techniques learned in graduate school
strike you as mere rhetoric, read later on in
this handbook what one person says about how
well her graduate work in English has served
her in her position with the Seattle city government, what Kenneth Haas says about the carry
over from his Ph.D. in English into his job as
a member of management at Korvette, or what
Blanche Adams says about the usefulness of her
English teaching experience in improving the
writing of executives in an accounting firm.[13]

It is important to emphasize that not all
the alternative positions for which your graduate work has qualified you involve being

writers, editors, information specialists, and
the like. Ellen Messer-Davidow, a graduate student in English now working on her dissertation,
serves as assistant to the president of the University of Cincinnati; she is one who believes
strongly that "most Ph.D.'s in English have acquired skills just as important as writing, and
perhaps even more marketable." And she goes on
to describe seven areas in which, simply as a
by-product of their graduate education, persons
with advanced degrees in English have knowledge
and expertise:

> 1. *Analysis and problem-solving:* at the
> heart of dealing with texts per se and
> with literary and critical works; funda-
> mental to managerial work of any kind--
> identifying the problem and formulating
> the solution, flowcharting it, utiliz-
> ing human, financial, physical, and in-
> formational resources, strategizing,
> and decision-making.
> 2. *Research skills and methodologies:*
> the *sine qua non* of managerial, as
> well as our disciplinary, work. With-
> out this skill, decisions never get
> made properly and projects never get
> done. One of the greatest lacunae in
> higher education management today
> exists between the people who compile
> data and the people who make plans and
> policy. Policy makers too seldom
> understand the details and method-
> ologies of data, and data compilers
> too seldom understand what to collect,
> for what purpose, and with what
> significance.
> 3. *Design:* an integral activity in
> the structuring of organizations, pro-
> grams, and projects; has no correspond-

ing term in our discipline, but we
practice it every time we deal with
plot structure, poetic forms and
weavings, and Aristotelian and other
critical thought.

4. *Human nature:* Individual and social
behavior is represented in the most complex and profound of ways in literature.
Understanding and intervening in the
dynamics of individual psychology,
small groups, interpersonal relations,
and organizational behaviors is the
fulcrum of managerial activity.

5. *Other-orientation:* Almost all work
today involves supervising people, relating to clients, working with colleagues individually and in groups.
Concerned as we are about the reader
of literature, about ourselves as students and critics of literature, and
about those we teach, we have acquired
other-orientation and many of the con-
comitant skills.

6. *Historical perspective:* We, who
work in a historically based discipline, have the perspective so patently
absent in the practice and theory of
management and, to a lesser degree, in
those social sciences which study and
affect the forms of work. For example,
much management theory and practice
proceeds today as if the Romantic re-
bellion had never happened, as if there
were no organic-humanistic stream of
thought running parallel throughout
the 19th century to the utilitarian-
bureaucratic stream. When Philip Slater
writes a *Pursuit of Loneliness* or an
Earthwalk, some cry up his originality;
we would wonder only when he had been

reading Wordsworth. When quality of
worklife programs begin to proliferate
in General Motors and the Washington-
based unions, we suspect that a reading
of Dickens or Gaskell or Lawrence might
have produced an earlier premiere.
When Volvo institutes autonomous work
groups and becomes a virtual magnet of
attention, we wonder why nothing was
known of the pre-industrial cottage
industry.
7. *Values:* The values which are our
strength are badly needed by all organizations. The value of an individual vs. an abstraction, the validity
of feelings and expression, the proper
place of the quantitative in the service of the qualitative, relish for the
texture of experience instead of pro-
tection or isolation from it--and, the
value of those good, old-fashioned
terms, morality and ethics. Organizational life is characterized by
compartmentalization of person and
segmentation of act; each person, en-
cased in her or his cellular interior,
is not responsible for the morality
and equity of organizational acts.
Each, antiseptically purified of emo-
tion, does not have to empathize.[14]

If upon reading Messer-Davidow's communication you realize that you have through your
graduate work developed even a few such compe-
tencies, you will have taken an important
step.[15] Another is to analyze not only what
you are able to do but what you particularly
want to do. During the 1960s many students
found themselves in graduate school without
knowing clearly why they were there. Some of

them, being in graduate English programs, felt
that of course they would ultimately be teaching
English, since that was the kind of career to
which such studies traditionally led. But today's job crisis makes it important to ask yourself some questions. Why did you originally
enter graduate school? What were you looking
for? What is it about teaching English in a
college or university that appeals to you?

The experience of being an instructor or
professor of English is, when one stops to
think of it, a fairly complex one, composed of
many different though intertwined strands. To
some people, it is the interaction with students
in class that is the important part. To others,
it is having like-minded colleagues with whom
they can share interests and ideas. Still
others may find that working in an academic
ambience, though not necessarily as teachers,
is what they particularly want to do. Of
course, to a few graduate students, the pull
of the subject matter on which they have been
concentrating is so strong, their emotional
and intellectual investment in "their" author
or period so great that they would feel pro-
foundly dislocated if they could not keep up,
through working in libraries, comparing manuscripts, and constantly searching for new interpretations, their close involvement with
Yoknatapawpha County or Regency London.

Each of these four parts of an English faculty member's role is certainly a genuine one;
and yet, aspirations to one or another of them
can often be satisfied in other ways than
through teaching in a college English department. Many other positions--teaching in continuing education or other alternative programs,
working on an academic journal, being a student
services counselor or information specialist on
a campus, or being on the staff of a university

press, for example--offer certain of the specific satisfactions that you may have thought in-
separable from an appointment to a college or
university teaching position.

Perhaps, however, you agree with one recent
job candidate who, as he insisted when he came
to the Placement Center, was determined "to
wait for a regular appointment to an English
Department, and was simply going to dig in my
heels and starve if need be" until he gained
the kind of job he felt he deserved. If you
feel as he does, you probably ought to ask one
or two members of your English faculty who know
your work well for a frank evaluation of your
chances as they see them. If they consider
your offerings as ones which may be in demand
this year or next for college positions, fine;
keep on looking, yet don't close off other options. If not, you may want to keep searching
anyway, for the hiring process today is full of
surprises, but you should certainly know about
alternatives. After all, as Prof. Linwood
Orange has pointed out, it is a fallacy to consider that "the primary, perhaps sole, function
of the college English professor is to perpe-
tuate his own species."[16]

If you decide to explore some of these
other ways of putting your graduate education
to practical use, it will help if you can re-
examine the bias in favor of the academic life
which you probably have acquired in graduate
school. Unfortunately, as it was pointed out
recently by Ruth Von Behren, a Ph.D. in medieval
history who is now management analyst for the
State of California, a person working for an
advanced degree in any one of the humanities
soon comes to share the view of most of his or
her professors that "an alternative to a teaching position is necessarily a job that is second rate or second best."[17] Actually, however,

a graduate degree in English is not a professional degree in the sense that law and medical
degrees are, nor need it be considered "wasted"
if one does not go into, or stay in, the teaching of college English.

The first and most important part of your
job search, then, is convincing yourself that
you are suited to, and might even enjoy, other
positions than academic teaching ones. Getting
your first such position, even if it is a temporary or part-time one, will probably show you
that you can build upon it and proceed from it
to others, just as Angela Hollis did. Talking
with people actually doing the kind of job you
are hoping for should help. So, too, should
reading about people who have actually made the
transitions described in the following chapters.

Once you have taken inventory of your assets
and have convinced *yourself* that you are a potential copy-writer, editorial assistant, public relations person, textbook adviser, free-
lance editor, or other nonacademic job-holder,
it is time for all of you, B.A.'s, M.A.'s, and
Ph.D.'s alike, to plan a campaign to use with
potential employers.

But you may well ask, *"What* employers?" At
first you may not know where to start looking
for them. When you begin the search for alternative positions, you enter a somewhat different
world, one seemingly with few if any rules, pre-
cedents, or specific job descriptions. In such
a world you will often have to assume the burden
of proof, sometimes showing a possible employer
both that he needs to have a certain job done
(his manuals edited, for example, or his employees taught how to write better, clearer
reports) and that you are the person to do it.
In the following chapter you will find a number
of strategies that have worked well recently for

other job-seekers.   Perhaps you can adapt some
of them to your own needs and temperament.

CHAPTER 3

Some Strategies for Job-seekers

I was getting stale in my job. Although
I had originally enjoyed my position
[as technical editor for a Northwest
branch of an organization doing contract research in the natural and social sciences], now after four years I
wasn't learning anything new, and I
began to feel less and less intelli-
gent. So I decided to enter a different field, looking for another job
while I still held this one. Having
come to the conclusion that public
relations offered the greatest challenge to someone interested in writing
and in social issues, I wrote up a
résumé and phoned six top people in
the city--vice presidents of banks
and of PR firms. I asked each one
not for a job but for ten or fifteen
minutes of his or her time to go over
my résumé with me and tell me what
else I should be doing to get into
my new field. Not one refused to see
me. I didn't stay more than fifteen
minutes anywhere. But each had some
good suggestions, and each knew four
to six other people for me to see.
Actually, by the time I had gotten

half way through this process, I began
to feel good about myself again. I
could see that I had something to
offer. After about three months I
found my new job, or rather it was
created for me; I am now an account
executive working full-time on the
public relations of a company manufacturing machinery to dispose of
industrial waste.--Comment from a
former editor, now in a public relations firm with offices in New York,
San Francisco, Portland, Seattle, and
Anchorage

In order to find a job or to change jobs you
need to have at least one fixed point that you
can count on. It may be time: be prepared to
spend from 90 to 180 days, says Richard Bolles.[1]
It may be money: if possible, gather together
enough, whether from savings or borrowings or
from a job you hold while you're looking for
another, to support yourself for that long. It
may be the very real security of knowing that
you *do* have a job, even if it's not what you
ultimately want. It may be belief in yourself
and what you have to offer.

The woman quoted above was fortunate enough
to have three of these assets working for her
throughout her search, and the fourth material-
ized as her campaign developed momentum: "I
really came to see that I had a lot to offer;
and, somewhat to my own surprise, I became very
sold on myself. You have to be, if you're going
to get a firm to create a new job for you.
Maximize your assets. Don't ask too nicely
or meekly to see people; it gives them too good
a chance to tell you to get lost."

Many people, both job-seekers and employers, whom I consulted offered similar advice. "Belief in yourself is the hardest thing for a job-seeker to develop, particularly a graduate student who has just been through the ordeal of his exams and his dissertation," writes a man who now has a college teaching and administrative position, "but one absolutely must find some way to re-establish his confidence in himself and to make it visible to others." "Where would I have been," writes a woman who suddenly found herself widowed and going back to work, "after being a happy housewife for so many years, if as I looked for a position I hadn't been on good terms with myself and felt that I could rise to the challenges of a new job as they came up?"[2] At the risk of sounding like an exponent of "positive thinking," I pass along these comments and urge you, as one of the most important steps you can take, to find ways in which you can come to think well of yourself and of what you have to offer. What particular ways you find and how you find them are outside the scope of this book.

In any case, you do have control over your own personal strategy in determining the best possible use of your particular assets. Many job-seekers who have found alternatives to teaching jobs have made use of one or more of the following ideas. Perhaps they may work for you too.

Remember that opportunities may well exist for which you are qualified. But you have to keep looking for them. Your stance has to be an active, inventive one; that is, you cannot afford to be content with asking at a placement center, "Are there any jobs advertised that I can apply for?" In addition to making such inquiries, you must keep alert to any news, anywhere, of new programs, agencies, or offices

where your services (as, for example, editor,
writer, publicist, researcher, program coordinator, teacher, or interviewer) might be useful.
Having discovered such a possibility, do all the
background research you can on the organization
and its needs.   Then, using Richard Bolles'
technique of "interviewing for information, not
for a job," ask to come in for a few minutes to
learn about opportunities in the field in which
the organization operates.[3]

   If you can apply this method with the flair
and the steady growth of self-confidence wherein
the woman quoted at the beginning of this chapter used it, you will have a valuable strategy.
If your temperament or your recent job-hunting
experiences have led you to be terrified at the
thought of being rejected or overly concerned
about seeming to impose upon other people's
time, perhaps you should discontinue, after a
fair trial, these requests for short interviews
with executives.   While it is helpful to be experimental in the ways you look for jobs, it is
also a good rule not to persist with any method
which you see as incongruous with your temperament and personal style.

   In any case, however you initiate your campaign to make contact with potential employers,
you will want to be prepared with a résumé and
specific examples of your work.   One hears a
good deal about résumés these days, and there
are firms whose staff members will be happy,
for a sizable fee, to write yours for you.
Actually, as both Bolles and Irish demonstrate,
you are the person best qualified to construct
your own.   If you have done the exercises in
Chapter 5 of *What Color Is Your Parachute?* you
will have several pages of information about
what you have done, plus some new insights.
For the specifics of presenting yourself on
paper, you should turn to some of the thorough

treatments listed in the notes and bibliography
of this handbook. There are, however, a few
general principles to bear in mind.

   • Be selective. You don't have to account
here for every minute of your time; you should
choose carefully which aspects of your education
or previous positions are probably the most relevant for the particular kind of job you're
looking for.

   • For most positions, prepare a résumé
rather than the traditional academic vita.
Unless your employer specifically requests a
curriculum vitae, running as its name implies
through the course of your life from your early
education to the present, construct a topical
résumé instead. Doing this will enforce selec-
tivity: you will group various kinds of work
you have done under such broad categories as
"Teaching Experience," "Administrative Experience," "Editorial Experience," or whatever categories best fit your life and the job for which
you are applying.

   • Consider having several résumés, one type
for each kind of position for which you are
applying. Many readers may want to have one
for jobs with publications, one for possible
teaching positions, one for business openings.

   • Remember that it is hard to be objective
about the way you present yourself. Write the
best draft you can for the various types of
résumé you may need, then go over it with someone else--a placement counselor, a friend, or a
person in the field of your choice who is willing to spend a few minutes giving you an objective opinion of what you have put down on paper.
But be sure to do your homework first; *have*
something on paper that is the best representa-
tion of your abilities and your experience that
you can construct by yourself.

   • If it is any comfort to you, *everyone*

finds it hard to write his or her résumé. Administrative vice-presidents, junior executives, and placement counselors routinely have a sympathetic colleague go over their résumés when they are changing jobs. We are all caught midway between the austere tradition in which we were brought up, which has all our lives been saying to us "Don't boast about yourself," "Actions speak louder than words," "Don't blow your own horn," and the opportunistic whisper in our minds which urges, "Now be sure to get all the mileage you can out of everything you've ever done." The solution may be to read what Bolles, Irish, Jacquish, or some other knowledgeable people in their field specify about résumé writing and to do the best you can; then, on the basis of the reactions of a trusted critic, consider revising. Finally, have your résumés reproduced in a format that looks professional, with clear, crisp typing and "plenty of white space."

• In any case, remember that nobody has ever been hired simply on the basis of a résumé, and nobody has yet won a Pulitzer Prize for writing the best résumé of the year. In short, the résumé is purely a means to one end: to get you an appointment for an interview.

• For almost any position for which you are applying, you should send a short, *individualized* letter of application along with your résumé and the application form. In such a letter you should not only refer briefly to your education and experience (without, however, simply recapitulating your résumé) but show their relevance to the current program of the department, office, or agency to which you are applying. By all means demonstrate that you have spent time learning about whatever is being done by that particular business or institution. A blanket letter which says merely,

in effect, "Here I am; I have these recent degrees and such and such experience," will seldom
make a possible employer tremendously anxious to
interview you.

   • No matter how effective your letter and
your résumé, you will probably at some stage of
most job explorations have to fill out an application form as well. Since you may be filling
out fifty or a hundred of them within several
months, it is easy to dismiss this part of the
routine as mere drudgery, hardly worth your
time or attention. Until you have been on the
other side of the hiring process, you may not
realize how even such a small matter as filling
out an application form can convey an impres-
sion of you to the employer, who--rightly or
wrongly--tends to think that it tells something
about your attitude toward the job you're applying for.

   After reading dozens of applications, nearly
half of which were from M.A.'s and Ph.D.'s, for
counseling positions at the University of Washington Placement Center, a colleague and I
developed a few dos and don'ts for job-seekers
to keep in mind. Although perhaps these suggestions should be self-evident, students we counseled have told us that they proved helpful in
cases where their papers had to be screened by
a personnel office before being sent to someone
in their own field who would do the interviewing
and selecting.

   1. First, an elementary suggestion: do fill
out *clearly* and *fully* the standard application
blank and any other forms you may be given. A
scribbled notation across your blank directing
the reader to "See résumé" seems too casual and
impatient, while faint or indecipherable writing
or typing on the form can make the reader feel
that you don't really care about getting the job
or that you cannot visualize how the application

looks to your reader.

2. Whether or not the blank specifies it, do attach your own résumé, which will give the reader additional information about you and your experience for which the form leaves insufficient room, and do enclose the cover letter mentioned above.

3. Do not have your file of academic references testifying to your excellences as a scholar or teacher sent from your campus placement center if you are applying for a nonacademic job; some employers would find it overwhelming or beside the point. It is better to have a special file of references for non-teaching positions, in which your professors or your former employers isolate, apart from any academic context, such points as your initiative and drive, your thoroughness, your adaptability, or whatever other virtues they see in you.

4. Do not send your academic transcript, particularly if you are a graduate student, to a nonacademic employer unless it is requested.

5. Job candidates often ask what to do about appearing "overqualified." Although there is no one easy answer to this question, the problem is often one of the candidate's attitude more than of his actual schooling or experience. Do not in any way let it appear in your application that you think your degree(s) are enough by themselves to qualify you for a particular position. You have to indicate one way or another that there is some connection between what you have learned or done and what the position calls for. By so doing, you will minimize the chance of your application's being thrown out on the grounds of overqualification.

• For nearly all positions involving writing, editing, or work with publications, most

of the employers consulted urged that you have
a folder of your own writing or editing, preferably done within the last two years, to show
at an interview or to leave if requested. This
work need not be ambitious or extensive; it
might include such things as reviews or commen-
tary (on books, films, drama, music, sports
events, art), course proposals, grant proposals,
reports to faculty committees on which you
have served, programs of conferences you have
arranged, program notes for a film series,
samples of your editing, letters to an editor,
publicity for an organization, newsletters, or
brief accounts of innovative teaching plans in
which you have participated. Whatever your
folder contains, it should demonstrate to a
nonacademic employer that you can write in
crisp, understandable language for a general
audience. If such writing has been published,
fine; if it has been mimeographed or Xeroxed
and distributed by an organization, that too
will show that you can finish what you write
and get it out into the world. The kind of
sample you should ordinarily *not* include would
be either a handwritten draft or an academic
term paper.

   • Keep a simple log or card file listing
everyone you phone, write to, or talk to in
your job search, even though you may not have
been formally interviewed. Putting down the
date when you made the contact and the exact
spelling of the person's name can save hours
later on. Putting down any suggestions made
or leads volunteered will give you a chance to
follow them up weeks later, when otherwise they
could have become vague in your mind.

   Aside from these specifics of interviews,
résumés, applications, and supporting material,
there are a few general principles which it has

helped a number of recent job candidates to
keep in mind.

For work with business or government, your
writing and research skills and any graduate
degrees you have may need to be supplemented
by some business or government experience or
training. Look around for short-term (sometimes
unacademic) ways of supplementing what you know:
internships, volunteer work, extension courses,
workshops, community college courses, as well as
a few university courses in fields new to you.

Remember that, despite the job shortage,
people do get hired, even in fields or by firms
where, according to rumor, "it is well known
that no hiring is being done." Vacancies do
occur because of employees' retirement, promotion, or illness; new programs develop through
the unexpected funding of grants or contracts;
top management sometimes has a chance to implement innovative ideas by creating positions
that personnel departments have never heard of.
Of those people who are hired, many of them
take a newly created or vaguely defined opportunity and gradually, after they get on the
job, see that it is redefined to fit their
capabilities and talents.

You should make both a long-range plan and
some contingency plans as well, so that if you
find yourself in a short-term peripheral job
you can turn it to good account. (You can, for
example, use such a marginal job to add to your
repertoire of skills, to try out new course
material, to tap as a source for articles, innovative programs, or a book). You can also
use almost any alternative job experience to
help qualify you for more permanent employment.

Usually you will not find your ideal alternative job to be the first one you get. Be
prepared to proceed by zig-zags, perhaps from
an hourly job in your chosen field to a sala-

ried, full-time one only vaguely related to your
chosen field, and then finally, with luck, you
might make a lateral move to a salaried job representing your first choice among alternatives.

A common criticism of twentieth-century
American society is that too many of us "tend
to define ourselves by our jobs." Unfortunate
as this tendency is, an even more self-defeating
one is becoming widespread. Too many people
looking for positions these days are defining
themselves by their joblessness. No matter how
time-consuming your job search may be, it is
still important not to focus all your thought,
and particularly all your conversation, upon
the state of being unemployed.

One good way of avoiding this temptation is
to continue, while you are job-hunting, at something connected with your profession. Teach
(if you enjoy teaching, even if it's only one
course, on an hourly or even a volunteer basis).
Write (and get published, even if it's only
minor book reviews, newsletters, pedagogical
articles, or Sunday supplement feature stories,
unpaid or underpaid). Be a free-lance editor
(even if you have only one client every few
months). Work on improving the reports and
internal communications of a business concern;
do tape-recorded interviews for a local oral
history project; help your favorite political
candidate by working on his or her public relations and speeches. Doing any of these
things will increase your sense of professional
continuity and versatility. Having such activities in your background should make you come
through at job interviews as a more interesting
person than you would if you were just one more
worthy, well-qualified, admirable but unemployed
English major or instructor. Such involvement
will, we hope, enable you to follow the precept
quoted in Chapter 10 from the publisher William

Targ: "You must make your presence and work contribution felt, but not your desperation."

When you *do* find the position you want, don't just settle in and take it for granted. See what you can write and add to your folder of examples of your work. Look ahead; keep your résumé and your placement file up to date. Ask yourself whether you have capabilities that aren't being used in your position and try to find ways of using them. Alternatively, ask yourself what you are learning in your current position that could add to your competence in the more nearly ideal position which may still lie ahead.

If these ideas seem self-evident to you, fine. You may not need this book. Go ahead and hunt for jobs following your own instinct. If, however, you want examples and a fuller explanation of how some of these strategies work in practice, you will find them in the following chapters.

CHAPTER 4

Will a Different Degree Help?

In the late throes of graduate work and
in the first ones of full-time teaching,
you could pick up certain repetitive
sentences from me and my colleagues,
particularly in late evenings: "You
know, it sounds crazy, but I've been
thinking of switching to law school"
or "What's three years out of a life-
time?" or "Do you realize what lawyers
make in New York?" . . . It wasn't
actually *being* lawyers that attracted
us; the *image* was invigorating.--Roger
Rosenblatt, literary editor of the
New Republic

One of the . . . reasons why most
people go back to school is . . .
to postpone decision, and create a
never-never land between one's past
and any future career. The "eternal
student" is becoming more and more
a familiar figure in our land.--
Richard N. Bolles, *What Color Is
Your Parachute?*

Far too little attention has been
paid to the human costs of prolong-
ing the educational process unnec-

47

essarily. The financial costs are
fairly obvious, but the sapping of the
individual's creativity by keeping him
in leading-strings when he ought to be
making his way as an active professional person or simply a mature citi-
zen is often overlooked.--Comment by
an American historian, December 5, 1976

Perhaps, rather than looking around for alternative ways to make use of your background in
English, you, like so many job-seekers with
graduate degrees in this field, are considering
starting all over again in a different graduate
or professional program. "I think I might as
well give up on English and get a degree in
something practical this time," graduate students often tell placement counselors.

Law school is probably the most popular
choice, at least in fantasy, and many readers
can empathize with the early daydreams of Roger
Rosenblatt and his friends. Somewhat less popular than going to law school, yet still exert-
ing a magnetic influence on many restless or
discouraged graduate students in English are
certain other graduate or professional programs:
librarianship, counseling, social work, public
affairs, business administration, or one of the
health sciences or health services.

Although there has lately been a good deal
of talk about "career switching,"[1] there is as
yet very little hard information about what
happens to young people who start preparing
for their second professional career before
ever actively commencing their first one. The
Harvard Office of Placement Services, for
example, has only recently begun to identify
people making this double post-graduate pre-

paration. In 1974-75, they note, there were six
Ph.D.'s at Harvard who had each gone on for
another graduate degree in a different field
from their first one: of these, three went to
law school and three to medical school. In
1975-76, there were six more Ph.D.'s working
toward an additional graduate degree: one Ph.D.
in English had begun the M.B.A. program; two
Ph.D.'s from other fields entered the Harvard
Law School; and one apiece entered medical
school, library school, or the graduate school
of business administration.[2]

Obviously it is much too early to predict
what returns these and many similar investments
made elsewhere—investments of time, money,
energy, and hope—will bring. But Edward Noyes,
director of Yale University's Office of Career
Planning, who has long had serious doubts about
the motivation of many students in going to
graduate school right after getting their bachelor's degrees, is even more concerned about the
new trend toward seeking a second kind of graduate or professional preparation simply as a
hoped-for answer to the job crisis. In fact
he shares Richard Bolles' concept of the "eternal student" as someone who may well be deluding
himself into postponing (or giving up too soon
on) job-seeking.[3]

Neither Bolles, Noyes, nor anyone else
means to say that such dual preparation is
never a good idea; under some circumstances,
as examples later on will show, it can turn
out well. Yet if you are beginning now to
think of "going back to school to get a different advanced degree, one in something *practical* this time," you should first of all try
to find out just how realistic your picture of
your entry into another field may be.

To gather solid information, you should
first explore the *Guide to American Graduate*

Schools,[4] then write to the official association
of your intended profession--The American Bar
Association, the American Library Association,
or other appropriate ones listed in Appendix
E--for career literature and for answers to
specific questions. You should also write to
or talk with a faculty adviser at each of the
schools to which you hope to apply. Then talk
to half a dozen students now working for the
degree you want to get, to people looking for
jobs in the field, and to those holding such
jobs. It is remarkable how many liberal arts
graduate students keep saying for years, "I'd
like to chuck it all and go to law school,"
without having made first-hand contact with any
source of data against which they can measure
the practicality of the idea for them.

    As you make personal contacts and write
letters, be sure to test certain assumptions
commonly held by graduate students and other
job-seekers looking at what they consider
greener fields. Without saying that these
five assumptions never hold true, placement
counselors and graduate admissions officers
nonetheless urge you strongly to see whether
you have any grounds for believing them true
in your particular case.

    1. "Once I've added a library (law, social
work, or other) degree--no matter where I get
it--to my background in English, I have a pass-
port to a whole new job market." But things do
not always work out this way. Through your
choice of institution you may already be limit-
ing your job target more than you realize.
First, there are differences in emphasis. Before you apply to a school of library science,
for example, find out whether it concentrates
on preparing its graduates to be school librarians, to work in large public libraries, or
whether, like the schools at the University of

Chicago, the University of California at Berkeley, and a few others, it prepares graduates to
become scholarly research librarians. Given
your advanced degree in English, you would probably want to work toward the last of these
goals. Schools of social work, and in fact
all professional schools, have their different
emphases, strengths, and weaknesses, a fact
sometimes overlooked by those longing to get
into the field and become accredited as quickly
as possible into a new profession. Second,
there are qualitative differences. Before you
apply to a particular law school, for example,
find out the percentage of its recent graduates
who passed their bar exams on the first trial,
as well as those who have been hired by law
firms in the area where you hope to work.

2. "The new field I want to start over in
is a highly practical one. There will always
be a need for social workers (or lawyers,
librarians, clinical counselors)." Don't take
this idea too much for granted. Call your
local branch of the Bar Association and find
out their latest figures on the number of newly
graduated lawyers who have passed their bar
exams and are still out of work. A representative of one law school said recently that
such candidates "were finding the job search
increasingly difficult, just as it is in any
profession." The new lawyers were waiting an
average of six to nine months before being
placed, with those faring best who were willing
to relocate to rural areas. [5]

Clinical counselors, too, however much they
may be needed, are not being hired in the numbers they were a few years back, and the files
of placement centers bulge with dossiers of job
candidates with doctorates in counseling, several years' clinical experience, and a string
of published research articles. When college

and university budgets are slashed, student
counseling centers are sometimes the first programs to be eliminated. As for social workers,
although their employment picture nationwide is
better than that of the counselors, nonetheless
most large cities have a backlog of unemployed
caseworkers and M.S.W.'s. Note, incidentally,
that social workers too are now writing and
reading books, pamphlets, and articles on career alternatives for people in their profession
who are trying to switch fields.[6]

It is important to keep in mind that even
with the most currently "marketable" of the
degrees often considered desirable by disen-
chanted English Ph.D.'s, master's degrees in
health planning and in business administration,
there is no guarantee that by the time you may
have finished one of them and are again on the
job market, the demand for them will have kept
up with the supply. Keep in mind, too, that
several successful job-hunters interviewed for
this book who could have persuaded themselves
to go back to graduate school and get an
M.B.A. worked their way without it to exactly
the positions they wanted in business or in
government.[7]

3. "If I could get admitted to graduate
school once, I can do it again--perhaps even
more easily now that I've finished one graduate program." This conviction may not be
borne out by the facts. As graduate schools
respond to university-wide cutbacks in funding
and to charges of producing more highly edu-
cated people than there are jobs for them,
inevitably admissions policies are tightened.
Where once your academic record and your graduate or professional school aptitude test
scores were the main criteria, admissions
committees today often take into account your
age, your "commitment to the profession," your

previous work experience, and your chance as
they perceive it of becoming an effective,
practicing member of your profession. (Although
admissions counselors at several schools of
social work told me that the candidate's age
and his long-range professional intentions after
getting an M.S.W. did not affect his or her can-
didacy, few graduate or professional schools
have such a lassez-faire policy.) Some health
science programs, besieged as they are by hundreds of qualified applicants for every available place, have turned down an applicant with
an excellent academic record in another professional field, insisting that he or she "already
has a profession."

In particular, do not count on the hope
that your having a Ph.D. in English may either
cut down slightly upon the requirements for a
degree in your new field or at least tip the
scales in your favor. One admissions officer
at a school of library science said that holding a Ph.D. in English or American literature
would be held as "neither a plus or minus, but
simply an irrelevancy. In this field, you can
go to school for twenty years or more, but it
doesn't necessarily qualify you for a job." An
admissions adviser in a counseling program said
that having a degree in English would count in
an applicant's favor only if a teaching assistantship had been part of the program. A
faculty member of a law school conceded that
people with Ph.D.'s in English would probably
make good lawyers, "since everything a lawyer
does, he does with words"; at the same time,
he said that having a graduate degree in English would count neither for nor against an
applicant to his school.

4. "If I could support myself through
graduate school once, I can probably do it
again." Here, too, careful investigation is

in order. You may be less likely to get a
teaching assistantship the second time around.
In particular, find out about any departmental
restrictions upon working part time along with
your studies. Although such work is often
possible, there are some programs, particularly
at many law schools, where it is forbidden.
"The three-year program leading to the degree
of Juris Doctor is a total commitment, a very
serious, difficult study," said an admissions
counselor at the law school of a large state
university. "The course work should take all
one's time and energy. Therefore the applicant
must register for full-time study and must not
take a paid part time job during the nine-month
academic year."

     5. "With my graduate degrees in English
plus my new degree in my second field, I'll
have a broad background that should make me
more valuable to employers, enrich my life,
and be a double insurance against disaster."
It is probably true that your second professional preparation *should* do all this and
more, yet in the present state of academia,
compartmentalized as it is, there is some
doubt that your double preparation *will* serve
these purposes.

     On the whole, placement counselors have
been finding that candidates with advanced
degrees in several subjects usually do no better
in the job market than those with one M.A. or
Ph.D. These counselors tend to think that there
is almost no candidate harder to help than the
one who took several graduate degrees in a row
without getting any practical or professional
experience along the way. William Bliss, director of the Yale Alumni Placement Service, goes
so far as to say, "In general, the 'professional
student' will never be a very good worker. The
Ph.D.-lawyer will probably have trouble finding

a legal job after law school."[8] Some employers
feel threatened by an applicant's double preparation; others tend to see him or her as
indecisive, or cast in the role of a loser.

Once you find a job in your new field, moreover, you may run into various kinds of academic
territorialism. For example, Theodore Greider
of New York University, writing in the *ADE
Bulletin*, points out that combining a Ph.D.
in English with an M.L.S. does not automatically
increase your chance for a satisfying career.
After making a survey of librarians at 122 institutions, Greider concludes that there are
real obstacles to be overcome by the "subject-
matter expert" wishing to become a scholar-
librarian. Many employers told him that Ph.D.'s
would probably move to other jobs as soon as
they could find them. "If good librarians with
relevant Ph.D.'s are available as applicants
for positions in reference, book selection,
cataloging, then they would certainly be seriously considered. On the other hand, I can
think of four who were with us for periods of
one to ten years (two in languages, two in history) who all moved out eventually to full-time
teaching posts." One cynical employer even
replied, "I will tell you that attaching the
least marketable products of various departments
of instruction to the library is something I
will personally resist. Let 'em drive taxis!
Many of us who hold subject Ph.D.'s also have
library school degrees and have librarianship
as our major commitment, not as a second-best
choice; . . . it would not surprise me if MLA
and other scholarly institutions were thinking
that libraries would be a wonderful place to
dispose of their surplus Ph.D.'s--a surplus,
one might note, the academic departments themselves casually and irresponsibly produced."
Another took the view that he did "not see a

great need for language and literature Ph.D.'s
except in those libraries where book selection
in these areas is a major activity."[9]

The attitudes, and especially the territorialism, uncovered in Greider's article are
paralleled in other fields: admissions counselors at law schools, for example, warn that
"nobody should go to law school as a second
choice"; and an adviser in a graduate school
of public affairs said that while applicants
with B.A.'s or M.A.'s in English would be welcome, those with Ph.D.'s would probably be
looked at with some skepticism. On the whole,
academics in one field tend to wonder why, if
a neophyte expresses extreme interest in and
commitment to their field, he or she didn't
start out there in the first place.

This is not to say that combining two fields
of professional training is impossible. Even
Theodore Greider, after outlining the many
obstacles which a Ph.D. in English may meet
as a beginning librarian, goes on to suggest
that, *depending upon one's particular interests
and temperament,* there may be opportunities:

> In a positive way, I can conclude by
> saying that librarianship can provide
> a most interesting professional career
> for the Ph.D. truly interested in
> books and their nature, the book trade
> and antiquarian trade, bibliography
> (national and international), the
> technical processes necessary to make
> books available to the academic com-
> munity, and the activities involved
> in assisting users of all levels of
> learning with the books that are at
> hand. Given a lack of interest in
> freshman themes and term papers, per-
> haps even a disenchantment with the

world of formal academia and its offerings, and given a willingness to pursue
a profession other than that of academic instruction, I think that the
Ph.D./M.L.S. will find a very considerable satisfaction in the various
pursuits of librarianship.

As one gathers from reading Greider's article,
the fusion of careers he is exploring is a
highly individual matter.

This important idea, the realization that
"in making any career change, what matters more
than any degrees is your understanding of what
you want to do," is the point that Donna Martyn,
director of the Harvard Office of Placement Services, urges you to keep in mind as you look at
law school, social work programs, schools of
librarianship, and all the other options.
"There's no magic, no invulnerability, in any
degree or any combination of them. Another degree will work for you only if the training
will help you to do a job you've set your sights
on."[10]

Thus if, during your first graduate work
or one of your early jobs, you envision what
you most want to do, and if it involves combining fields, taking another graduate degree
might be practical. Four cases (not, however,
involving people in English) will help illustrate this point. A young woman who received
her first degree in music, majoring in the
flute, worked for a year as public relations
coordinator for a civic opera company, then
went back to school for an M.B.A. so as to combine her musical and her administrative interests. She is now happily established in her
third year as business manager for the symphony
orchestra of a large western state. A young
lawyer who became interested in American history

during his military service went back to school
to get a Ph.D. in American constitutional history, which (after meeting some skepticism at
job interviews as to why he made this shift) he
is now teaching as an assistant professor at a
university. A Ph.D. in nursing research became
so much concerned with the differences among
various cultures in their attitudes toward
health, hygiene, and medicine that she went to
graduate school for a second Ph.D. in anthropology; she uses the materials of both disciplines in her interdisciplinary research. And
the late Prof. Evelyn Clark of Vassar College,
who had received her first Ph.D. in classics
and had taught it for some years, became so much
interested in contemporary history during World
War II that she felt irresistibly drawn to take
a Ph.D. in it. Subsequently she taught history
at Vassar for many years, gaining added perspective, as she saw it, through her classical
background.

These inner-directed people each had a plan;
their second period of graduate study helped
fill a need which their own work and thought
had generated. They didn't shift fields because somebody told them to, or because an
occupational forecast told them that there
would be more jobs in their new areas of interest during the coming decades. In fact, they
didn't so much shift fields as enlarge their
fields so as to be at home in two areas which
they made adjacent.

The point which William Bliss, Edward
Noyes, Ivan Settles, and other counselors emphasize is that, while there really are many
opportunities to apply to other fields some of
the skills learned as a graduate student of
English, you may be able to do so more easily
than you think without yielding to the tempta-

tion to arm yourself with another graduate or
professional degree.

Career-switching is becoming much more
common today than it was even a generation ago.
Indeed, job counselors have recently predicted
that many people will have three or more separate, though related, careers one after another
during their working lives. But such switching
need not involve entering upon another complete
course of professional training. Those who have
finished one graduate degree tend to get into a
frame of mind in which they think that anything
else they do must involve a program of the same
extent and thoroughness as that of their graduate program.

Actually, there are alternatives to such an
ambitious plan. Assuming that you want to
build upon and use, not abandon, your preparation in English, you can either supplement it
with shorter, less academic courses or you can
manage to get enough work experience in your
chosen field to decide whether you actually
want and need formal preparation.

For example, if you find that you want to
combine your writing training with an interest
in film-making and make documentaries for educational or environmental or medical agencies,
you should ordinarily not insist on getting a
degree in documentary film. You should instead, following the example of many professionals in the field, concentrate on learning about
subject areas (education, environment, or whatever), and meanwhile take several good practical
courses in film-making; what you will need is
the basic technique, not another degree. (Excellent film-making courses are now given at
M.I.T., Boston University, the University of
Indiana, the University of Washington, U.C.L.A.,
at certain community colleges, and, of course,

around the country at specialized schools such
as the San Francisco School of Art and
Photography.)

In addition to film-making, there are
several other courses that English M.A.'s and
Ph.D.'s report as being valuable. Some of
these are noncredit courses, some are offered
by continuing education programs, some are
undergraduate courses, and some are given at
community colleges. Graduate work quite properly makes students afraid of superficiality;
but this fear can be carried too far. Your
reasons for taking some of these shorter, less
academic courses would be different from your
reasons for having entered graduate school, for
now you would be trying to acquire just enough
familiarity with a subject, its vocabulary, and
the best books to read about it so that you
could go ahead on your own.

Among the courses that people to whom we
talked had found valuable supplements to their
graduate training in English were:

Accounting. Taking one basic introductory
course has been recommended by people in publishing as helpful for aspirants to this field,
even for editorial positions.

Advertising and layout. These would be
helpful not only to those hoping to enter advertising (see Chapter 9) but also to anyone who
edits a newsletter or does publicity for a
visiting speaker or an organization, or works
as a campus information specialist.

Basic computer language. This is useful
for, and increasingly understandable by, people
doing editing in fields which are becoming more
and more quantified, such as nursing and health
services research, sociology, and history.

Editing and copy-editing. This background
would obviously be useful for anyone entering
the fields of journalism or publishing, and good

too for those who want to stay in teaching or
do academic writing.

Grant proposal writing. Short courses
given in this make it much easier to draft proposals for yourself or for the organization you
work for; moreover, once you have gotten this
expertise, your services are often in demand to
use professionally for others (see Chapter 8).

Graphics courses have helped people with
graduate degrees in their entry into publishing.
The expertise acquired here is also immensely
useful if you are in an organization, an academic department, or a learned society which
issues a newsletter.

Introduction to health services. This
course, along with world health, would be particularly helpful for anyone beginning to do
editing in health care fields.

Photography. Having taken a basic course
in black-and-white photography is an asset for
those who want to work on magazines or newsletters. A course in film-making can start you
toward assisting with and ultimately making
documentaries in connection with whatever position you may find as writer, editor, educator,
journalist, information specialist, or PR
person.

Publication procedures. Such courses,
though not always easily available, may be a
good entry into the world of publishing (see
Chapter 10).

Reading development. There are various
institutions such as the Warren Reading Foundation of Seattle specializing in research into
reading problems as well as instruction in how
to improve students' reading ability at all age
levels. Having taken a course at such a school
or in Michigan State University's reading instruction program could be a helpful addition
to your preparation for some types of community

college teaching or for working in a college's
"individual development center" or "study
skills center."

Technical writing and technical editing.
These would be immensely helpful for work as
editor or writer in connection with business,
industry, or public agencies.

Urban planning. Although the whole program
leads to a degree, taking one or two introductory courses would be an excellent background
for a position as writer or editor with some of
the many public or private planning agencies.
These agencies prepare feasibility studies and
impact statements, as well as material addressed
to the general public; there is a constant
need of people who can help them write prose
that is clear, logical, and interesting.

Writing for publication. Such courses,
given with varying emphases in noncredit
studies, in communications, and as part of
technical writing and editing sequences, have
obvious uses in almost any position for which
you might apply. They will also help you in
building up the folder of samples of your writing which nonacademic employers keep telling us
that people with degrees in English should be
able to show them.

Some of the content of these courses could,
it is true, be learned on the job. But if you
take one or two of them, you will have a springboard from which to go ahead and learn still
more on any job to which they are applicable.
And, perhaps more important to you just now,
your having taken a few such courses will show
an employer that you are interested in applying
your writing and research skills to his needs.
Of course, if you get into a field such as publishing and find that you would like to work in
such a specialized area as law in relation to
publishing, then after you have gotten a foot-

hold in publishing and know that you want to
stay there, it might be realistic to go back
to school and get a law degree as "mid-career
training." Such a return would represent a
combination of your already well developed interests rather than merely a search for an
added credential.

Roger Rosenblatt, in his speculations on
the value of a literary background, considered
and then rejected the idea of going to law
school. His conclusions may be worth keeping
in mind. Inevitably, he points out, a person
who has studied literature intensively lacks a
complete education, for no education can be complete. Yet the study of literature, Rosenblatt
is convinced, teaches us a great deal. He urges
us all, therefore, to acknowledge that a graduate degree in English is a good one, and then to
see how each of us can build upon it in our own
way.[11]

CHAPTER 5

Nontraditional Teaching

The profession is inbred, and . . .
adult education programs will, besides
providing jobs, get it in touch with
the population at large. Both stand
to gain from the encounter. For now,
graduate students are pinched from
both sides. We fear being disqualified from community colleges; we fear
being underqualified for four-year
colleges.--Stewart Justman, *College
English*

A good many teachers in English and
history and psychology, far from feeling displaced in [the] new academic
terrain [of continuing education pro-
grams], are settling in. And not just
or only because there are no positions
elsewhere. These are men and women
who are not in holding patterns, waiting to land on more fertile ground.
They are happy and productive where
they are.--Daniel Fedo, *The Chronicle
of Higher Education*

Possibly you have an advanced degree and, far

from wanting to switch to another field, hope
to stick as closely as you can to your original
goal of teaching college English. In that case
you might look at the many opportunities offered
by the current variations of the teaching of
English, as in new or emerging academic teaching specialties, English teaching opportunities
outside the United States, or instructing in
English through continuing education programs,
community colleges, in-service courses, "universities without walls," and other nontraditional
programs.

Of course, many readers of this handbook
are already aware of these less traditional
kinds of teaching. A considerable number of
people with graduate degrees in English, however, do come into placement centers not knowing
what other kinds of English teaching positions
there could be except teaching in a four-year
college or, alternatively, a high school. If
you are one of these people, the following discussion, though far from exhaustive, may suggest
a few leads for you to follow up on your own.

NEW OR EMERGING SPECIALTIES

Though it is natural to look primarily or
even exclusively at MLA job listings with their
emphasis on traditional period and genre
courses, it is also possible to go further. You
could, for instance, browse through college and
university catalogues, programs of English meetings, and articles in *College English* to see
just how wide a range of courses is being given.
Some courses, like technical writing, technical
editing, English as a second language, women
and literature, and children's literature,
everybody knows about yet not everyone is able
to teach. Interestingly enough, among the
English candidates who have used the University

of Washington Placement Center, many of those
who have recently received job interviews and
offers were those who were prepared to teach
one of these fields.

Scientific and technical communication, one
of those specialties which is currently receiving increased attention, is, according to two
of its practitioners and professors,

> a relatively new professional field.
> Its basic function is to convey sci-
> entific and technical information
> clearly and accurately through vari-
> ous media to a wide spectrum of
> readers who range from the general
> public to experts in such fields as
> the sciences, engineering, medicine
> and social sciences. [1]

As Paul V. Anderson of Miami University pointed
out at the December 1976 meeting of the Modern
Language Association, "ever since World War II,
industry and government have been asking, with
increasing frequency and firmness, that colleges and universities provide more instruction
in writing to students in science and technology."[2] Prof. Merrill Whitburn of Texas A&M
University, Prof. Myron White and Prof. James
Souther of the University of Washington, and
other faculty members in the institutions now
having programs in technical writing and technical editing cite numerous examples of graduate students in English who, after adding some
work in technical writing to their regular program, began to receive job offers. Many of
these English Ph.D.'s are now teaching both
technical writing and traditional college composition or literature courses. [3]

Children's literature, too, is an expanding
field, despite the patronizing attitude with

which some people, both within and without departments of English, look upon "kiddy lit." (For those of you who need to be convinced of its importance, read what Prof. Carol Gay of Youngstown [New York] State University has to say about its functions.[4])

If you are interested in developing the specialty called English as a second language (ESL), you should know that although there are sometimes jobs for people with B.A.'s in English, you will be in a stronger position if you have also had a minor or at least some course work in one or more of the following: anthropology, comparative foreign area studies, education, linguistics, psychology, sociology, or speech and hearing science.

There are entry-level positions in this field requiring a B.A. in English or in a modern foreign language, with special training in teaching ESL listed as desirable but not mandatory. There are some positions here in the United States, especially in community colleges or special ESL institutes (such as the one at Seattle University, Seattle, Washington), teaching English to recent arrivals from other countries; more positions, however, are overseas.[5] If after getting some experience teaching such classes you wish to go on and become a specialist in teaching others how to teach ESL, you will of course have to take at least an M.A. in the graduate program of one of the increasing number of colleges and universities who offer teaching English as a second language.[6] Among these institutions, to give only a few examples, are Iowa State University, Ames; University of the Pacific, Stockton, California; University of Minnesota, Minneapolis; Trinity University, San Antonio, Texas; University of Northern Iowa, Cedar Falls; Southern Illinois University, Carbondale; San

Francisco State University, California; and the
University of Washington, Seattle. For other
similar programs be sure to look in the catalogue of colleges and universities in your area.

Other new courses too are beginning to be
in demand. Native American literature, for
example, or popular culture, or fiction of the
British Commonwealth are three such offerings,
particularly apt to be found in the branches
of the state university systems of California
and of New York.[7] Some fields you can perhaps
prepare by yourself, through your own reading
and exploration; for others you may want to
enroll in or audit courses.

OPPORTUNITIES FOR TEACHING ENGLISH OUTSIDE THE UNITED STATES

One obvious application of courses in
teaching English as a foreign language is to
go abroad and teach native students who want
to learn English. Even without special TEFL
training, however, you may have chances to
teach English language and literature at various levels in schools and colleges abroad.[8]
Among the countries that offer good opportunities for American teachers of English are
Japan, Taiwan, Hong Kong, and Iran for English
language or literature; and New Zealand and
Australia for English and American literature.[9]

In East Asian countries, particularly in
Japan, there is a steady demand for language
instruction in colleges, universities, and
schools, as well as in private language institutes run somewhat on the principle of the
Berlitz schools. Language departments and
placement centers in the United States period-
ically receive requests from Japanese private
schools and institutes for English teachers.
Although some of these requests are for persons

with special training in TEFL, others call for
only a B.A. or M.A. in English or another
modern language plus, ideally, some teaching
experience. The few Ph.D.'s who apply are made
very welcome, since the doctorate is still considered a prestigious addition to a teacher's
preparation. Knowledge of Japanese is definitely not required of teachers of English in
Japan because teachers are encouraged to use
the oral-aural method and to speak only English
in the classroom.

Although the pay may not be high and the
work is demanding, accepting a year's contract
gives one a chance to live in a thoroughly different environment and to be exposed to a new
language and culture, as well as to the eager-
ness of the Japanese people to learn English.

If you are simply looking for a way to
support yourself while you enjoy the experience
of living in a foreign milieu, then teaching
English to adults (businessmen and women and
professional people, usually in classes held in
their offices or places of business) in Tokyo,
Nagoya, or other large Japanese cities has much
to be said for it. There is also an active interest in English and American literature on
the part of many young Japanese; if they read
our authors at all, they are apt to ask more
detailed questions, particularly about Fitzgerald, Hemingway, and Faulkner, than our undergraduates often do. If you have an opportunity
to teach a course in recent American literature
at any of Tokyo's colleges or universities, you
will find class discussions lively.

Other teaching opportunities abroad may be
found in UNESCO-sponsored schools, for which
you can consult the list of vacancies, updated
monthly, in most placement centers. There are
occasionally regular appointments available,
usually for an initial year or two with further

possibilities open, to teach American or British
literature in a college or university. For information about the latter, you can get names
and addresses of the fifty Tokyo colleges and
universities at the Japanese consulate in many
large cities. You can also consult placement
center listings for New Zealand universities
for a list of openings at any of them. For
teaching job advertisements in any of the British Commonwealth countries, look in Section IV
of the Sunday *New York Times,* and don't overlook
the "Education" columns in the London *Times
Literary Supplement.* [10]

Recruiters come to the West Coast college
and university placement centers at least twice
a year in search of teachers for Australian
secondary schools, and although neither the
Australian nor the New Zealand universities
send recruiters, the school representatives
can give inquirers considerable information
about their country's system of higher education, where to apply, and what specialties may
be in demand. The actual hiring for both Australian and New Zealand universities is largely
done by correspondence. Sometimes, however, a
faculty member on sabbatical leave from one of
these universities will be deputized to interview candidates for positions.

On the whole, American college teachers who
have gone recently to either Australia or New
Zealand send back favorable reports. Schools
and colleges have high standards but apparently
put less pressure on faculty, both in terms of
class schedules and of publication, than do
American ones. In New Zealand at least, tenure
may come sooner and with less personal stress
than it often does here. Faculties are cosmo-
politan, being a mix of persons from Canada,
the United States, England, South Africa, Australia, and New Zealand, plus a scattering from

continental Europe. Opportunities for research
in the national libraries are good. The main
disadvantage would appear to be a lower salary
scale than ours and the distance of Australia
and New Zealand from America and Europe.

All in all, almost any kind of teaching in
a foreign country is, as Victor Kolpacoff of
the University of Washington's English Department points out, an excellent thing to do just
after you finish a degree. You plunge directly
into teaching, sink or swim, and you have a
chance to see whether the classroom is where
you want to spend the rest of your professional
life.

ALTERNATIVE INSTITUTIONS AND PROGRAMS

Community Colleges

Now that the physical expansion of community
colleges has slowed down, the job crunch is as
pronounced there as it is everywhere else. As
one commentator puts it, "After a decade of
growth, suddenly the bloom is off the boom."[11]
Accordingly, full-time positions in English
at most community colleges are almost as hard
to come by as positions on the regular promotion ladder in four-year institutions, and for
various reasons they are much sought after.[12]
It is therefore only part-time community college teaching jobs that I am considering in the
category of "nontraditional teaching." These
positions too are becoming scarcer, although
opportunities to teach one or two sections of
English composition have been known to open up
during the last few days before each quarter
begins. Ideally, you should have your résumé
and letter of application in the hands of both
the English department chairman (or in some
colleges the humanities division chairman) and

the college's personnel office several months
in advance, but you should also be within reach
of the placement office just before and after
the beginning of a quarter. Changes in enroll-
ment sometimes mean that part-time teaching
vacancies can occur and be filled within a
single day.[13]

When you apply to teach in a community college, do remember that here, as everywhere, the
more individualized your letter is, the better.
Show in it that you know something of a particular college's aims and of its clientele. Do
not make the mistake of thinking that all community colleges are the same, or that all English courses they offer are vocationally
oriented or remedial. At Queensborough Community College, Bayside, New York, which has been
called "one of the best two-year colleges in
the nation," two-thirds of the student body
continue to four-year colleges and earn bachelor's degrees. Mort Young, commenting on educational standards nationwide, singles out
Queensborough as giving "academic courses on
a par with those given in four-year colleges."[14]
Other community colleges around the country,
among them Bellevue, Shoreline, and Green River
in the Puget Sound area, Foothills in the San
Francisco Bay area, and Columbia-Greene, Hudson, New York, to take only a few examples,
offer English courses comparable with those
given in the freshman and sophomore years of
four-year colleges.

Qualifications for community college teaching are ordinarily an M.A. plus two years'
teaching experience. Holders of Ph.D.'s are
acceptable, though not actively sought after.
Holders of masters of arts in teaching and of
the new degree of doctor of arts in teaching
are warmly welcomed. These official requirements are of course only the minimum. For

part-time no less than full-time instructors,
English departments are looking for people who
have not only excellent academic backgrounds
but a wide range of interests and a communicable
sense of the excitement of their subject.[15]

Those who have taught English in both four-
year and two-year colleges have often found
that there is less difference between the two
kinds of schools than one might imagine. In
the community college (and again, I am talking
now about the ones in or near a large city) you
will find that classes are lively; your English
colleagues are enlightened; and academic standards can be exactly as high as the instructor
chooses to make them.

The one serious flaw in the community college rationale in many areas of the country,
according to those who have taught in one, is
the funding structure. Because of the relationship of the individual colleges to the statewide
system, a potential financial crisis always
looms ahead. As the administrators of many
community colleges interpret the financial picture, the colleges' instructional budget can
best be balanced by hiring half or two-thirds
of each faculty on a part-time, quarter-to-
quarter basis, with hourly wages, for "class
contact hours" only. At one Puget Sound area
community college, there are usually around 220
part-time faculty members and 80 full-time ones,
including administrators. Many of the part-time
faculty have considerable experience; all those
who teach the college transfer courses have
M.A.'s, and a number are Ph.D. candidates or
hold Ph.D.'s; yet neither their professional
qualifications nor their successful teaching
can lift them out of the expendable part-time
category when instructional funds are lacking.[16]

Despite this critical drawback, you may
find part-time teaching in a community college

extremely satisfying because of your colleagues
and because of the close contacts with students
made possible through small group discussions
and frequent individual conferences. And the
community colleges' philosophy of trying first
and foremost to reduce the distance between the
student and the subject matter can lead to valuable insights for any instructor, experienced
or inexperienced.

Continuing Education
Courses at Four-year Institutions

Few if any continuing education programs,
whether at a community college, a four-year
college, a university, or New York's New School
for Social Research, have full-time teaching
opportunities. At the University of Washington,
as at most state universities, appointments to
teach must be approved both by the appropriate
academic department and by those in charge of
the noncredit studies curriculum. Qualifications for noncredit course teaching often
involve having a Ph.D. or at least an M.A.
(for those teaching academic subjects), plus
considerable experience in teaching adults. In
short, as Constance Wells, director of noncredit
studies at the University of Washington puts it,
you need to be full of "*informed* enthusiasm for
your subject."[17]
While the salary for this type of teaching
is, like that at the community colleges, paid
at the "class contact hour" rate, there is
somewhat less chance that instructors will put
in what amounts to full-time work for part-time
pay. With most noncredit courses there are no
department meetings to attend, no grades to
give, and only a few conferences--those volun-
tarily arranged by the instructors of special
classes such as writing workshops.

Courses in the credit divisions of most universities tend to be taught by their regular faculty members. To apply to teach in one of them, first study the catalogue and the quarterly lists of current offerings; then plan a course or several alternative ones not already given that you would like to give. Include a prospectus of such courses with a letter of application, and take or send it with your résumé to the director of continuing education of the institutions which interest you.

There are also from time to time a number of vacancies among full-time administrative positions in continuing education and elsewhere. Such positions, involving directing or coordinating all the continuing education programs of an institution, are listed in college placement centers in nearly every issue of the *Chronicle of Higher Education,* and often in Section IV of the Sunday *New York Times.* There will be an expansion of such programs in the next decade, Wells predicts. In similar vein, the authors of "All Education Is 'Adult Education'" point out in the *AAUP Bulletin* that even now there are all over the country "proportionally fewer college students of traditional college age [than there were thirty years ago] and more adults of twenty-five and over."[18]

In-service Courses

Although the typical continuing education course draws its clientele from the general public, there is a growing trend among business and professional groups toward sponsoring courses in writing or communications for their members. The Boeing Company has given in-service courses in expository writing and in English as a second language to groups of employees. The U.S. Civil Service Commission in

Seattle has two full-time staff persons, one of
them an English M.A., who co-ordinate short
courses and workshops in writing for government
employees in the Puget Sound area. Other civil
service regions have similar staffs and programs.

Other in-service courses are held on university campuses for classified and exempt staff
employees. The University of Washington program includes report writing and other classes,
for which instructors, some of them graduate
students or recent recipients of degrees in
English, are hired on contract.

Actually there are many expanding possibilities. New York City, Chicago, Boston, and
Cambridge all have a number of such workshops
and courses, some sponsored by adult education
centers and others by government agencies or
businesses. In downtown Seattle a new institution, City College, offers English teachers a
chance to teach college English to people
already engaged in a business or profession,
as do the Seattle Campus of the University of
Puget Sound and the Sand Point Naval Base.
There are some newly funded short-term teaching
opportunities too under the Comprehensive Education and Training Act (CETA); these positions
offer the challenge of teaching writing or literature to a wide range of persons not usually
served by college instructors. [19]

There are other groups, too, not often
taught by college English instructors until
now, because the need has only recently been
recognized. Within and without the university
community, groups of professionals--physicians,
health services planners, graduate nurses,
psychiatrists, and others--are beginning to
hire instructors to design and teach classes
for them in expository writing, academic and
professional article writing, and related
areas. These people need no further academic

credit; they are highly trained in their own
fields, even though relatively inexperienced
in writing. They realize that they need practice, and they are willing to pay for individualized instruction in small groups.[20]

Today the emphasis in adult writing classes
has changed considerably from the former remedial one. For example, in a university community, physicians, professors of fisheries,
education, or engineering, and staff members
working on documents and procedures for the
academic administration, as well as others
editing journals--all these and other professional people, some with Ph.D.'s--have been
students recently in noncredit writing classes.
Some of them are specialists in one or another
of the natural sciences who have found themselves editing journals without being sure what
criteria they should use for the revision of
articles submitted to them. Others have been
physicians whose accelerated undergraduate programs allowed them no writing courses, yet
their awareness of style makes them hope to
avoid their colleagues' overuse of jargon.

Such students come to class not only to
hear what the instructor has to say about points
of usage and organization but also to find a
much-needed forum where they can share concerns
and exchange comments about their problems in
writing and editing. Instructors of such
courses enjoy the rare privilege of seeing that
what they teach matters "out there, in the real
world."

Other kinds of courses for nonmatriculated
students are being talked of, and in some cases
implemented. As a former U.S. commissioner of
education pointed out not long ago, the 1960s
were the days of physical expansion of campuses,
while the budget cutbacks of the 1970s may give
educators a chance to forget about bricks and

mortar and reach out beyond their campuses to
people who simply want to learn, wherever they
are.[21]

In such a spirit, Yale, Dartmouth, Swarthmore, and many other institutions are offering
to their graduates annual short courses and
conferences, sometimes called "Alumni Colleges,"
often held far from the parent campus in cities
centrally located where there are enough alumni
to warrant them. Someone has to design the
curricula for such courses, to work out the
reading lists, to co-ordinate the details. If
you have already had some experience with continuing education, why shouldn't you get in
touch with your own undergraduate college, or
with some other institution which hasn't yet
offered such a program, and see whether you can
be the one to do the planning?

Another kind of teaching opportunity that
would fit in with this growing widespread urge
to cut through the red tape of registration,
matriculation, and credits lies in a trend
toward the establishment of drop-in centers
for individualized instruction in writing.
These centers, variously known as writing
clinics, individual development centers, or
writing workshops, are being tentatively set
up at some of the community colleges in the
Puget Sound area and elsewhere. They have
several points in their favor: they exemplify
the unstructured, problem-focused kind of writing instruction which Kurt Vonnegut, Jr., has
recently proposed as the only really useful
kind;[22] they draw students when they are
struggling with a specific writing dilemma
and are naturally most receptive to help; and,
since these centers have the magic aura of
"innovativeness" about them, they are sometimes
more apt to receive funding than is a regular
instructional budget.[23]

Other new types of extension programs, sometimes called "universities without walls," are
talked of glowingly by nearly every community
college administrator. The concept has been
implemented by Whatcom County Community College,
Washington, a two-year college designed to be
without classroom instruction or a resident
faculty. At the four-year level, Dr. William D.
Rearick, vice-president of Seattle Pacific
College, has recently endorsed a similar plan.
He feels, as he said on September 12, 1975, at
a faculty retreat, that "there has been too
much emphasis upon degree programs and upon the
matriculated student. We need to recognize and
cultivate programs . . . for non-degree learning."[24]

In somewhat the same spirit, Antioch College
in Ohio has just announced a fairly ambitious
program of granting "external degrees" for academic work done in various cities throughout the
country and supervised by persons affiliated
with Antioch. Other colleges are expected to
follow suit in the near future. Provided that
you have already gained some conventional academic teaching experience *and* provided that you
really see the value and possibilities of this
kind of course, there might be a chance for you
to become involved in teaching some of them.

Here, of course, as with many alternative
jobs, there is no neat list of vacancies to
apply for. The administrator probably will
not realize how useful you could be until you
turn up with a sheaf of program ideas and a
résumé showing good academic credentials. If
your record also demonstrated some successful
experience in teaching in untraditional settings, it could be very persuasive.

In themselves, part-time alternative positions can be immensely satisfying. At the same
time, it is essential to look ahead and see

where they may lead. According to evidence con-
tinually coming in to the various placement
centers, in the world of college teaching even
hard work, excellent credentials, good student
ratings, and the support of your department may
not be enough to win you advancement from part-
time to full-time status *at the same institution*. Although such a promotion *can* take place,
it is statistically unlikely, and the worsening
state of instructional budgets makes it even
less likely in the near future.[25] So, instead
of pinning your hopes on gaining a full-time
position at a place where there may never be
sufficient funds in the budget, why not see how
you can deliberately turn your part-time or
peripheral experience to your advantage in other
ways? Otherwise there is always the danger that
your sense of hard work unrewarded may lead you
into a chronic state of frustration or, as
social workers put it, into becoming "an in-
justice collector."

Instead, however, you can look upon these
alternatives as transitional stages in your
career, stages which in various ways can contribute to or even shape what you do later.

First of all, part-time teaching will provide you with a sense of continuity with your
graduate work and teaching. Even if you decide
to switch to a nonteaching field for your main
employment, the challenge of meeting a college
literature or writing class once or twice a
week can give the focus to your reading and
thinking and the chance to interact with students that is important to anyone who enjoys
teaching.[26] If, on the other hand, you are
trying to wait out the job crisis until more
teaching openings come along, you will find it
better for your morale to be teaching at the
college level, though but one course, than not
at all. Certainly if you are teaching a single

course and enjoying it, you are automatically more employable than you would be if you were completely out of a job.[27]

Again, through one of the ironies in which the whole employment situation abounds, while part-time or extension teaching will not often lead to a salaried, full-time position at the institution where you are, it can sometimes lead to job offers from other places.[28] When someone from another institution is interviewing you, the mere fact that you have successfully taught certain courses can seem more important than your status while teaching them.

Fourth, many of these alternative jobs give you great latitude to experiment, to work out your own course plans and materials, to rethink old courses or try out new ones. It is easier to do this in situations where you feel that your stay is temporary than during your early years in a full-time position, where you may be concerned about departmental approbation every step of the way.[29]

Still another advantage of some of these teaching alternatives is that they may bring you a new point of view or a new interest. Teaching English as a second language, for example, whether you do it here or abroad, will probably involve you in so many questions from your students about rules that you may have taken for granted, and about exceptions to those rules, that class discussions will stimulate or renew your own interest in grammar and linguistics.

It is also possible that experiences in alternative teaching may lead to writing that would be professionally helpful. If you teach English or American literature abroad, the contrast between the way you think of the authors you teach and the way students from a different cultural tradition see them could suggest a

number of articles for you to write. If you
teach English as a foreign language, the improvements in methods or materials which occur
to you may lead to your writing a new textbook
or designing one of the "self-paced instructional packages" currently welcomed by educational publishers. Again, wherever you teach
abroad, you may be lucky enough to find materials for research involving English or American
authors who have had some connection with the
region, or whose manuscripts or early editions
have been gathered there in a library.[30]

If, however, you are teaching continuing
education courses, the issues raised by the
needs and expectations of your adult students
and by your attempts to meet those needs could
result in your originating a new text, or in
writing articles for such journals as *College
Composition and Communication* and *College English* about the issues involved. Or, conceivably, you might eventually develop your own
courses and your own clientele, so that such
an enterprise turns into a career. In Seattle,
Gordon and Mary Anne Mauerman have accomplished
this during the past seven years with their private adult school, The Writing Shop. Similar
independent writing programs flourish as summer
workshops at Port Townsend, Washington, at
Penticton, British Columbia, at Banff, and
elsewhere.[31]

Finally, some of these alternative formats
for teaching may contribute, directly or indirectly, to nonteaching careers. Several
years of teaching in another culture could be
an asset in your attempt to enter into such
positions as a foreign student counselor, a
minority affairs counselor, or an Affirmative
Action staff member on a college campus. Your
overseas teaching might also be a preparatory
step for a position with the central Fulbright

Scholarship Office in Washington, D.C., or the
American Field Service Committee, or the Con-
sular Service, or indeed for almost any position
involving working with people of differing backgrounds and traditions. If you are applying to
business firms with overseas branches, it would
interest them to know that you had lived and
worked successfully for a year or two outside
of the continental United States.

Likewise, teaching technical writing or
editing could lead to doing such writing, editing, or consulting for business or industry
(see Chapter 11). Teaching courses designed
from the feminist point of view would help prepare you for an administrative position in one
of the expanding women's studies programs or
departments. Having taught in community colleges or in continuing education programs and
having become thoroughly familiar with their
clientele could help qualify you as a student
services counselor (working in a placement or
financial aids office, for example) at a two-
year or four-year college, or perhaps a member
of the college relations office of a university.
Again, depending upon your other experience,
teaching in such programs might help you toward
a position in a publishing firm specializing in
innovative textbooks and programs.

Then too, such experience might also help
prepare you to direct a continuing education
program. People looking toward an administrative career in this field should certainly have
demonstrated successful teaching in continuing
education. In addition, says one university's
director of noncredit studies, ideally

> they should have language skills and
> a strong academic background, as well
> as experience in one or more of the
> following fields: publicity, media,

educational research, management,
market research, or counseling.
They should be keenly observant of
what the population is like, and
willing to experiment with uncon-
ventional formats for courses without
feeling that in so doing they are inevitably lowering their standards.[32]

Finally, some readers of this handbook may be
glad to know that an increasing need is just
now being projected for continuing education
administrators and staff members with advanced
degrees not, as formerly, in education or educational administration but in the various
subject disciplines.[33]

CHAPTER 6

A Campus Is Not Only for Teaching

. . . You may find that, for one reason
or another, you have neglected to consider a route or position for which you
are qualified. The question to ask
about every channel, therefore, is
"why not?" You may discover that more
paths are open to you than you had
thought possible.--Margaret V. Higginson
and Thomas Quick, *The Ambitious Woman's
Guide to a Successful Career*

Of the approximately 10,000 employees of the
University of Washington, there are some 3,000
faculty members and 7,000 staff members. On
the campuses of smaller private colleges the
proportions differ: Wheaton College in Massachusetts has about 112 faculty members and 136
staff, and Linfield College in Oregon has about
80 faculty members and 80 staff.[1]
Very often it is staff members who represent the institution to the public. As a dean
of a west coast liberal arts college points
out, it is members of the staff rather than the
faculty members who on the whole are responsible
for internal and external communications, explaining what the various parts of the institu-

tion are doing. It is staff members who help
students decide what courses they should take
as undergraduates, how they can best finance
their education, and, often, what positions they
should hunt for after graduation. On university
campuses it is often staff members who implement
college or university policy in specific instances, as, for example, determining what students, under the faculty rules, can be admitted
to the graduate and undergraduate schools.

Staff jobs, then, although different in
methods and focus from teaching ones, need not
be considered unimportant, dull, or divergent
from the ongoing goals of the university. And,
since a number of staff positions attract people
with advanced degrees and many others involve
considerable knowledge of the academic world,[2]
the weekly or biweekly bulletins of the staff
employment office of the educational institutions in your neighborhood are certainly worth
your continuous attention. Unlike teaching positions, staff positions may become vacant at
any time of the year and may be filled at any
time--usually from three to four weeks after
the deadline for receiving applications has
closed, although special circumstances may make
"exempt" positions take longer.[3]

It must be admitted that nonacademic staff
jobs are not for everyone. As Donna Martyn of
the Harvard Placement Office has observed,
those who do best at these jobs are apt to have
gotten a start as undergraduates by "picking up
little bits and pieces of administrative experience,"[4] as dormitory or house tutors, class
officers, or members of campus business enter-
prises. Then too, there is the question of
how plentiful nonacademic staff positions are
these days. At a small college, as Prof. Neal
Woodruff of Coe College warns, the number of
such jobs can fluctuate widely with the ups and

downs of the budget. On the other hand, as
William Bliss points out, "a big institution
will have a lot of jobs; Yale is now the largest
employer in New Haven."[5]

The following brief survey of typical college and university offices and of some of the
staff positions connected with them touches on
merely a few high points of several representative types of positions on public and private
campuses. Although the titles differ from campus to campus, jobs like these open up at times
at most universities, four-year colleges, and
community colleges.

Academic adviser. To apply, you should
have a bachelor's and a master's degree, one
or both from the school to which you are applying, and it will of course be an advantage if
you have teaching and advising or counseling
experience. Currently, academic advisers sometimes hold Ph.D.'s. You must have the ability
to retain, apply, and communicate a complicated
set of rules and requirements as you deal on a
one-to-one basis with students and their quan-
daries about their academic programs. Obviously
it will help you both get and hold such a position if you enjoy conferring with students and
if you see what you accomplish thereby as being
important.

Documents and procedures analyst. According
to the job specifications for a "Procedures
Analyst I" at a large university, this position
requires one to "perform the research, analysis,
and writing necessary to produce basic operating
procedures" for the administration of the university. One may also "assist in writing and
editing statements of administrative policy."
Applicants must have at least a B.A. with emphasis in business, communications, public
administration, or a related field. Obviously,
English can be considered a "related field."

An "Analyst II" should in addition be able
to "develop varied and complex policy statements; . . . analyze and design forms used in
conjunction with procedures." According to
a staff member of the Documents and Procedures
Office at the University of Washington, "a
successful Procedures Analyst must (1) think
clearly; (2) write concisely; (3) relate well
to other people; (4) have some understanding of
business administration concepts; (5) be able
to see both the forest and the trees."[6] The
fourth criterion, incidentally, need not rule
out people with backgrounds in English.

Editor. Persons applying for jobs under
this category may work on a college or university internal newsletter, on public relations
assignments interpreting the university to the
media or directly to the community; they may
work on a scholarly journal as assistant to a
faculty member, or may be the project editor
assisting a principal investigator who has a
government grant or contract. In many states,
editors under the state civil service systems
have grades of I, II, III, and occasionally IV.
A few others working for departments of health
sciences or health services in some universi-
ies have the status of nonteaching faculty
rather than of staff. For individual job requirements, see the specific job advertisements
in the staff employment bulletin in the college
or university nearest you. For comments from
representative editors, see Chapter 8. In general, writing ability, an eye for detail, and
an ability to organize are the main qualifications. Several campus editors who responded to
the survey described in Chapter 8 hold English
Ph.D.'s, and a good many have M.A.'s in English
or communications.

Employment representative. At many staff
employment offices there are people who inter-

view candidates for certain jobs after they have
passed through the preliminary screening process
for various types and levels of campus employment. Representatives for "professional and
supervisory classifications" should have had
some graduate work and/or professional experience. Holders of an M.A. in English might do
well in these positions, even though no such
training is required.

Financial aids counselor. In this job, one
interviews students with financial problems,
helps them determine their eligibility under
the various university, state, and federal rules
for student aid, and assists them in finding
alternative sources of help. A counselor who
worked in this office at the University of Washington for a year after receiving an M.A. and
before moving to the Placement Center reports
that it was an extremely interesting job for
anyone who enjoys dealing with individual students on a short-term basis.

Grants and contracts office staff members.
People in this type of office help faculty
members and administrators with the writing of
grant proposals and the obtaining and administering of grants and contracts from the federal
government and from foundations. Ability to
write clear expository prose and to analyze
statements is one of the main requirements for
these positions. The University of Washington
Grants and Contracts Office has five people on
its staff, each of whom came to it with a quite
different background, one of them with a graduate degree in English. Since the whole field
of grant-writing and administration is a new
one, and since most of what is done must be
learned on the job, there are no prescribed
requirements.

Information specialist. This position in
its various grades is not always very clearly

differentiated from that of editor. Its main
duties consist of gathering and writing up material bearing upon the activities of a segment
of a university, such as the university hospital, or a single department, such as an educational assessment center.[7] Those who come to
such positions with a background in English
tend to feel that it is far from wasted, as
several information specialists point out in
Chapter 8.

Minority affairs counselor. If you have
had experience working with minority groups here
or overseas, and particularly if you are a
member of a minority group, you might look
into any minority affairs vacancy which comes
up. It would help in such a position to have
the writing, analytical, and speaking skills
which you will have developed through your work
in English.

Placement counselor. At the placement centers of most universities and many colleges
there is a staff of several counselors in addition to the director. Usually each counselor
concentrates upon one or two kinds of jobs:
college and university teaching and alternative
positions; liberal arts and public service
vocations; secondary education and library
positions; primary school teaching; or scientific and technical positions. Much of the
counselor's work involves skills which graduate
students and instructors of English would have
had a chance to develop. As a placement counselor, you would listen to job candidates who
came to your office; you would direct them to
resources within the placement center, the
libraries, elsewhere on your campus, or elsewhere in the community. Most of all, you would
try (without assuming the role of a clinical
counselor) to help applicants to take advantage
of resources within their own experience and

education which they might have overlooked. You
would write statements and reports of many
kinds, correspond with candidates, and evaluate
the written recommendations in candidates' con-
fidential files. Finally, you would give talks
to small groups of students about the placement
and job-seeking process.

If you enjoy interacting with a wide range
of people, and if you find satisfaction in ex-
pressing yourself in speaking and writing even
though the end product never appears in published form, you may find being a placement
counselor absorbing. It can call upon nearly
all the qualities which you have been using in
teaching, and it can help develop further many
of your best energies and talents.[8]

Publications office. Most large universities have editorial and printing facilities for
university publications such as catalogues,
brochures, timetables, directories, and newsletters. By working in one of these offices in
any capacity, including a secretarial position,
you would learn a great deal about graphics,
page format, layout, and typography which could
be extremely helpful if your ultimate goal is a
job with a publishing house (see Chapter 10).
The same point applies to any kind of work you
might secure in a university press.

School and college relations office. Since
the function of this branch of a university is
to create liaison among schools, colleges, and
the university, members of its staff must be
able to speak easily before groups, write reports, plan public relations, and interpret a
university's requirements to students as well
as to high school faculty and administrators.
If you feel comfortable in dealing with the extensive details of course distribution requirements, entrance requirements, and the like, you
might find this work extremely interesting.

Women's programs in continuing education.
These offices, increasingly common on college
and university campuses, not only counsel individual women students (and particularly older
women who have returned to the campus after a
long interval) but act as resource centers for
the vocational or personal concerns of any woman
student. They also sponsor several courses in
which English instructors help students explore
literature with an emphasis on its personal
impact. There are several opportunities for
people with graduate work in English here, and
more resource centers for women are opening up,
under different names, in four-year and two-
year colleges.

On the whole, there are several elements
of your English undergraduate, graduate school,
or teaching background that could be applicable
to various staff positions. First, your
information-gathering and interpreting techniques, even though originally designed for
other materials, can be useful here. Second,
your writing ability will be extremely helpful.
You can write clearly and concisely, help others
to do this, and compose reports, policy statements, and news releases.
Moreover, if you have been an English
teacher, you will have learned to talk easily
before groups of people in class, as well as
with individuals who come to your office hoping
that you will solve their problems. Finally,
you will have learned, through regular conferences with students, how to offer information
and to explore alternatives with others, while
at the same time leaving the problem-solving
initiative with the students themselves. It
is this tightrope which all student service
counselors and many other university staff members must always walk.

To apply for such positions, you must be sure to look at the staff employment bulletin or its equivalent on your campus the day it comes out, each time it appears. After finding out where the vacancies are, you are ready for the routine of making an application, as outlined in Chapter 3.

You may, it is true, sometimes find a few positions with rather fluid job descriptions and less formal rites of entry. "Temporary" positions for instance, or innovative or newly funded ones, may from time to time be filled simply because someone in authority has administrative needs which he or she finds you are qualified to help meet. It was this kind of many-faceted job that Ellen Messer-Davidow, a doctoral candidate in English with a background in writing and in working for social change, found herself holding when she became communications coordinator and one of the special assistants to the president of a midwestern university. There she has applied the research and problem-solving skills she developed in graduate school to working on internal and external communications for the administration, serving on a task force making a ten-year financial study of the institution, carrying on staff work for a national administrative search, and doing review and recommendations on policy.

Messer-Davidow and others with degrees in English have found personal satisfactions in holding a staff job.[9] It can be interesting to see from a new vantage point how a college or university works. It can be satisfying to feel that you have some hand in carrying out policy and representing an institution to the public. It is also instructive to join the eight-to-five world in which most people outside of college teaching live and work. And, once

you are on the staff of a college or university,
you are apt to hear easily about other openings
to which you can move. Professionally, the main
advantage is probably that some of this experience will help qualify you for a wider spectrum
of subsequent positions in college administration, business, government agencies, or
publishing.

CHAPTER 7

Free-lance Editing

Take the manuscript of a book. Set it
firmly upon a desk or table so that it
cannot slip or slide. Pick up a pencil.
Start reading through the manuscript,
and as you read correct typographical
errors and note passages that may con-
fuse a reader and usages that may cause
trouble for a printer. You are doing
copy editing. . . . If the task sounds
easy, you do not understand it. There
are many complications, not the least
of them being that it is a task without thoroughly set limits. . . .--
William Bridgwater, editor-in-chief of
the Columbia University Press, *Editors
on Editing*

The term "editing" is a catch-all. To some
people it means the process of mechanically
correcting spelling, punctuation, and typographical errors which Bridgwater touches upon
in the first part of the comment quoted above.[1]
To others, editing calls up visions of Maxwell
Perkins' role as midwife to the manuscripts of
Thomas Wolfe's novels.

Throughout this section, the word "editing"
will indicate the kind of work done through one
or two arrangements: either directly assisting
an author by helping him or her revise a manuscript before sending it to a publisher or,
instead, working for a publisher on an already
accepted manuscript.

"But how do I get to be a free-lance editor?" you may ask. "Do I, as an English major
or graduate student, already know enough to be
one, or are there special kinds of expertise
that I have to acquire? If there are, where
and how would I learn them?"

If you have found satisfaction not only in
writing but in revising and improving your
undergraduate or graduate papers until they
are exactly the way you want them, if you really
enjoy rearranging sentences and seeing that
there are transitions between paragraphs, you
probably have a certain aptitude for editing.
If in addition you have been a teaching assistant or instructor in freshman composition or
other writing classes, you have probably tried
to help your students learn to become their own
editors; so you may find that you do for the
writing of adults in various fields what you
have tried to get your students to do for themselves. The more deeply involved you become
with editing, the more you will learn.

There are good courses in editing available,
some of them in continuing education programs
and others as part of writing and editing sequences such as the ones at the University of
Virginia, Pennsylvania State University, North
Carolina State University, the University of
Puget Sound in Tacoma, Washington, the University of Redlands in California.[2] Technical
editing, too, is often taught in conjunction
with technical writing. There is a growing
demand for these courses. Yet many editors

when queried say that they have learned most of
their craft on the job. "Each manuscript I deal
with is unique," writes a free-lance editor with
eight years' experience, "and I've learned what
I know now largely through wrestling with the
problems each one presents, looking at authori-
ties such as *Words into Type* or The University
of Chicago *Manual of Style* to see what they
suggest, then turning to books already published
in the field in which I'm editing so as to see
how they apply the style books' principles."

In any case, if you hope to get started as
an editor who works directly with authors, you
will need to widen the circle of writers and
researchers you know and to be systematic about
turning your editing skill into a professional
activity instead of a casual favor for a friend.
In any university community and in most cities
there are experts in their own professions who
realize that their manuscripts need editorial
help with problems ranging from organization
and style to punctuation, footnote form, and
other details of copy editing. Many physicians,
nurses, social workers, sociologists, urban
planners, and others would like such help. In
particular, as Barbara Cox points out in her
article, "The Author's Editor,"

> most scientists who publish in profes-
> sional journals work for large insti-
> tutions, especially university medical
> centers. The physician in a large
> medical center may see patients most
> of the time, and the basic scientist
> may spend the largest part of his
> time in the laboratory, but each must
> write if he is to reach out to his
> colleagues. . . . Yet . . . the aver-
> age scientist is not trained to write.
> Consequently, he tends to tackle the

> job inefficiently. . . . Writing in-
> volves a linear thought process,
> wherein the words are placed on paper
> by a system of priority. Yet many
> scientists are relatively nonverbal.[3]

At first, of course, scientific writing may
make you hesitate. Some of the terms may seem
formidable, the journals may often prescribe
what may strike you as a rigid formula for organization, and these periodicals' ways of
citing references may come as a surprise to
someone used to the MLA Style Sheet. Indeed,
the whole enterprise may seem alien to you.
But look into it a bit before you dismiss the
possibility. The scientists are asking for a
nonspecialist to read their work to see that it
reads clearly, that the structure is logical,
and that there are transitions whenever needed.
The nonspecialist is extremely useful, as well,
in detecting and eliminating redundancy.

Actually, once you start exploring the growing body of articles and manuals dealing with
scientific and medical writing, you may be surprised at how often the familiar precepts of
Strunk and White's Elements of Style are in-
voked. The further involved you get with scientific articles, the more you will find that
their authors are presenting you with the same
problems which beset nearly all writing: the
ongoing struggle of every writer toward clarity,
flow, emphasis, interest, and ultimate
readability.[4]

Of course, not all your clients will be
scientists. Some will be planners, educators,
or people from one of the other professions
whose language has become so inflated and confused that, according to Edwin Newman, we now
live in

a world in which things that are good
for society are positive externalities
and things that are bad are negative
externalities, in which unemployment
is classified as an adverse social con-
sequence, . . . rationing becomes end-
use allocation, stressful situations
arise in the nuclear or matrifocal
family, and people in minigroups or,
if the shoe fits, maxigroups are in a
state of cognitive inertia because
self-actualization is lacking.[5]

Fortunately, many professional people caught up
in jargon of this kind have begun to realize
that their language needs help. And a good
editor *can* help--not only with an individual
manuscript but often with long-term writing
problems.[6]

In addition to scientists, planners, educators, and members of other professions, you may
attract nonacademic clients too. "An editor,"
as Helen Taylor of the Viking Press points out,
"is a plastic surgeon to books by 'unprofes-
sional' writers. Book writing these days isn't
limited to people trained in literary matters.
That's where the editor comes in. It is he who
cuts . . . dead wood, organizes and tightens,
reshapes sentences, puts in the grammar and
punctuation, and still retains the author's
book too, though the author often doubts it
while the process is going on."[7]

If you are interested in such work, whether
for academic or nonacademic writers, your next
step, after telling writers you know that you
enjoy editing manuscripts and are qualified to
do so professionally, might be to place ads in
the student newspaper of the college or university nearest you, to leave word with depart-

mental secretaries about the services you offer, and to put notices on bulletin boards of offices where writing is done. Once you have completed your first half-dozen editing jobs, colleagues and friends of your clients should have heard about you, and you may soon find that you have taken on a specialty and an identity.

There are problems, of course; editing is not all clear sailing. You will usually need to have a preliminary conference with the author to see what his expectations are and whether they mesh with yours. With some clients you may have to spell out the point that you are not ghost-writing, offering secretarial services, or acting as a literary agent. In your own interest, too, you should evaluate the manuscript carefully to be sure that the author's problems actually are those of exposition and of mechanics rather than ones involving the methods of a quantitative discipline in which you are untrained.

It is a good idea to do a one- or two-page sample of copy editing to show to the author before either one of you commits yourself to a long-term arrangement. It is of course your responsibility to arrange with the author the rates and times of payment. A recent book by Carol L. O'Neill and Avima Ruder, *The Complete Guide to Editorial Freelancing*, offers advice about the practical details involved.[8]

If you decide to do free-lance editing, probably one question that will occur to you as you sit with your first manuscript spread out before you is that of your role, your relationship to the author and his or her material. Will your own interest in writing, your experience with undergraduate or graduate papers and perhaps many other kinds of writing, help or hinder you? May your own sense of style lead

you to make individualistic changes in the
manuscript?

There *is* this danger. You should keep in
mind the succinct advice of Francess Halpenny
of the University of Toronto Press that "it is
one of the oddities of the editorial function
that it is most successful when it is least
observed."[9] Halpenny's warning was echoed recently by Emily Johnson, who through her years
as director of scholarly journals at the University of Washington often served as unofficial
liaison between writers and copy editors. In
particular, as she enjoined a group of copy
editors to whom she spoke, editors should remember that their function is to

> read the author's manuscript thought-
> fully, first going over it as a whole,
> scrutinizing sentence structure, gaps
> in thought, transitions, agreement of
> text with charts and graphs, overuse
> of jargon. . . . You must be able to
> say "I am nothing," for really, you
> *aren't* anything on that editing
> job. . . . Your job is not to get the
> author's ideas expressed in the most
> beautiful words possible; it is to
> see that he says what he has to say
> with the fewest obstacles in between
> him and the reader. The hardest thing
> about training editors is to get them
> to respect someone else's by-line.
> They've got to learn that they aren't
> supposed to function as creative
> writers; they should just get their
> satisfaction in being paid for their
> work--and, if they're lucky, in find-
> ing that the author has given them a
> kind word in the Acknowledgments.[10]

In case you feel that such words represent
an exceedingly austere ideal, you may want to
look again at Barbara Cox's discussion of what
the "author's editor" should do and be. Viewing the author-editor relationship as a sym-
biotic one, she suggests that "the mere availability of an editor does not guarantee his
usefulness. . . . A creative interaction must
take place between author and editor, and this
is a learned process."[11] Author and editor
should definitely meet together, Cox thinks, so
that the editor can clarify any of the major
objectives of the manuscript which may not have
emerged unmistakably from the text. As a result, the editor can if necessary carry out
"intensive analysis and revision—ranging from
necessary organizational changes to simple
grammatical corrections." Eventually the author
and the editor "become [so] familiar with each
other's work styles," that in the end "the
written product represents the synthesis of two
minds—the professional scientist and the professional communicator."[12]

There is, of course, no one ideal stance
for the copy editor. Although if you become
one you will usually subordinate yourself as
completely as Halpenny and Johnson suggest,
occasionally, depending upon the nature of the
writing project and the extent of your experience, you and the author may achieve the de-
sired working synthesis Cox describes.

Yet no matter how good your rapport with
your author may be, you will find that free-
lance editing is the kind of work you do on your
own, without colleagues around you, or a fixed
daily schedule to keep. Some free-lancers enjoy
this independence; others, wanting to have peers
to consult with and some sense of belonging to
a professional organization, form partnerships
or groups. In the *Literary Market Place*

there is a listing of many such groups. Although there are predictably more in the New
York City area than elsewhere, no part of the
country is without them. Some of them special-
ize, among them the Academic Marketplace, Inc.,
Lavallette, New Jersey; Effective Learning,
Inc., Mt. Vernon, New York; and Mathco, Rock-
port, Massachusetts. Others, such as the Associated Editors, of Stamford, Connecticut, the
Author Aid Associates of New York City, Edit-
cetera of Berkeley, Editorial Services of La-
conia, New Hampshire, the Broome Agency, Inc.,
of Sarasota, Florida, and Edit, Inc., of Chicago, Illinois, deal with a wide range of manuscripts, as do the three whose staff members I
know, Haskells Editorial Services and Editorial
Consultants, Inc., of Seattle and Editorial
Associates of Palo Alto.[13] The diversity of
groups suggests that there is considerable need
for such services. The apparently short life
span of some of them, however--to judge from
changes in their listing in the *Literary Market
Place* from one year to the next--suggests that
these consulting services could benefit from
members with, in addition to their knowledge of
editing, practical experience in advertising,
public relations, and marketing.

  The Complete Guide to Editorial Freelancing
deals intensively with the second kind of free-
lance editing touched upon at the beginning of
this section, the one in which the editor does
not work for the author but for one or several
publishers. Usually such copy editing is done
at an hourly rate on manuscripts the publisher
sends the free-lancer.[14]

  Although most publishing companies have
staff members who do the bulk of the copy editing, proofreading, and indexing, many of the
larger houses also have a list of free-lancers
on call. In this way the publishers save money

by having extra part-time staff available at
peak seasons; moreover, they have a large talent
pool representing different fields of special
knowledge.[15]

To find such a copy editing job, you should
send to publishers a letter of inquiry, including a brief résumé which emphasizes any special
field of knowledge you have and any credentials
relevant to editing, i.e., work on publications
or experience teaching English in high school
or college. If, having spent some time as an
"author's editor," you can cite several published authors for whom you have worked, you
may be in a strong position to get a manuscript
sent you for editing, on trial. In O'Neill's
and Ruder's book there is a detailed yet enter-
taining treatment of the paths of entry, the
pitfalls to avoid, and the pleasures of such
editing.

If you succeed in getting on a publisher's
free-lance list, the chief measure of your
success will be your receiving more assignments
from the publishers. You may also be asked not
only to copy-edit but to proofread and, occasionally, to do research, write captions, compose jacket copy, or make an index.

As a matter of fact, indexing, though sometimes included as a part of the copy editing
process, is a specialty in its own right and
deserves a word of explanation for those who
are interested yet have never been involved in
it. At first it may seem deceptively simple
to index a scholarly book of about three hundred pages. You need merely to have available
your full working days for approximately a
week, several packs of 3x5 file cards and alpha-
betical dividers, a good-sized table on which to
spread out and classify the entries as you make
them, and a copy of Sina Spiker's pamphlet,
Indexing Your Book.[16] You will, incidentally,

also need excellent eyesight and unflappable nerves.

By the time you have gone through the successive steps which Spiker explains, have made perhaps a thousand small decisions, have typed up the final entries from your cards, and have spot-checked them by using the index yourself, you may well agree that the operation is no simple or mechanical one. For one thing, the time element introduces a sense of urgency into the whole proceeding, for the publisher's deadlines usually allow only a week, or at the most two, to be spent indexing a single volume. This time crunch arises because it is obviously impractical to begin an index until the page proofs arrive from the publisher, but by that time other phases of production are so nearly complete that the publisher seldom can wait long for the index without seriously threatening his schedule for completing the book you are working on, and sometimes those stacked up behind it as well.

Despite these constraints, indexing offers certain challenges and satisfactions. And both indexing and free-lance editing can be modestly lucrative as well as interesting for those of you who are addicted to everything connected with the written word.[17]

Although you will never become rich or famous through a career of free-lance editing, there are several advantages to considering it in at least one stage of your career: you control your own hours and conditions of work, you learn a great deal through your exposure to a variety of authors and their manuscripts, and you develop a gradually increasing mastery of the editing process. Then, too, experience in free-lance editing can lead into many related careers. Among former free-lance editors interviewed during the course of writing this book,

I found eleven in full-time careers in fields of
their choice: three editors for private research institutes, two editors on a university
staff, two working for publishing houses, two
editors for HEW projects, one an account executive for a public relations firm, and one on
the editorial staff of *Ms. Magazine.*

CHAPTER 8

The Institutional Editor

The English writing and literature
courses that I took for my B.A. and
M.A. have been very helpful for editing; . . . the production details of
publication I have learned wholly by
working experience. Teaching English
was even better preparation for editing, though I didn't realize it at the
time.--Questionnaire response from
Jean McAlpine, assistant director for
communications, Sea Grant Program,
Albany, New York

Do what you're interested in.
Volunteer if you can afford it. Try
to create a job for yourself or to
get the kind of skills you need to
get to the place you need to be.--
Questionnaire response from
Antoinette Wills, Washington
Council on the Humanities, Seattle
Project

Be creative, do interviewing,
use resource books and other materials at public libraries, go to
seminars, get out and scrounge!
For certain jobs, all [your] so-

called useless degrees *do* have value,
but usually in a different setting
from the one you originally expected.
Believe me, the world still needs
people with your skills.--Comment
from community services coordinator
at a city public library

Assuming that one way or another you have
developed expertise and you hear of a vacancy
as editor or information specialist on the staff
of an institution--a university, a museum, a
hospital, a research project, a foundation--what
might the job involve if you applied and got it?
Would the duties be largely routine ones, or
would you have a chance to use your own judgment? What qualifications are apt to put you
in such positions? If you don't see specific
vacancies advertised, how do you find out about
such work? And what advice do people already
holding such positions have for job-seekers?
     In a questionnaire sent out to editors and
information specialists working on a wide variety of institutional projects I asked such
questions; the following digest of the fifty
replies received may suggest possibilities to
some of you.[1]

DUTIES OF EDITORS AND INFORMATION SPECIALISTS

These two job types not only include many
different functions but overlap somewhat.
People working in either of these positions
may gather information or do background research on new developments; may write or edit
an internal newsletter for one department or
school of a large university; or may produce a
bulletin for the alumni of a university, the

patients of a hospital and their families, or for the general public.

To read the fifty responses to my first question ("Briefly, what is your job title and what are your current duties?") is to find out that editors and information specialists, whether they work for a university, a hospital, a nonprofit agency, or elsewhere, do almost everything that could possibly be called communication.

Among them they direct publicity campaigns for large hospitals, write news releases for daily and weekly papers, do radio and TV news scripts, edit technical manuscripts for medical journals, read proof, coordinate production arrangements with publishers, assist faculty members in running conferences, write and edit college publications relating to admissions and transfer policies, work with authors on book-length manuscripts, write brochures, edit footnotes and bibliographies for style, take photographs, get out newsletters telling either the members of one profession or the general public about recent developments within a field, and write and edit grant proposals.

Not only are their functions varied but almost every person replying reported doing several related kinds of work in his or her job. Clearly, the work week of an editor or information specialist does not consist of simply sitting at a desk and making marks with a blue pencil upon a manuscript that someone else has written about discoveries that still another person has made. The tasks performed--telling the public about the latest International Arctic Ice Experiment voyage, explaining the new equipment for radiation therapy in a university hospital, or interpreting the impact of new legislation on colleges and universities--call for judgment, acquaintance with the community, writing skill, and often a familiarity with more than one of the media.

QUALIFICATIONS FOR EDITORIAL
AND INFORMATION SPECIALIST POSITIONS

In view of the nonliterary, often scientific or technical, subject matter of much of the material gathered or edited by the respondents to the questionnaire, one might assume that many of them would have a graduate or undergraduate degree in one of the sciences. Actually, however, of the fifty persons replying to my questionnaire, twenty had bachelor's degrees in English, fifteen in journalism, four in classics, three in French, two in music, and one apiece in sociology, Biblical history, linguistics, economics, electrical engineering, and psychology. Of these, twelve had gone on to get M.A.'s in English; seven persons had master's degrees in journalism or communications, two in library science, one in history, and one in music. There were also five Ph.D.'s represented: four in English, one in history. Obviously, then, applicants with a background in English are in a reasonably strong position.

The consensus among both employers and employees is that most of the vocabulary of a technical subject has to be learned on the job, and that the editor or information specialist is hired mainly for his or her skill in digging out, sifting, and organizing material and writing it up clearly and effectively. Having had contact with the scientific or technical field in which one is going to work is of course an asset, but it is definitely not the main criterion. A former assistant professor of English now holding an editorial position with a university school of nursing points out: "My study and teaching of English really has prepared me

well for my present job. Even though some of
the problems I face in my work are unfamiliar
at first, I can usually figure out how to proceed by extrapolating from the basic principles
of organization and good writing I've been working with for years."

In addition to asking what degrees they had
taken and what their major subjects were I asked
for the amount and type of relevant experience
(editing, writing, teaching, other) that each
person had had before beginning his or her current job. As for the amount, answers varied
widely: eleven people had had two years or
less; seven had had twenty or more; and each of
the years between was represented by either one
or two people.

In answering the question about kinds of
prior experience, respondents listed their
earlier jobs as shown in the following table:

Other editorial work	23
Teaching (English, 10 persons; journalism, 3; Latin, 2; and women's studies, 1)	16
Newspaper work	13
Writing (free-lance)	9
Advertising	7
Research	4
Public relations	4
Proofreading	3
Secretarial work	3
Work on staff of a magazine	2
No previous job-related experience (first job after college graduation)	2
Library work	1

Needless to say, this list represents a few
loosely defined jobs, a certain amount of over-
lapping, and many instances of persons who men-

tioned more than one kind of relevant position.
What the answers to this question lack in pre-
cision, however, they make up in demonstrating
the wide spectrum of skills valuable to an institutional editor or information specialist.

There is, obviously, no one best route to
a good editing or writing position. As one
example of the zig-zags often taken by successful careers, Warren Downs, now writing news releases, radio environmental news scripts,
articles, and booklets about marine subjects
in his position as associate editor of the University of Wisconsin Sea Grant College Program,
majored in cello as an Oberlin undergraduate,
then earned a master's degree in music at the
Eastman School of Music before getting a second
master's in journalism at Wisconsin and stepping
into his present job.

On the whole, it would seem that many editors and information specialists have arrived
at their present jobs with broad and varied
backgrounds but with an emphasis upon English
(or upon other languages) rather than upon technical fields. Many of them have had more scholarly and academic training than their present
positions might seem to demand, yet incidental
comments on the questionnaires revealed more
satisfaction than frustration. In fact the
respondents, who have been in their current
jobs anywhere from two to eighteen years, appreciate them and want to keep them. As one editor
said, "We who already have such jobs tend to
cling to them with clenched teeth, because we
like our work."

Despite their protectiveness of their positions, however, many people responding to my
questions were articulate and expansive in
telling how they heard of their positions and
in passing along general advice to readers of
this book.

WAYS OF LEARNING ABOUT EDITORIAL POSITIONS

When asked "How did you find out about your current job opening?" the respondents mentioned several different channels. Out of these, there were five main ways in which the fifty successful job-seekers questioned had first heard about their present jobs:

1. *Through their own inquiries*

Telephone inquiries	2
From sending a query letter before moving to the area	1
Personal visits ("banging on doors, and luck," as the respondent put it)	1

2. *Through normal channels--advertisements and posted vacancies*

From university staff employment office listings ("Sometimes the system *does* work!" reflected one of these job-seekers. Among these 11, 4 reported that their names had been kept on file and that they were called back 6 months later for other jobs than those to which they had applied.)	11
From newspaper ads ("contrary to the conventional wisdom," said a surprised job-finder)	2
From a state employment office listing	1

3. *Through personal or organizational contacts*

> From friends, who knew of opening
>   and told respondent to apply   10
> From respondent's employer, who
>   knew of upcoming vacancy   3
> From organizations to which re-
>   spondent belonged (in two
>   cases, it was the "Job Bank"
>   and in a third, the "Rent a
>   Writer" system of Women in
>   Communications)   3
> From respondent's faculty ad-
>   viser, who knew of opening   2

4. *Through internal promotion*

> From the fact that a new job for
>   which the respondent was
>   eligible opened up in the
>   same agency or department   4

5. *Through evolution of respondent's present job*

> From a less responsible and rather
>   vaguely defined one   <u>10</u>

>   50

Some of the above ways of finding out about vacancies--such as reading ads and institutional employment listings--are so obvious that one tends to take it for granted that they won't work. Yet sometimes they do.

Two of these sources of job leads, the third and the fifth, deserve a word of comment. In learning about job openings from friends, you may expect either too much or too little. Ordinarily, such a lead doesn't (and of course

shouldn't) imply that you will be given prefer-
ential treatment over other candidates in job
selection; it is simply a great help to have
upcoming vacancies, which one otherwise might
not hear about until it is too late to apply,
called to one's attention.

As for job evolution, many job-seekers don't
believe in this possibility until they see it
happen, but several respondents to the questionnaire *have* seen it happen. For example, a research publications editor of AIDJEX (the Arctic
Ice Dynamics Joint Experiment) writes: "The
man organizing this project told me that there
was a fuzzily defined half-time position in the
budget for doing something that was neither secretarial nor administrative, probably for passing information among the various researchers.
I wanted a half-time job, so I applied. Later
the job got classified as Editor I and now it's
Editor II, full time." Another editor at the
same level, doing writing and rewriting of medical research articles, said that his job had
originally been listed at the student employment
office as a part-time electronics one. After he
got started in it, as he was pleased to find,
the writing part of it slowly developed. A
woman who now edits the medical articles of
eighty physicians in the medical research department of a large hospital started out in a
secretarial position in that hospital. When
the administrator for whom she was working
realized that she did far more than type, that
she had a good sense of language and sentence
structure, he encouraged her to try for a new
editing job as it was created, and he helped
get the job properly defined.

Other examples of having a job evolve to
fit one's talents appear in the response of
Antoinette Wills, a Ph.D. in history who had
been working as a volunteer for the Washington

Council on the Humanities. As she writes, "My
involvement in WCH projects led to the WCH's
asking me if I would help put together a proposal to the National Endowment for the Humanities for the WCH-Seattle Project. I was present
at the creation of my job opening."

A final example from the questionnaires is
interesting both because of the way it shows an
excellent position evolving from an unpromising
source and because it points up the fact that
sometimes it's not a bad idea to apply for a
position for which one is "overqualified."
Shirley Hudgins, for the past three years
happily established as editor and communications
coordinator of the UCLA Sea Grant Institutional
Program, where she works with radio, television,
and newspapers, came to her job via a secretarial route. She had received both a B.A. and an
M.A. in English at the University of Rhode
Island, where she had also taken almost enough
zoology courses for an undergraduate major.
After teaching freshman English at Rhode Island
for two years, she moved to California; there
she worked for a year in the Script Department
at MGM Studios, and then for a company that
made records for the automobile industry. Her
editorial position evolved in the following way:

> Out of work and hungry, I saw an ad
> in the Los Angeles *Times* for an execu-
> tive secretary working with oceano-
> graphers. I'm not a secretary by
> inclination or training, but the magic
> word "oceanographers" made me answer
> the ad. I was obviously not qualified
> for the position, but the USC Sea Grant
> Program, just beginning to grow, liked
> my background in the sciences and Eng-
> lish. They needed at least a part-time
> editor for their scientific documents,

so I began as part secretary/editor to
the head of Advisory services. After
I had held that dual position for
about six months, they created the
full position of Editor for me.

Hudgins' luck in finding that a job she didn't
really want evolved, after six months of hard
work on her part, into a position she considers
ideal inspired her to offer readers this advice: "Investigate anything that sounds interesting to you. Even if the exact position that
you would be looking for is not available, check
into it anyway. The ideal job usually doesn't
just appear, anyway, so try to figure out where
you could fit in, and perhaps do what you want
without their [the employers'] knowing it."

ADVICE TO JOB-SEEKERS FROM
EDITORS AND INFORMATION SPECIALISTS

Like Shirley Hudgins, most respondents volunteered suggestions to readers of this book.
Among these comments were seven recurrent
themes.
    1. *"Get some 'real world' staff editing or
writing experience somewhere (either on your
campus paper or outside), and parlay that as
best you can."* An editor from Delaware writes,
"Get some hands-on practical experience—something marketable." Look for internships
(summer, short-term, or any informal arrangement
that you may be able to promote, yourself) to
give you experience working on publications.[2]
Magazines published by nonprofit corporations
sometimes offer these internships, as do research centers. Established periodicals such
as the *Atlantic Monthly* have had summer traineeships for college students. The University of
Washington has offered internships for members

of minority groups to give them an introduction
into editing and publishing procedures.[3]

If in order to get practical experience you
have to offer your services on a volunteer
basis, several respondents urge you to do so to
whatever extent you can afford. As a public
relations director of a large hospital suggests,
you should aim to "get broad, varied experi-
ence--available through volunteer work with
nonprofit agencies--with progressively more
advanced administrative responsibilities." "I
often find work," writes Jean McAlpine, an editor in Albany, New York, "by joining an organization I am interested in anyway (e.g., the
League of Women Voters) or volunteering for a
local candidate I like. Some referrals and
moonlighting have resulted."

2. *"Write a lot of nonfiction and get it
published,"* urges a research publications editor at a state university. And, she continues,

> while you are an undergraduate or a
> graduate student . . . leave enough
> time to turn out a lot of published
> material and/or to work on publica-
> tions (no matter how small). The
> market is so tight that you either
> must have terrific tenacity or ex-
> perience. . . . When in school, . . .
> we lose sight somehow of the everyday
> work problems. Editing a newsletter
> does indeed pale when compared to
> great literature. To eat after gradu-
> ation, however, it is best to spend
> some time working on those little,
> time-consuming newsletters or stories
> or articles that could and should be
> done . . . while you are taking courses.
> Write--get it down on paper, and sell
> it. Nothing better to get a job [with]

than being able to lay something down
on the table. Find a good editor who
will tear your copy apart. Then put
it back together again.

As the director of publications and information services of the University of Washington
College of Engineering points out, the field
which includes being an editor or information
specialist "is still one in which jobs are usually awarded on the basis of performance--what
you have done--rather than on academic preparation. I would suggest compilation of a portfolio. To get experience, do volunteer work.
Many, many agencies, associations, churches,
etc., have writing and editing tasks for volunteers. Good places to get a start, to accumu-
late concrete products to show to a prospective
employer." And a communications officer who
manages information activities for a research
advisory services program in Cambridge, Massachusetts, makes the point that the liberal arts
subjects you have studied "are *not* useless . . .
if the student sees them as mainsprings for
thought, excellence in writing, and self-
education," and suggests that you "put the
latter skills to work--in journalism, public
information, etc., *in any field of subject-
matter.*"
    3. *"Make personal contacts,"* urge many re-
spondents. "Visit offices and departments who
use writers and editors, perhaps even convincing
those not advertising for editors/writers that
they need them. Be sure to take or send examples of finished work everywhere." In getting
in touch with people in your field, writes a
manager of information and publications for a
research center, "be organized and persistent.
Decide the field or fields you want to be in and
find out from people there what's needed and how

to go about it. *Anyone* will see you if you're
looking for advice, not a job. Follow up. Be
sold on yourself. Be sure to sell your *self*,
not a list of qualifications."

Another kind of contact which many find
helpful to morale and sometimes indirectly useful in their job search is with professional
organizations—either national ones such as the
American Medical Writers' Association, the National Association of Science Writers, the National Association of Press Women, the Society
for Technical Communication, Women in Communications—or local ones, which will be found on
most large campuses and in most cities.[4] Some
of these groups publish bulletins and journals,
offer annual prizes for good writing in their
fields, and sponsor speakers and workshops.
Watch local papers for announcements of these
workshops and of open meetings; attend and see
whether they interest you, and learn what the
qualifications are for membership. (Student
memberships are often inexpensive and offer a
good way to get in.) All these groups offer
the newcomer a chance to talk with established
professionals in the field. And all of them
offer a demonstration of the fact that there
are other *kinds* of standards of excellence than
those of the world of academic and literary
scholarship.

4. *"Develop a subskill,"* advises an information specialist. "In my case, the fact that
I have written or co-written (successful)
funding proposals has brought me about fifteen
requests from people needing to write them.
I don't particularly relish that specialty,
but I *could* make a career of it if I wanted
to, having had the experience." Other sub-
skills mentioned as back-ups for general
editing included technical editing, indexing
book-length manuscripts, graphics, photography,

"professional secretarial training, which makes
a better springboard than most people realize,"
and "exposure to computer science." As Barbara
Gill, formerly of Tymshare, Inc., Cupertino,
California, wrote:

> Even an introductory course in
> computer science, or any other oppor-
> tunity to do some data entry and
> understand the basic concept, is
> valuable in technical writing and
> editing. Some smaller organizations
> train people on the job if they can
> show the basic aptitude and famili-
> arity with data entry, research design,
> data analysis. The lingo is what's
> important in getting hired. Also, any
> demonstration that you are . . . con-
> cerned with detail, methodical about
> written presentation. . . . Teachers
> are often sought for technical writing
> and editing because there is a large
> component of training in much of the
> documentation.

5. *"Be willing to take a nonwriting job and
try to get it turned into a writing one"* was a
common piece of advice. Said a campus information specialist with an M.A. in English:

> There are always openings on campus
> for typists and office assistants.
> If you get into an office or a de-
> partment that puts out printed mate-
> rial and you happen to have editorial
> skills, sooner or later they'll ask
> your help, and maybe you can get re-
> classified. I know a number of Infor-
> mation Specialists who got started
> that way. One thing to avoid: don't

get in an office where you'll never have
a chance to do any writing, such as Payroll or Purchasing. Look out for job
openings that wind up as dead ends.

One journalist went even further: "Take anything that interests you," he urged, "even men-
ial labor or clerical work, to establish your
record as a productive and reliable employee."
    6. *"Don't be afraid of technical language,"*
writes an editor in anesthesiology in a teaching hospital.

> From the point of view of a health
> sciences . . . position, it is impor-
> tant that one not be afraid of tech-
> nical language and also be able to
> work with the quite structured format
> of technical writing. Two former
> editors . . . continually had problems
> with authors in that they tried to
> change technical writing into creative
> writing, and in this process changed
> the context of the material. This . . .
> put doubt in the authors' eyes as to
> the usefulness of departmental editors.
> I think that there is a lot of need
> and potential in the medical/scien-
> tific area for editors, and awareness
> of the field's specialized nature is
> necessary.

    7. *"Major in English but minor in some spe-
cial field of interest or expertise (environment, marine affairs, biology, music, education)
as an undergraduate,"* says Warren Downs of Madison, Wisconsin. "Or, at least, if you are already a graduate student, read up on one or two
such areas and take courses in them. Employers,
I think, are looking for people with both writ-

ing/editorial skills *and* strong interests in
their [the employer's] field." Similar comments
stress "free-lance writing after pursuing a
specialty" and "free-lancing with educational
institutions as a source." Areas particularly
recommended as needing writers currently, in
addition to the ones picked out by Downs, include art, urban affairs, labor, commerce,
investments, and health sciences.

Here, then, in institutional editing or
writing, is a type of work involving many of the
skills you have probably acquired through your
major in English. Such jobs, while scarcely
plentiful, do exist in fairly large numbers in
state universities, hospitals, and nonprofit
foundations and agencies. Despite the impact
of widespread budget cuts upon the hiring process, institutional positions as editors and
information specialists seem to be here to stay.
As Vice-president Margaret Chisholm at the University of Washington said recently, "institutions such as universities need to strengthen
their interpretive role if they are to survive."[5] If you work as a writer, editor, or
information specialist for a university--or for
a college, hospital, or a civic or research
organization--you can have the personal satisfaction of helping along that survival, even in
a small way. You will also find that you have
chosen a career which not only makes use of all
your talents but develops new ones. It may
help qualify you, too, for other, related
careers in editing, writing, and publishing.

CHAPTER 9

Possibilities in the Media
and Related Fields

In 1974 the number of persons employed
in various segments of communications
was as follows: technical writers--
20,000; newspaper reporters--40,000;
advertising--170,000; public relations--
100,000; photographers--80,000, and
radio and TV announcers--19,000.--
1976-77 *Occupational Outlook Handbook*

I guess newspaper journalism consists
of (a) finding things out, and (b)
telling other people about them. I
believe that newspaper employers take
it for granted that people with degrees in English probably can write,
but they worry about part (a), which
strikes them as the more important.--
John Schacht, School of Communications,
University of Illinois

For radio and TV, the prerequisite
that comes to mind is great energy.--
Dean Woolley, personnel director,
KING Broadcasting, Seattle

[Magazine writers have] to be able
to manage an argument--which is actually not too common a skill.--

David Brewster, publisher, *The Weekly
of Metropolitan Seattle*

Of all the professions involving the use of
words to communicate information, journalism is
probably the most visible. There are approximately seventeen hundred daily newspapers in
the United States today, as well as thousands
of weekly papers, and of trade, consumer, and
other specialized publications which count as
newspapers.[1]

Obviously the communications industry today
is an enormous, complex, and constantly evolving
one. It would be futile even to try in this
chapter to give an introduction to the whole
field and its many specialties and subspecial-
ties (a job best accomplished in such books as
Wilbur Schramm's *Men, Messages, and Media*).[2]
Instead the aim here is simply to discuss
whether people with a background in the academic
study of English literature or writing can make
their way into the related yet different field
of journalism, and if so, by what means.

As advisers in the University of Washington
School of Communications are quick to point out,
the field is a highly competitive one. Yet
there *are* openings: a study made by The Newspaper Fund, Inc., reveals that "in a typical
year 3,600 people enter newspaper editorial departments for the first time." And not all
these positions go to people who have majored
or even minored in communications as undergraduates. Of these 3,600, the Newspaper Fund report
continues,

about 2,800 . . . are from journalism
departments or schools, about 500
have other liberal arts degrees, and
about 300 come directly from junior
colleges, high schools, or from dropping

out of college. These . . . figures
exclude newsroom employees hired from
other newspapers, media or occupations.[3]

In a recent editorial in *Press Woman,* Jean
Wiley Huyler cited the best available figures
on future employment on newspapers:

The 1976-66 *Occupational Outlook
Handbook,* produced by the Department
of Labor, states that employment in
communications will increase about as
fast as the average for all occupations
through the mid-1980's, predicated on
the state of the economy. . . . Most
jobs will be due to the need for replacements. Beginners with exceptional
talent are likely to find favorable
employment opportunities, especially
on small town and suburban dailies
and weeklies. Others, however, face
stiff competition, especially on large
city dailies.[4]

Thus there may be room for some of you with degrees in English, provided that you meet the
newspapers' other requirements. What are they?
When asked what kind of people their papers
were looking for, Tom Bryan, personnel manager
of the *Seattle Times,* and Gerald Hedman, his
counterpart at the *Seattle Post-Intelligencer,*
said that their papers want bright, fluent,
hard-working people with B.A.'s (not necessarily
in communications) and one to two years' newspaper experience elsewhere.[5] These criteria
seem in line with ads in *The New York Times* and
other metropolitan papers for their staff positions. While having a master's degree will certainly not disqualify a candidate, most papers
would consider master's degrees in political

science, economics, art, business, music, or one
of the health sciences more helpful than an advanced degree in English for a newspaper writer.
    According to Prof. John Schacht, a Ph.D. in
English who spent some years as a working journalist and now teaches in the University of
Illinois School of Communications.

> The [newspaper] employer suspects that
> the English major is interested chiefly
> in "books," and that although the grad-
> uate student has already done a lot of
> reporting (i.e., through his research),
> it's been mainly in English and Ameri-
> can literature, which is a bit special-
> ized for his reader's tastes. Also,
> the employer suspects that the English
> major, particularly with advanced de-
> grees, won't stay long in journalism
> if he can find work elsewhere.[6]

So, if you are looking for a job on a newspaper,
it is up to you to offer convincing evidence
that your interest is a genuine one rather than
being a temporary by-product of the teaching
job shortage.
    Regardless of how many degrees you have,
says Tom Bryan, if you want your application to
be taken seriously by a city daily, you should
have proven yourself by having worked for a
year or two on smaller nonmetropolitan papers.
In the Pacific Northwest, these would include
the *Bellevue Journal-American,* the *Everett
Herald,* the *Bremerton Sun,* the *Vancouver* (Washington) *Columbian,* the *Eugene Register-Guard,*
the *Wenatchee World,* the *Bainbridge Island Review,* or the *Lewiston* (Idaho) *Tribune.* In the
Midwest, consider trying to get experience on
such papers as the *Champaign-Urbana Courier* (or
any of the Lindsay-Schaub chain), the *Moline*

Dispatch and the *Rock Island Argus*, the *Quincy
Herald-Whig*, the *Peoria Journal-Star*, the *Rock-
ford Star*, or the *Mexico* (Missouri) *Leader*.
Look for comparable papers in other areas of
the country. Such smaller papers, being less
departmentalized than the big dailies, can offer
a new reporter a wide variety of experience, as
well as time to learn from veteran staff members. On the larger metropolitan papers, as
one assistant city editor pointed out, "the
pace is so fast that nobody can afford the time
to train beginners, no matter how good their
background."[7]

All this is not to suggest that the only
value of working on a small paper is as a stepping stone to a large one. As Prof. William
Johnston of the University of Washington's
School of Communications explained, most of the
job vacancies today are on the smaller papers,
and "small" papers--ranging from tiny weeklies
to larger "nonmetropolitan" dailies--are often
the communications hub of their communities.
Having fewer other competing media in their
areas, they are read more carefully by their
subscribers. These papers usually tend to be
very well staffed, with more people (in propor-
tion to the size of their circulation) digging
up information than on a large city daily.
"It's these small local papers," says Johnston,
"that really have the clout in community
affairs."[8]

You might also find that a small metropolitan "alternative" newspaper like the *Seattle
Sun* is a congenial place to work, as does Brandt
Morgan, a creative writing B.A. who after two
years in the Peace Corps and two years of free-
lance writing joined the *Sun*'s staff. True,
your employment future there could be precarious, according to Alan Fiskien, a young man
just five years out of Yale who is the *Sun*'s

publisher. Fiskien says that most such small
papers, which start out to serve the needs of a
specific geographical area within a city, fail
within six to sixteen months. (The *Sun*, modeled
loosely on New York City's *Village Voice*, has
lasted four years so far.) In any case, the
reporters who work for such papers can find the
satisfaction of digging deeply into social and
political issues that their readers care about.[9]

Somewhat similar opportunities can sometimes
be found on small papers serving a minority
group within a big city. As Miyune Tsudakawa
of Seattle's *International Examiner* said in a
panel discussion with Jane Hadley of the *Sun*,
"the community press is very important--
disproportionately so considering its circula-
tion--because they cover news that the main
daily papers don't deal with.[10]

Everyone I consulted in the newspaper field
agrees that the most important thing in your
favor when you apply for a newspaper job will
be your experience. Says John Schacht:

> The college paper should serve
> pretty well here. At the *Daily Illini*
> and many other campus newspapers of
> large universities, there's no pro-
> blem about working part-time, almost
> at one's convenience. Previous ex-
> perience shows that the applicant's
> interested. If he hasn't any experi-
> ence, the employer--no doubt unfairly--
> will ask in astonishment, "Why not?"
> (I guess this is a hangover from the
> *Front Page* era, the idea that any
> potential newspaper man or woman
> simply can't stay away from a news-
> paper office of some sort.)

If, however, you have been so busy studying

or doing other work that you have not had one or
two years' experience on either a campus paper
or a small town or city paper, Tom Bryan suggests that you stress in your application any
recent, substantial work you have done on business house organs, professional newsletters, or
the staff of an advertising or promotional
agency. If you apply on the basis of such reporting and writing experience, Bryan and others
urge you to have a file of work published within
the past two years ready to take around with you
to interviews.

Another entering wedge, if you don't have an
undergraduate major or minor in communications,
adds Bryan, would be to enroll in a few courses
at your nearest school of communications; most
schools have certain courses open to nonmajors
on a "space available" basis. You could help
considerably in preparing yourself, he believes,
by taking from nine to fifteen credit hours of
classes in reporting and advertising. Such
course work might open certain doors to you
which would often be closed to an English major
or graduate student who had not demonstrated
such an active interest in newspapers. Johnston
urges you to take newswriting and reporting:
"These two courses alone will give you a basis
for deciding whether you want to go on in newspaper work."

Whatever your background, you do have to
know, and to demonstrate that you know, the
basics of reporting in order even to be
considered.

If you decide to apply for a newspaper position, you will find that some--though far from
all--vacancies are widely advertised. Campus
placement centers and classified ads in the
newspapers themselves are the obvious places to
look first. Watch, too, the lists of "jobs,
internships, and scholarships" posted on the

bulletin boards in the school or department of
communications on any large campus. Get in
touch with your state newspaper association,
which has lists of openings. Become familiar
with the several dozen journalism periodicals--
among them *The Quill*, *The Columbia Journalism
Review*, *Editor and Publisher*, *Journalism
Quarterly*, and *The Press Woman*--in the communications section of your university or public
library. Though they don't all carry regular
job listings, browsing in them will lead you to
get acquainted with the field. And be sure to
check that bible of the newspaper world, *The
Editor and Publisher Yearbook*.[11]

When sending résumés or letters of application for a communications position you should,
according to editors Burt Bostrom and Ron
McIntyre, list any courses taken in communications, political science, economics, history,
or English. Give job descriptions and time-span
covered for any work in communications. Indi-
vidualize your letters; show that you've read
the paper to which you're applying and know the
kinds of readers the paper has. Better still,
say Bostrom and McIntyre, take enough time to
study each paper so that you're "familiar with
its organizational structure, format, style of
communication and the geographical area it
serves for size and audience makeup." Study
the community itself, too, several editors
suggest. Finally, try "to be in constant touch
with your college placement office, to sign up
for interviews with . . . media groups and
large corporations. . . . Don't overlook those
who may not seem to be involved with media but
who do own newspapers, broadcast stations, or
magazines."[12]

When you succeed in getting an interview,
take samples of your writing in addition to the
few that you may have sent with your applica-

tion. But be prepared to have an on-the-spot
writing test as well. As one editor explains,
the published samples with your by-line are an
indication of what you can do; at the same time,
the interviewer doesn't know the circumstances
under which these stories were written, or how
much they may have been edited by someone else.
Therefore a newspaper personnel department often
will give applicants a test which helps establish what kind of writing they can do under
pressure.[13]

Both Schacht and Johnston believe that it
is important to see and get to know editors in
the region where you want to work. "I think
I'd try to phrase my letter," Schacht suggests,
"so that it doesn't demand a reply--which may
be 'no.' I'd say something like 'I'd like to
come in and talk with you' rather than 'May I
come in . . . ?' And I'd go in, even if I'd
been turned away." Johnston adds:

> I'm a strong believer in getting
> your feet in that door. You can nag
> and persist about *interviews* whereas
> you can't about jobs. When you get
> in the editor's office, you aren't
> just seeking an immediate job but
> you're making contacts for life. If
> the person who interviews you says
> that there's no job at the moment,
> you can say "I understand, but I'm
> going to be bugging you again in six
> months." Journalism is a craft--a
> calling--it has a *mystique*. An
> editor often finds a young person
> *from his locality* (the *local* part
> here is very important) rather per-
> suasive. A person who already knows
> the town where the paper is can cut
> down his training time by half.

Apart from the matter of applying for and getting interviews for newspaper jobs, there may be a question in your mind--as in the minds of some of the employers Schacht mentioned--whether your work in English has qualified or disqualified you to be a working journalist. Would there be a lot for you to unlearn? Could you make the transition?

According to Craig Sanders, who first headed the English department and now heads the communications department at Bellevue Community College (Washington), students of English language and literature are particularly well suited to working on newspapers: "Through their courses they've become interested in anything-- history, biography, events, people, ideas, opinions--and they've developed ability to analyze and organize. And if they haven't developed fluency they should have. What they have to learn when they start writing for a newspaper is mainly how to cast their ideas in simple, objectified form and to write short, punchy sentences."[14]

Adds Johnston: "Journalism is essentially a generalist's business, but you have to be able to learn about a lot of things." And Schacht points out:

A newspaper person has to develop
curiosity about a lot of things which
he or she probably didn't follow too
closely as an English teacher. . . .
What sort of things? In highfalutin
terms, societal institutions and
their interrelationships; in plain
English, how things work--the city
council, the school district, the
lumber industry, the numbers game
setup in the ghetto, the local basket-
ball team. . . . As a desk man and

certainly as city editor, I had to keep
telling myself that whether or not a
new factory was located here was important and whether soybean supports went
up or down was important, even though
I'd started out not really caring much.

As for unlearning your academic habits, you
do obviously have to get used to a different
time-span; from starting out on a story, getting
the information, writing and—occasionally—
rewriting, the cycle from start to finish is
usually one of hours rather than weeks or
months. (Woodward's and Bernstein's relentless
year-long pursuit of their quarry can be considered an exception.) Persons who have gone
into journalism from academia, however, find
the change of pace less threatening than one
might expect. Says Schacht: "You just learn
to do it by practice. The pressure—within
limits, I suppose—should be an enjoyable part
of the job. I think most newspaper people enjoy
the verbal legerdemain of turning out finished
(if generally very minor) bits of writing in
nothing flat: really nothing to it, they say,
blushing modestly."[15] One other mental adjustment you would have to make is in your sense of
your audience; a journalist doesn't have the
luxury of the scholar, who can write for people
with pretty much the same preconceptions that
he does.
      Certain psychological benefits may be by-
products of a switch to the world of newsprint:
not only the exhilaration of learning to turn
out stories in nothing flat but also a satisfying sense of completing something each time you
turn in a story. According to Linda Daniel,
who taught writing at the University of Washington for four years before becoming first a re-

porter and now the assistant city editor of the
Seattle Times,

> when you're a news reporter, your
> responsibility is to get your story
> filed, and that's it. But when you're
> teaching, you always feel responsible
> to your students. There's always
> something more you could be doing.
> You could prepare more, think up
> better assignments, find more exam-
> ples--there's literally no end to
> what you could do to make things
> clearer--or more challenging--to
> your classes.[16]

Somewhat similar is the point made by a Ph.D. in
English who supports himself by writing for the
Wall Street Journal while working on his own
novels in his off-duty time. Having taught
English full-time in a community college for
several years, he prefers his current job.
Teaching, he found, required so much involve-
ment that he felt too drained to do his own
writing; journalism, he says, suits him better;
"Now when I'm free, I'm really free."

Obviously the switch from the college lecture room to a newspaper office isn't for everyone. On the whole, if you are going to make
such a switch, the earlier in your career the
better. "It's a young person's business,"
Johnston says of journalism. Nonetheless, I
talked with four men who made such a change
after finishing Ph.D.'s in English, and another
who did so when his doctorate was nearly complete. There may be many more.

One new development affecting newspaper
employment is the technological revolution now
under way--"the cold-type revolution," it is

often called. Briefly, this phrase refers to
the changeover, which started in the late 1960s
among smaller papers, from "hot type" to "cold
type." The term "hot type" indicates the old,
traditional method of a linotype operator setting lead type line by line. Using "cold type"
involves setting "type" on film via computerized
tapes; ultimately the reporter will be able to
punch out, and correct, his or her story directly on a video display terminal, thereby
becoming his own typesetter.[17]

This new process, one widely heralded among
newspaper management, is increasing the speed
of newspaper production and (after the huge initial investments in equipment have been amor-
tized) should significantly cut down the costs.
It is important for those of you who may be
trying to enter the world of print journalism
to consider what is happening, says Johnston.
While changing to the cold type process means
cutting down on the number of employees in the
composing room, it is suddenly putting more of
a burden on the reporting staff. No longer can
they count on knowledgeable human intervention
in the composing room to correct inaccuracies
and verbal slips in their copy: the reporters
themselves must be able and ready to type out
each story exactly as it will appear. So, says
Johnston, "if the detail-conscious printer is
being carted out of the picture, each writer
must become more detail-conscious."

Citing the example of one medium-sized newspaper where the switch to cold type led to
eliminating eleven positions in the composing
room, Johnston said that the paper was now trying to get four more people on its reporting
staff. There is a new demand for reporters who
can write precisely, can edit themselves as they
go, leaving no loose ends of punctuation, word
arrangement, spelling, usage, or agreement of

tenses, for a nonexistent copy-editor or proofreader to tie up. As Johnston remarked, his
own journalism students are being forced to become more detail-conscious; at the same time,
he suggested that English majors should be encouraged by the new possibilities opening for
them.

If, however, you think it's too late for you
to backtrack and get the kind of preliminary
experience which most newspapers want you to
have before they hire you, don't overlook two
part-time possibilities, doing special assignments and free-lancing.

As Prof. Elizabeth Turpin of Texas A&M University found in a job survey she made in 1974,
teachers of English are occasionally hired for
special quasi-journalistic assignments such as
"writing for a TV documentary, developing encyclopedia articles (requiring coordination with
other writers), seasonal promotional work . . .
for manufacturers, merchandisers, and associations. Other temporary work includes summer
positions relieving regular copyeditors for
vacations, administrative/editorial coordination
of series of publications for which no full-time
regular employee is hired . . . governmental
agency projects . . . and other specific projects with a beginning and end defined.[18]
Naturally, the more evidence you have (in terms
of previous performance) of your professional
competence, the better your chances of being
hired for these special assignments.

As for free-lancing for newspapers, there
is always the chance that if you have the time
and energy you may be able to write and sell
occasional Sunday magazine section feature
articles, book reviews, travel articles, or
other short pieces. Although this market is
not particularly easy to crack, many people
who would not consider themselves outstanding

writers have done it. For some, taking a class
in writing for publication will stimulate the
release of ideas you were aware of but wouldn't
otherwise have taken the time to work up into
articles. For others, a book like Peter Elbow's
Writing without Teachers can be a catalytic
agent.[19]

Betty Woolley, a Mercer Island, Washington,
free-lancer, got her start through a college
literature class in which she found that she
particularly enjoyed writing term papers. After
graduating with a major in English she wrote a
lot on her own, took a writing course with a
practicing novelist, and began to send in short
humorous pieces to Seattle papers. She has now
had many of them published in the *Seattle Times*
and elsewhere; she also writes a weekly column
for a suburban paper. Before Woolley submits
material to a new market, she reads a number of
back issues of the paper carefully, then sends
a query letter; once she's been accepted by a
paper, she simply sends off her 500-word pieces
as she finishes them. And usually they are
published and paid for. Her advice? "After you
get an idea, write it up *quickly*--before it gets
cold. Put it away for a few days, then have
someone else read it to see whether you've
gotten across your point. Then jump in with
both feet and send it in."[20]

Beginning free-lancers should own a copy of
the latest edition of *The Writer's Market*, with
its listing of newspapers and other media who
buy free-lance investigative articles, fillers,
and feature stories. Beginners have stiff competition, for a great many established journalists do free-lance writing in their spare time.
Yet if you are willing to start with small newspapers, house organs, special-interest papers,
and other media that offer little pay except the
satisfaction of seeing your writing in print,

you may find these to be an entering wedge.
Don't ever count on free-lance writing as a
career, however; those who know call it "a
marvelous avocation, but a perilous vocation."
Nonetheless, almost anything you do in this
field can help other parts of your career. For
example, the discipline of writing for a wide
nonacademic audience and against a deadline will
make you more versatile as a writer and, if you
stay in teaching, probably a better instructor.
Having such articles or reviews published from
time to time will help build up the portfolio
of recently published examples of your writing
that so many employers expect to see. And
finally, such experience can also help toward
establishing your qualifications for a job as
information specialist or publicist with a
business firm, a government agency, or a nonprofit foundation.

POSSIBILITIES IN RADIO AND TELEVISION

Many free-lance writers for other media look
hopefully at radio and TV writing as possibilities. Established professionals in the field,
however, while admitting that entry into it is
possible, offer cautions.
Cracking the market for radio scripts is far
easier, they say, than selling TV scripts.
While you can deduce the requirements for most
radio programs by listening to them for a while,
TV programs come and go more rapidly; by the
time a newcomer has written and submitted
scripts for a series, it could either have been
canceled or else had its direction completely
changed. Most TV producers, moreover, are wary
of scripts not submitted through established
literary agents. Anyone who is really convinced that he wants to write for TV should try
to meet with a production staff; scripts for

most TV programs are done by writers who live
near the studios and work closely with the
producers.

As the compilers of *The Upper Left-Hand
Corner* suggest,

> there is a small but growing market
> in the field of community and educa-
> tional television. The pay is low,
> but the field is open to new people
> with good ideas. Write directly to
> stations in your own area and talk
> to the producers of programs for
> which you would like to write. (If
> you have an interesting idea for a
> community television program, you
> may find yourself acting as the host
> as well as the writer.)[21]

Persons working in radio and TV have pointed
out that the best chance to move into their
field in most regions is through doing background research for television news and specials
such as investigative documentaries. According
to Seattle Channel 5's Jean Enersen and others,
it's harder to break into either radio or TV
than it was five or six years ago, but it can
sometimes be done if you are ready and able to
do behind-the-scenes investigation and writing.
If, for example, you develop an idea for a program or a series of programs, or if you appear
at just the right time when someone is needed
to do background research in a particular area,
there are chances.

Some liberal arts graduates have found that
they can best get a foot in the door by volunteering to arrange for and announce programs of
classical music for small FM stations. The pay
is at first nonexistent, then minimal, but
there is great variety of experience. Others

have found William Johnston's advice useful.
"Go to a small town," he urges, "and get yourself a job on a small, three- or four-person
station. There you'll learn to do everything--
sell air space for commercials, probably write
them as well, announce the news, plan programs--
the whole works. Keep at it for a year or so.
Work and hope."

Dean Woolley, personnel director for radio
and TV at Seattle's KING Broadcasting Company,
says that when they hire new staff members,
they have few preconceptions about their background. Their present staff "represents a wide
spectrum in education, experience, and life-
style, including people from 19 to 84 years
old." Ideally, however, says Woolley, if she
were asked to pick out the single best preparation for a radio or TV career, she would pick
out a broad liberal arts background, followed
either by an internship in a university's
school of public affairs or by experience in
practical politics.[22]

Apparently it was the second kind of credentials that got one newcomer to TV her job
recently as a KING television news reporter in
Seattle. A young woman with a liberal arts
background and experience working for Seattle's
public prosecutor was hired for KING's "Action
Northwest" program, on which she does investigative reporting and then goes on the air with
her findings about a variety of local problems.
"I hadn't had TV experience or any courses in
broadcast journalism," she told me when interviewed. "My employers like people who know an
area well. Some knowledge of how things work
in a city is more useful to them than having
someone right out of college with a brand-new
communications degree. My advice to people
trying to get into this field would be to sell
yourselves; be able to say to your possible

employers, 'I know about education in this city;
I know what the housing problems are; I know
about business in this city. . . . I can do
stories for you because I know people in these
fields and they will talk to me.'"[23]

Although, as Dean Woolley says, nearly
everyone applying for a job at KING hopes eventually to go on the air, the company employs
over 220 people who are never seen or heard by
the public at all, along with about a tenth of
that number who are well known to the public.
In the news room some of these invisible but
important staff members serve as reporters,
camerapersons, producers, graphics specialists.
In the programming department there are film
editors, set designers, graphics experts, and
the production director.

Any basic courses you may have taken in any
of these fields can help as an entering wedge,
even though much remains to be learned on the
job. An entry-level position mentioned by
Woolley as a good one was selling FM advertising
time. For anyone combining a knowledge of classical music with sales experience, such a position would be a chance to get on a radio staff
and begin to learn the ropes while in a relatively pressure-free job. Such salespersons
deal for the most part with owners of small
businesses, helping them decide what kind of
exposure they want and what kind of program will
best spread their chosen image. Once a person
has joined a radio station staff, chances for
moving to other positions within the company
are good. As Woolley said, "This is one field
where the 'foot in the door' tactic really
works."

Whatever job you start with in this field,
Woolley and others agreed, you need versatility.
"Everyone may have to pitch in at any time and
do whatever needs to be done," she explained.

This is one reason why in her interviewing of
candidates for any position she gives them a
typing test. "In radio and TV," she contends.
"typing ability need *not* relegate you to clerical jobs; it is simply your life-preserver many
times a day; no matter whether you're a new reporter or the vice president in charge of production, you will often want to type up, revising as you type, your own ideas or your version
of new material that is being discussed. Anyone who stood on his or her dignity and refused
to type his own stuff because it was a 'clerical' job wouldn't last long."

To sum up, the prerequisites for success in
radio would seem to involve qualities of personality and temperament as much as they do experience and education. "The prerequisite that
comes to mind is great energy," says Woolley.
"Be able to cope with yourself. We need self-
motivated people, who don't pay too much attention to the idea of an eight-hour day."[24]

WORKING FOR A MAGAZINE

Reputedly hard to enter and perhaps (according to a few pessimists) too precarious to
worry about entering is another branch of the
communications industry, magazines. With the
recent death or transformation of so many national magazines (*Life, Collier's,* the *Saturday
Review of Literature, Look,* and the *Saturday
Evening Post,* to mention only a few), and with
mounting outcries from publishers about the
havoc caused by rising postage rates, you
should not be surprised to hear some knowledgeable people advising you to stay away from
magazines altogether. Yet, in Seattle alone
within the past year two new periodicals--one
with a wide general appeal, *The Weekly,* and one
directed to a specialized professional audience,

The Nurse Practitioner--have gotten off to a
good start. Nationwide, new magazines, both
those of general interest and those aimed at
special groups, have emerged fairly regularly
within the past six years (the best known include *Ms. Magazine* [1971], *To the Point International* [1973], *Moneysworth* [1974], *Working
Woman* [1976]).

"How do you get a position on a magazine
staff?" job-seekers ask. "Do you have to be an
established writer? Or is there any other recommended route?" Here, even more than for most
positions, there is no single best way. Occasionally, if you're a college student, you can
win a contest and become a summer "guest editor." You can be a graduate student in political science who happens to send some poems to
the *Atlantic Monthly* and their acceptance in
turn leads to an entry-level position and ultimately to an associate editorship--as happened
in the case of one of the *Atlantic*'s editors.
You can read an ad in a newspaper, apply when
you're fresh out of college, and get the job--
as several members of the staffs of *Mademoiselle*
and of *Ms. Magazine* have done. You can use your
experience on one magazine to get yourself a job
on another or to serve as your backlog of knowledge if later you decide to start your own
magazine.

Members of the magazine staffs I talked to
agree on two things: that the requirements of
magazine work differ from those of the other
media, and that you should start by getting any
periodical experience you can, if necessary on
a small one as a volunteer or an intern. Your
background in English should lead easily into
copy-editing and, with any luck, ultimately into manuscript evaluation, editing, and rewriting. Aside from that, whatever you can learn
about page makeup and about various printing

processes is a plus, even for work on the editorial side. As a writer-researcher for a
general publication, you have to know how to
get information from people's lips as well as
from libraries. If you want to work for a
scholarly journal, your graduate-school train-
ing--even if in a different field--can be immensely helpful.

One suggestion for working your way onto the
staff of a scholarly or professional journal is
to convince an overworked and understaffed editor that he needs your kind of general assist-
ance--even on an hourly basis--for proofing,
evaluating manuscript overload, copy marking,
or rewriting. A graduate student in journalism
at Indiana University approached the editor of
the *Phi Delta Kappan,* the national journal for
educators that was headquartered in her university town, with a proposal for hourly editorial
assistance. After a summertime trial period on
the *Kappan* staff, she was given a contract for
half-time duties as assistant editor, while she
completed her master's degree. By the second
year she had received higher levels of responsibility, pay, number of hours, and kinds of
assignments. By the end of her third year the
job had become a full-scale professional one.

If you hope to get into the editorial rather
than the production part of a magazine staff, it
certainly doesn't hurt to have published articles of your own. The best way, says John
Schacht, is to concentrate at first on the
smaller magazines. Of the students in his
course at the University of Illinois in free-
lance writing for magazines, he estimates that
at least half get something published in a
magazine while they are still in the course.
Having studied *The Writer's Market* so as to
know where to send their work, they get it
accepted by a variety of lesser known but widely

read weeklies or monthlies, among them *Focus/ Midwest*, *Chicago Sun-Times Midwest*, *Chicago Tribune Magazine*, *Illinois School Board Journal*, *Graphic Arts Monthly*, *The Aquarium*, *Bicycling*, *Quill and Scroll*, *Air Progress*, *Vend*, *Chicagoland*, *Christian Century*, *Jewish Frontier*, and the *Journal of Popular Culture*. As Schacht says, "The main point in freelancing, and almost the only point, is to figure out what readers of a particular magazine are interested in--then write it. Any magazine editor I've ever heard talk about freelancing has said this, or something like it: 'If you want to write for my magazine, *read* my magazine.'"

David Brewster is a former English major turned magazine editor. In fact, he took an M.A. in English at Yale before he came to the Pacific Northwest to join the staff of *The Argus*. Recently I asked him how he had picked out his staff of nine for his new venture, *The Weekly*. What kind of person had he been looking for? Established writers, subject-matter specialists, "names," or what?

> Our major need [said Brewster] was for
> subject area specialists--people know-
> ledgeable in one particular field such
> as politics, entertainment, food, the
> Women's Movement, the environment. . . .
> Over and above that these people had
> to be good researchers for complex
> issues of the kind that engage wide
> public attention. As writers, they
> had to be able to manage an argument--
> which is actually not too common a
> skill. Having this ability sets
> successful magazine writers off from
> the newspapers' investigative reporters,
> who have to concentrate on objectivity
> above everything. The successful maga-

zine writer has to find out what
people are potentially interested
in, to collect facts, opinions,
hypotheses, to be aware of nuances
on all sides, and then ultimately
to take his own stand. The magazine
writer's feat is much like that of
an actor--he or she must be able to
go on stage and be inspected by an
audience while doing his job.

Although Brewster was not actively looking
for more staff members, he had advice for those
hoping to get into the magazine field.

First, have a good broad Liberal Arts
background. But don't *lean* on your
degree or degrees. You have to have
done *and published* some writing that
you can show when you apply. When I
was getting together my *Weekly* staff,
far too many people wrote me offering
nothing but impressive résumés, references, and future intentions. It
doesn't matter as much where you've
published as *that* you've published,
that you've developed some expertise
in writing for an audience. So sit
down and write. Then get your pieces
placed (and don't overlook "little
magazines," university magazines, and
periodicals put out by foundations
and special interest groups that can't
pay anything. They're a good place to
get started).[25]

THE FIELD OF PUBLIC RELATIONS

Job-seekers should also consider looking
into another field, that of public relations,

which according to the *Occupational Outlook Handbook* employed more persons in 1974 than did any branch of the media. The rapidly expanding field of public relations is currently rather loosely defined, both in its scope and its methods. Some people lump it together with advertising, and others consider the public relations consultant as a person who whitewashes, in some secret and probably disreputable way, the activities of his or her clients. But Jerry della Femina, head of the influential Madison Avenue PR firm of Della Femina, Travisano & Partners, told a seminar of the Public Relations Society of America, "There's nothing mysterious about what a PR person does; it's all based on a lot of research and a lot of hard work."[26]

The PR field lacks a single formalized kind of training or means of entry. To be sure, there are excellent courses with labels like "Theory and Practice of Public Relations" which you can take in almost any university's school of communications; yet only one of the ten practicing public relations people I talked to had taken one. Apparently people come into the world of public relations after being newspaper reporters, teachers, editors, or writers in other fields.

Occasionally if you have a job or close contacts with a business whose workings you come to know extremely well, you may start doing small pieces of newspaper publicity about it and in time be able to turn yourself into a full-time PR person for this specialized area. A young woman who writes press releases, brochures, newsletters, and trade journal articles for heavy industry (logging, concrete, fiberglass, and general construction) got into public relations in such a way. As she says, since nearly everyone in her family worked in heavy

industry, she became so saturated with this
information that it was easy to start writing.
Now, with her own one-woman agency, she
has branched out into other business areas.[27]

Other people go from reporting or teaching
into public relations simply by taking on a few
people or organizations as clients, setting up
their own one- or two-person consulting firms,
then acquiring more clients. At a recent conference on careers in the media, several of
these PR persons told aspirants to their field
what they saw as the requisites. According to
Fern Olson, who two years ago founded the three-
person firm of Harmony Graphics, Inc., the requirements for a PR career are curiosity, enthusiasm, and a background in journalism.
"There's no such thing as a 40-hour week in
this business," she reported. "You have to be
flexible in everything, and willing to stick
with an assignment until you get it done,
whether it's daytime, evening, or a weekend."[28]
A woman doing free-lance public relations
pointed out that "you always have to keep com-
batting the negative image of PR. In each job
you do, you may have to establish your credibility all over again. In publicizing a project for a social service agency, for in-
stance--*you* know you're a professional reporter and PR person, but to the social workers
you may seem an outsider, an amateur, because
you haven't a degree in social work or public
administration."[29]

A former English teacher who became a
free-lance consultant after twenty-five years
of newspaper reporting told a group at a workshop on jobs in communications: "there is a
big field in PR; people *do* need you; many businesses and nonprofit organizations are looking
for freelance PR people, among them public information agencies, school districts, small

theaters, and organizers of special events."
She feels that a background combining teaching
and journalism gives one most of the necessary
skills to be a public relations consultant, and
that the rest are best learned on the job.
But, she warned,

> you constantly have to discipline your-
> self. You must know practically
> everything connected with the agency
> or business you're writing about. If
> it's an organization, go to its regu-
> lar meetings; sit in on the board
> meetings. If it's a business, use
> its products, check its competitors'
> products as well; and read all the
> company reports. Tailor your mate-
> rial each time for the medium you're
> using. And make your work more pro-
> fessional by going to the annual
> seminars held in most large cities
> by the Public Relations Society of
> America; you'll learn a lot.[30]

While some people set up this way on their
own as consultants and are hired by new or
small businesses, most public relations today
is carried on by large firms specializing in
public relations for their client business
firms, though sometimes also working with advertising firms. (Fewer and fewer firms today
do *both* advertising and PR.) The Public Relations Society of America performs an important
function by trying to educate the public, teaching that public relations isn't all a matter of
press releases, press parties, and hoopla, designed by apologists for the sins of their
clients. Instead, says an account executive
for a large PR firm with offices both in New
York and on the West Coast, public relations

firms increasingly perform an educational role
in campaigns for ecology, improved health care,
or peaceful social change.

Furthermore, the profession, increasingly
sensitive to criticism of late, is developing
a social conscience. At a recent Public Relations Society seminar, for example, Tony Ward
Smith of Tony Ward Smith and Associates
attempted to define the responsible role of
the public relations profession. He speculated
upon what he and his colleagues should do in
presenting images of medical institutions and
health care plans to the public in this time of
controversy over abortion, physicians' and
nurses' strikes, and the right to terminate
life support systems of the terminally ill.
Smith concluded that in his profession "our
efficiency in delivering messages has outrun
our ability to decide what the messages should
be . . . . Since institutions tend to develop
tunnel vision, we unfortunately tend to develop
it too--but we must develop peripheral and even
periscopic vision."[31]

A woman who recently joined a large PR firm
with offices in New York City and on the West
Coast is typical of those who realize the positive potential of public relations. As account
executive for a new firm manufacturing water
treatment systems that eliminate industrial
wastes, she sees her firm as "actually *doing*
something about waste treatment," and thinks of
herself as helping bridge the gap between the
industrialist and the public. She writes press
releases and articles for trade journals, helps
with sales presentations, decides which exhibits
and trade fairs her client should be represented
in, and in general "finds out where her client
wants to be and then helps him to get there."

When I asked her if she had had a background
of courses in communications, marketing, or

technology, she explained that she had no course
work beyond that for her B.A. at Wellesley College, where fourteen years ago she had majored
in Biblical history and taken more than enough
English courses to have had a second major in
English. It was mainly her previous position
as editor-in-chief for a research organization
that had gotten her the new PR job; she felt
that "even in today's highly specialized world,
experience counts more than academic credits."
Nothing in her past professional life quite
prepared her for some of the changes she had
to make in her new job, she admits, particularly
the difficulty of writing in a different style
from her previous academic one:

> You've been doing it one way for
> years, and suddenly it's all wrong.
> All at once your writing has to be
> very simple, very terse, in highly
> compacted sentences for press re-
> leases. Yet it still has to be in-
> teresting. Somehow you have to
> help the reader find out that the
> *ideas themselves* are interesting.
> Nonetheless, even though the first
> two months on the PR job were almost
> as disorienting as my first two
> months in college, the new job is
> very exciting and very much worth
> while.

To enter the field of PR, she prescribes
involvement

> in doing PR for political campaigns,
> or as a volunteer for some organiza-
> tion or cause that excites you. PR
> is one field in which nobody cares
> where you get your experience. If

you're a woman just thinking about
returning to the job market, you can
start getting experience wherever you
are. Publicizing events for your
P.T.A. is PR; so is writing newsletters
for the A.A.U.W., the A.C.L.U., your
church, or any other group you believe
in. Jump in and get some practice and
build up a bunch of published work that
next year you can show employers.
Meanwhile, if you want to do some
reading, there's the *Public Relations
Quarterly* and the book that's considered the bible of PR, Cutlip and
Center's *Effective Public Relations*.[32]

This method of breaking into PR was one that
Jerry della Femina agreed with. He thought that
anyone interested both in people and in ideas
could get into PR if he had enough determination. (He himself came into it from advertising, and got into advertising--with no college
credentials--by sheer persistence. Having
worked at every manual job he could find for
seven years while he wrote ads and other copy,
he got a few ads placed now and then on a free-
lance basis and showed them to employers as he
made the rounds of New York offices.) When I
asked him whether academic people, former
teachers and graduate students, would be passed
by as "overqualified" in PR, he said:

No--not if they're really interested
in the kind of thing that PR does,
and see its possibilities. Nobody
is overqualified for anything--unless
he thinks he is. You can put all
you've done and all you know into
almost any job--if you see the possibilities. But tell your English

types that they've got to be "street
wise," not just "book wise." Tell
them that they've got to read all sorts
of people writing today, not just the
great ones. Tell them to read Jimmy
Breslin and Hunter Thompson. Tell them
to keep their eyes and ears open for
everything that's happening.[33]

Distinct from public relations yet drawing
upon many of the same kinds of skill is the advertising business. L. Roy Blumenthal defines
the two so as to point up the difference:
"Advertising is the use of paid space or time
for the presentation of a sales message. . . .
Public relations is the use of all communications media for the promotion and furtherance,
subtly or overtly, for a commercial property or
a cause without the use of paid space."[34]

Among several advertising people interviewed, Steve Seiter of McCann-Erickson had
fairly specific advice for job-seekers. First
of all he warned that employers are turned off
by vague expressions of "interest in advertising." The more you know about what subspecial-
ties exist within this huge field (writing, art
direction, account management, media, and
others), the better your chance of getting a
job. Copy-writing is probably the closest to
the background of applicants with degrees in
English, although account management is a possibility for those who, in addition to having
writing ability, can deal with clients and
their business problems.

To work with one of the larger ad agencies
you need previous experience. Ideally, urged
Seiter, you should take an introductory course
in advertising in a university communications
department, then get as much work in English
and as varied writing experience as you can.

Before you apply for a job in advertising, try
to get involved in editing a newsletter, getting
out house organs for business, pamphlets, brochures for organizations, or press releases for
a political campaign. Next, if you are geo-
graphically mobile and are definitely interested
in advertising, you might consider trying to get
into one of the training programs given by some
of the New York City firms such as J. Walter
Thompson or Ogilvie and Mather.

Meanwhile, if you are applying to an ad
agency in person, approach your interviewer with
a résumé and samples of your writing. In this
field (unlike many of those discussed in this
book), employers look for creative writers who
demonstrate their enjoyment in working with
words not only in straight exposition but in
poetry and fiction.[35] One young woman who was
recently hired as copy-writer for a group of
women's clothing stores got the job, improbably
enough, on the basis of a fanciful semi-
autobiographical novel she submitted along
with her application. If the agency considers
that an applicant shows writing talent, they
are sometimes willing to do the rest of the
training on the job.

Here, as everywhere, it is essential to get
firsthand information from people now in the
field or those who have recently worked in it.
Talk with former ad agency people on the faculty
of the school of communications nearest you.
Look for notices of lectures and symposia sponsored by Alpha Delta Sigma, the advertising
fraternity: many of its events which are open
to the public are highly informative. Go to
any open lectures or discussions sponsored by
the American Advertising Federation. Read some
of the recent analyses of the impact of advertising, and make up your own mind about the
charges leveled by Vance Packard and Ralph

Nader. Plan hypothetical ads for new and exist-
ing products. Outline some of them and get
criticisms of them by people in the field to
whom you talk. When you have steeped yourself
in the background of the field, have decided
what part of it you are most interested in, and
have thought about what contribution you could
make, you will have learned how to present yourself to a potential employer, and he or she may
appreciate your knowledge and energy.

Most of these fields just discussed--print
journalism, radio, TV, magazines, PR, and ad-
vertising--are changing rapidly as a result of
"cold type" techniques, increased computeriza-
tion, paper shortages, postal rate increases,
the takeover of many publishers by conglomer-
ates, and shifts from traditional to new marketing methods. Generalizations made today, in
1977, may have to be completely recast within
two years. Meanwhile, any investigating that
you are able to do on your own will be likely
to turn up more information.

When he last visited the University of Washington campus, the British poet and biographer
Robert Gittings commented upon the apparently
fixed boundaries in the United States between
the academic world and that of the media:

> It seems unfortunate that in America
> one finds such stratification, such
> sharp boundary lines, between people
> in different sectors of the literary
> and intellectual world. Over here
> you tend to get your feet firmly
> placed on the rungs of one particu-
> lar ladder--whether teaching or
> reporting or publishing or whatever--
> and you hardly ever seem to look
> back or to consider any other possi-
> bilities. In Britain, on the other

hand, it is easier to go in and out
of academia, sometimes writing for
the BBC or for a magazine of general
interest, sometimes teaching or writing a scholarly biography.[36]

It is just possible that the present widespread uncertainty about careers could have one
beneficial result: more open-mindedness among
both the academic and the communications professions about one another. Whether or not
such open-mindedness eventually becomes common
in America, your cultivating it should help you
in your own job search.

CHAPTER 10

The World of the Book Publishers

You must make your presence and work
contribution felt, but not your desperation. Your ambitions must be
registered, but not with a pile-driver
impact.--William Targ, senior editor,
G. P. Putnam's Sons, letter to *Publishers Weekly*

Vacancies do occur, of course, and
the best advice I can offer university graduates is to be persistent
about knocking on doors. One
shouldn't assume that all jobs are
in the east--a number of regional
textbook houses have grown up in
recent years, and there are trade
publishers outside New York as well.--
Ashbel Green, vice-president and
senior editor of Alfred A. Knopf
and Company, letter to author

The publishing industry in some areas
is doing pretty well--despite the
words of gloom. . . . A person who
is *convinced* he has to get a job with
us at least has a chance.--Alfred
Schenkman, Schenkman Publishing Company, Cambridge, Mass., letter to author

Although nearly everyone in the field of English
feels an affinity for the world of publishing,
editors are quick to point out that affection
for the printed word is not enough. In fact,
T. D. Wittenberg, editor-in-chief of Bobbs-
Merrill, goes as far as to write, "I would urge
you to dissuade those people 'who just love
books' from seeking employment in the publishing
industry. What we really need today are hard
workers who can bring the books out on time and
under budget."[1]

In an attempt to find out what qualifications are prized by publishers and what if any
means of entrance into the book trade there are
for holders of degrees in English, I recently
conducted, through the Placement Center, a survey of 125 publishers across the country. The
seventy responses received, many of them abound-
ing in specific detail, add up to the message
that entry into the world of American publishing
in the 1970s is indeed possible, although it
takes persistence, considerable preliminary exploration of the industry, and luck.

From among the many practical suggestions
made by the editors and publishers who answered
our questions, certain main points emerge.
First is the insistence that applicants should
not blindly go looking for "a job in publishing," but should try to learn about the industry
as a whole, and to learn at least of the exist-
ence of the many positions in it besides those
involving manuscript editing. Philip D. Jones,
director of the University of Texas Press,
writes: "Ninety-five per cent of the people
who have come to my office for advice over the
years respond 'editorial' when asked what sort
of work they want to do in book publishing.
When asked what kind of editorial work they
want, virtually none are aware that there are

various kinds such as copyediting, project editing, acquisitions editing."

Other respondents, such as John Harney of
D. C. Heath and Carol Meyer of Harcourt, Brace,
Jovanovich, mention the range of noneditorial
positions in publishing, among them "sales,
publicity, promotion, advertising, production,
contracts and permissions, royalty accounting,
data processing, and subsidiary rights." In
general, it cannot be too strongly recommended
that you make an *informed* job campaign.

Among ways of acquiring such information,
one of the easiest is systematic background
reading. For familiarity with copy-editing
practices, you can go to The University of Chicago *Manual of Style*, 12th edition, as well as
to *Words into Type*. For an overall view of
publishing trends, you should keep up with *Publishers Weekly*. You should also explore several
of the descriptive accounts of the publishing
business written by insiders in recent years--
books such as Herbert Bailey's *The Art and
Science of Book Publishing*; John Dessauer's
Book Publishing: What It Is, What It Does;
Chandler Grannis' *What Happens in Book Publishing*; and Gene Hawes's *To Advance Knowledge:
A Handbook on American University Press
Publishing*. [2]

In addition, Robert T. King, director of
the University of South Carolina Press,
suggests that job-seekers make inquiries of
both the Association of American Publishers
(AAP) and the Association of American University Presses (AAUP), "simply saying that one
is interested in a career in publishing and
would be grateful for information."

Next, browse. Go to bookstores and look at
publishers' catalogues. Form some idea of the
kinds of books that different publishers bring
out. Follow the advertising of the various

firms in *The New York Times* Book Review Section
and the *New York Review of Books*. Talk and
listen to publishers' representatives when they
visit your campus or one near you. Talk to anyone else involved in the making or selling of
books. Be sure to go to the paperback exposi-
tions sponsored annually on many campuses by
groups of publishers. And, of course, begin to
form some specific questions in your mind—not
just about job openings but about publishing
trends—to ask publishers when you eventually
find yourself having an interview in one of
their offices.

In addition, you may be able to take one of
the courses in publishing procedures offered by
various colleges and universities. The best
known of these courses, the one given each
summer at Radcliffe College under the direction
of Mrs. Diggory Venn, is one that Don Ellegood
of the University of Washington Press particularly recommends. There are comparable courses
given annually by the University of Wisconsin,
the University of Oklahoma, the University of
North Dakota, New York University, the University of Denver, and Hunter College. In January
1976, another such course took shape at Pacific
Lutheran University, Tacoma, Washington.[3] In
addition, several other publishing houses, particularly among the university presses, occasionally sponsor internships.[4]

While the respondents to our questionnaire
were predictably divided about the value of such
courses, more than half spoke well of them. A
senior editor of Houghton Mifflin, for example,
said that although what one actually learned
through such a course might be picked up on the
job, at least through hearing the twenty lectures by representatives of twenty different
publishers, one could get a good idea of the
whole range of publishing jobs and know better

where one might fit in. Carol Meyer of Harcourt, Brace, Jovanovich was also impressed by
the broad survey of publishing houses that such
courses could give a student; she pointed out,
too, that many people already working in publishing enroll in such courses to advance their
skills and that meeting these people can be
helpful to newcomers. It seems obvious, too,
that your simply having finished such a course
can indicate to prospective employers that you
have made a certain commitment to a publishing
career.

A second qualification for entry into publishing, according to forty-five of the seventy
editors responding, involves having at least
some business experience. Even for aspirants
to editorial posts, publishers stressed the
value of firsthand knowledge of such business
areas as marketing, advertising, bookstore
sales, textbook sales, and sales management.
Publishers answering my questionnaire also
noted the advantage of taking introductory
courses in accounting or basic computer language and of having office and general secretarial
experience.

Even for editors, it was emphasized again
and again, experience in bookstore sales is extremely helpful. A senior editor of Houghton,
Mifflin pointed out that so distinguished an
executive as Alfred Knopf began his career at
the cash register of a Doubleday bookstore; so
too did a number of Houghton, Mifflin's top
editors. George Ernsberger, former editor
at the Berkley Publishing Corporation, explains, "The reason that bookstore selling is
useful is that it forces the seller to consider
the wants and interests of people unlike himself." Almost any kind of selling experience,
in fact, is considered a plus and should certainly be mentioned in your résumé.

Actually, your bookstore or other selling experience need not have been extensive, so long as you have had enough to learn what it is like. Similarly, a few basic courses in business will often do the job; you do not have to study business administration in depth. On the subject of business courses, William Sommerfield, speaking from his experience as an editor of a New Jersey textbook firm, has this to say:

> If a young person wishes to ultimately get into the administrative end of this business, he/she must be well grounded in both marketing/ business procedures and literary skills. . . .
> Publishing is carried out in the world of business, and any editor worth his blue pencil must be able to joust with a profit and loss statement and calculate costs with the best of the bean counters. . . . Without these skills, your creative offerings will be drowned in a sea of ledger books, financial reports, and general accounting problems. I would insist that everyone with aspirations towards the world of publishing take at least one course in accounting.
> Publishing is usually carried out in the environment of the firm encumbered by the organizational problem surrounding this group process. Each aspiring editor or publishing executive should sample the academic wares of either the marketing department or management department in the school of business.
> Publishing, as a rule, suffers

from the lack of empirical data upon
which it makes its decisions. All of
us could stand the services of an editor who could apply some basic market
research techniques.

Aside from these practical considerations,
students sometimes wonder whether there is any
particular major or degree which will help their
entry into publishing. In general, most publishers feel that having a broad liberal arts
background with one or two fields of speciali-
zation is a good idea. On the questionnaire,
when asked what majors and what degrees applicants should have, employers expressed these
preferences:

Undergraduate major:

English	26
Communications	11
Modern languages	9
History or poli-	
tical science	2
Science	1
Education	1

Field of graduate study:

English	16
Communications	10
Modern languages	5

Although two editors said that graduate degrees in English would be of no help "and might
even be a detriment," nonetheless many of the
editors mentioned as *desiderata* the kinds of
things one learns in graduate work in English.

William Sommerfield thought that applicants for
educational publishing houses should be "well
socialized into the world of academia" and have
a good grounding in literature; Thompson Webb,
Jr., of the University of Wisconsin Press
thought that "to qualify for editorial work at
a scholarly publishing house some education at
the graduate level is needed. . . . For editors
the commonest (and probably the best) educational background is literature—English and
languages."

Several correspondents pointed out that
although they had master's degrees in English,
they were hired because they had worked at
diversified unacademic jobs. What they had
learned in graduate school, however, helped
them later, after they had gotten into
publishing.

Contrary to what one sometimes hears, a
graduate degree will not automatically make
publishers consider you overqualified. Whether
it is considered an asset or a liability depends upon your own attitude. Says Luther
Nicholls, West Coast editor for Doubleday, "If
you have an M.A. or a Ph.D., don't flaunt the
degree as such, but be sure to bring out, in
your letter of application and your résumé, any
expertise, academic or otherwise, that you've
acquired in a subject field."[5]

Emily Johnson, former director of the University of Washington's Office of Scholarly
Journals, who has counseled a number of people
now working in publishing houses, urges that
you include in your résumé *anything* at all that
might conceivably have relevance to publishing.
If you have been a teaching assistant, research
assistant, or a reader for a course, for example, include the fact, with the name and number
of the course. If you have worked your way
through school in a library, you may have

learned a great deal there (as she herself did)
which can be helpful in publishing. Also include your thesis title and the name of the
chairman of your committee. Mention undergraduate or graduate course work in composition,
translation, foreign languages. Be prepared
in an interview to discuss your undergraduate
major and minors, and to tell in what way graduate work may be helpful to you in the publishing world. If you have a background in science
or in modern foreign languages, put it on your
résumé, and be prepared to enumerate courses.
Johnson also suggests that you classify all
course work in four basic areas--science, social
science, humanities, business--and list them in
some detail.[6]

Concerning the logistics of job-hunting,
she advises writing a letter to the publishers
who interest you in a specific region, telling
them that you are intending to move to the area
and will be in town for such and such days in
the near future. Say that you will, on arrival,
phone them for an appointment, and when you get
there, do so. If your letter and résumé have
done their work well, the publisher will usually
see you even though he may have no definite
opening at the moment.

In addition to his professional qualifications, an applicant's personality will usually
enter the picture. As Thomas Weyr points out
in a *Publishers Weekly* article, executives in
this field "are looking for things in people
that are largely intangibles, such as personality, manner, a special curiosity, rather than
specific skills. By and large, requirements
tend to be vague."[7] Weyr and several of the
editors in the survey made the point that most
people who get ahead in this field enter it
young (somewhere between the ages of twenty
and twenty-eight). Said Norma Mikkelsen of the

University of Utah Press: "We each have to be
versatile, efficient, interested in the books
and their authors rather than individual
egos. . . . We are looking for a set of personality or 'working' traits that would enhance
the personality of the Press." In a somewhat
similar vein, John D. Moore, editor-in-chief of
the Columbia University Press, writes, "Much
depends upon how well one communicates with
others orally as well as in writing. Human relations skills count heavily in most jobs here,
as in other industries."

It might be a good idea, therefore, as you
put together your résumé, to list any partici-
pation in a professional group effort such as
working on a committee, being on the editorial
board of a publication, doing student advising,
or working in a political campaign. As should
be obvious, evidence of successfully carrying
out one or two such responsibilities is worth
distinctly more than the customary protestations
that you "want to work with people."

The application process for a publishing job
differs considerably from the procedure in
applying for a teaching one. For example, publishing vacancies are advertised, if at all,
much less widely than teaching jobs. In response to my question to publishers: "Would
you please put the UW Placement Center on your
mailing list for news of job vacancies as they
occur?" many people replied, "We have no such
list." Most news of publishing vacancies
travels by word of mouth. Among the few printed
sources, the most valuable ones are the advertisements in *Editor and Publisher*, in *The New
York Times*, and in the "Weekly Exchange" section
of *Publishers Weekly*.

Accordingly, the publishers answering my
questions agreed with Emily Johnson on the value
of making the rounds of publishers' offices *in*

person. As J. Kenneth Munford points out, even
if aspirants do not find a job, such visitors
"will pick up benefits through serendipity.
They see something of how editorial offices and
shipping rooms operate. They become acquainted
with some of the people in the field. They can
begin to judge better where their true interests
lie." And Kathleen Macomber of Pantheon Books
advises: "The job-seeker, carrying a well
written résumé, should go to the personnel
offices of the firms he would choose to work
for first, then make the rounds of all the major
firms." Luther Nicholls, however, dissents from
part of this advice.

> Don't go through the Personnel
> Department of most big publishers
> or you'll end up with a clerical job
> that lacks variety and a chance for
> promotion. Write to the editor of a
> specific department of a specific
> firm, having looked up his or her
> name and title in *The Literary Market
> Place.* Then send a letter of appli-
> cation with a brief résumé which
> stresses both your writing and your
> business experience. You might in-
> clude one or two examples of short,
> nonacademic pieces of writing. Better
> yet, visit a publisher's office, leave
> these samples, and shortly afterward
> ask for an appointment.[8]

Donald Stewart of the American Library
Association is another editor who highly en-
dorses the value of candidates' having available
a portfolio of work done, preferably published
work. To build up this folder, he suggests that
graduate students not underestimate the value of
appearing in small regional or special-interest

journals, even in those that do not pay their
contributors.

Many editors agree that one shouldn't wait
to talk to publishers until one can get to the
East Coast but should visit regional publishing
houses. As Robert Roy Wright, managing editor
of the Association Press in New York writes, "I
do understand the attraction that New York City
has. But you should remind your students not to
overlook the fact that a great deal of publishing is done in many other places throughout the
country."

In this connection, publishers from all
parts of the country wrote that since they had
no funds to pay the travel expenses of applicants from other parts of the country, they
were forced to limit themselves to interviewing
people who could somehow get to their offices.
Weyr's *Publishers Weekly* article emphasizes the
chance element in getting publishing jobs; and
a woman editor of an eastern university press
underlines it. "Timing is everything, it seems
to me," she writes. "An applicant has to be in
the right place when a publisher needs someone
with his or her skills. An application six
months old is not going to be very seriously
considered, on the basis that, if good, [the
applicant] is hired some place else."

The applicant does not have to depend solely
on timing, however. Says one editor, "Publishers, like other businesses, tend more and
more to hire people through employment agencies,
who do the initial screening. Several specializing in publishing personnel are regularly
listed in the 'Weekly Exchange' section of
P.W." Twenty of our correspondents, moreover,
volunteering the fact that they might have openings in the coming year, said they would be glad
to receive letters and résumés.[9]

Assuming that you do hear of an opening in

a publishing firm and are finally offered a position, should you be selective in what you
accept? According to most of our correspondents, no. They advise that, simply to get in
publishing, it is practical to accept almost
any job with any publishing house. Milburn
Calhoun, president of Pelican Publishing Company,
says the crucial question about an applicant is
"What is his attitude toward the job? (If he
isn't ready to sweep the floor if it needs it,
he should stay in the governmental sectors.)
Is he willing to begin with any job available?"
     The two most often mentioned starting points
in publishing are secretarial jobs and textbook
sales. Although supporters of the women's move-
ment have recently been vocal in warning women
not to start as secretaries if they have long-
range plans to do anything else, apparently secretaries are more apt to be on a genuine promotion ladder in publishing offices than in many
other fields. Helen Stewart, formerly of the
Rutgers University Press, insists that she has
"never known anyone with real editorial or promotion skills relegated to a secretarial job
for long. No sensible publisher overlooks
underpaid talent in the office."
     Linda Liesem, placement specialist for
Doubleday, goes even further:

        Most of our entry level jobs are
     secretarial in nature and are filled
     by people with B.A.'s (occasionally
     M.A.'s) in English or a communications
     related field. A major prerequisite
     is the ability to type at least 45
     wpm. While these secretarial jobs
     in our editorial, subsidiary rights,
     or publicity departments may not
     offer the challenge and responsibility
     most graduates seek, they do provide a

prepare one for the next step up. In
the editorial department the line of
progression (for which there is, however, no fixed time schedule), is as
follows: editorial secretary, assistant to the editor, editorial assistant,
associate editor, and editor. There
are corresponding steps in other departments.

Again, William Targ, senior editor of G. P.
Putnam's Sons, urges job-seekers:

If you want to learn the book business and get ahead in it--in any area
of it--take a secretarial job if you
have no specialty. . . . An editorial
secretary can learn about authors' behavior; about manuscripts and proofs;
advertising, publicity, review media,
manufacturing, jacket copy, etc. All
one has to do is keep the eyes and
ears open--and the pores. *Being well
read doesn't hurt.*[10]

And, finally, Truman Talley, of Weybright
and Talley, brings out an additional advantage
to entering publishing as a first-rate secretary. He finds this position "most important
because [it is] most misunderstood, looked-
down-upon, *and therefore an open door.*"
The other most often mentioned entry point,
working as a "college traveler"--a sales representative for a publishing company who may spend
up to half of the month visiting college campuses in a five- or six-state area, and the
other half working in the firm's regional or
main office--used to be a masculine province.
Recently, however, such positions have opened
up to women.[11] Don Ellegood at the University

of Washington Press recommends such positions as
a very good way to get started, and William
Sommerfield considers "these people usually. . .
the most knowledgeable as to the many ramifica-
tions within the industry." The editor in
chief of the Pitman Publishing Company agrees
with him, reminding us that such positions
"offer an easy entry point and can lead to any
other department," while Theodore McConnell of
the Fortress Press is firmly convinced that
"if editing or managing is one's goal, sales
is the best way to learn what is needed."

If you do take an entry position in publishing, however, be prepared for long hours and low
pay--even lower, in many publishing positions,
than in college teaching. A University of Washington professor of English, who worked in
both advertising and magazine publishing in New
York City before getting her Ph.D., agrees that
jobs in these related "glamour fields" combine
hard work and starvation wages. "It takes unusual commitment and dedication to pursue a
career in editing or publishing," she warns.
"Yet after the first two or three years, the
work can be highly rewarding and exciting."

Once the entry-level job is attained, what
kind of position should one aim for ultimately?
According to many editors, it is the textbook
departments that will probably do best in the
near future. If one's own firm has no such
branch, one should try to get into a company
specializing in high school and college texts.
(Since there is continual "cross-hiring" in the
industry, a lateral shift from one firm to
another is much easier to manage than is one's
initial entry into publishing.) Senior editors
at Houghton, Mifflin and elsewhere explain that
textbook sales are what are going to keep publishing alive in the seventies and eighties if
anything does. While we talk of editions of

trade books in thousands, editions of texts
usually come out in hundreds of thousands.

Other areas to watch are some of the offshoots of conventional book publishing, i.e.,
paperbacks, says Maria Carvainis of Avon Books,
or mass market publications, or "support" industries for book publishing, such as the re-
viewing media, or printing, binding, and distribution; or law as related to publishing; or
magazine or newspaper publishing. Also, as
Donna Martin, managing editor of Sheed and Ward,
points out, "there are house organs, trade
magazines, and alumni magazines all over the
country which give a young person a great opportunity to learn much about editorial and production techniques. . . . Many of these positions pay better than book publishing *per se*
and [one] might even find he or she preferred
a career in one of these fields." According
to George Ernsberger of the Berkley Publishing
Corporation, so many people have recently
switched from trying to get into publishing to
making an effort to get into television or
films, that the "flood has lessened, and it is
probably less difficult now than in the past
for a talented young person to get into publishing, with some hope of having a decent
career."

People with advanced degrees in English
have what Maria Carvainis sees as a basic advantage: "a good solid knowledge of books
past and present." And, as Harry Kaste remarks, "even in these times of retrenchment,
there is a continuing demand for editors with
special subject-matter competence." Teachers are
sometimes in demand; a Xerox editor says that
their paperback book club staff includes many
former teachers, functioning now as acquisitions editors and educational advisers, and an
editor at the University of California Press

points out that "for editorial procurement,
specialists in different academic disciplines
may be needed." The longer you are in the
field, the more your ability to organize material, to assess books quickly, to write, and
to copy-edit will be called upon.

If you have innovative ideas about new
courses, ways of teaching, or textbooks, you
should explore the list of educational publishers, many of them small experimental firms,
mentioned in *New Roles for Educators* by Weathersby, Allen, and Blackmer.[12] In educational publishing firms, as in university
presses, what Philip Jones of the University
of Texas Press says is worth remembering:
"Although advanced degrees may not help you
very much as you try to enter publishing, . . .
having them can be extremely useful later on,
as you work your way up the ladder of
promotion."

In the Pacific Northwest, there are fewer
large, well-established book publishers than in
many other regions of the United States. Nonetheless, at a time when many of the big East
Coast publishers either are having financial
problems or are being bought up by conglomer-
ates, those we consulted within the Pacific
Northwest were helpful in responding to our
questionnaire and reasonably optimistic about
the continued expansion of regional publishing.
Dan Levant, owner-publisher of the Madrona
Press of Seattle, commented that "this is a
good time to be starting--or working in--a
small regional publishing firm. Those of us
who are involved in this kind of small-scale
enterprise feel that we have a chance to help
reverse the trend toward monolithic publishing
corporations and to make our own decisions as
to what books we bring out, taking into account
other things than merely the balance sheet."[13]

As for the overall picture, it changes from
week to week; it has changed several times as
this chapter was being compiled. The best advice is probably to keep up with the *Publishers
Weekly* for new developments, to believe that
here is one field in which a "foot in the door"
policy works better than it usually does in
college teaching, and to adopt the mixture of
cynicism and hope of many of the correspondents
quoted in this chapter. They are aware of the
constraints within which their industry must
work; they know that no editor can ignore what
the ledgers tell him or her; still they do not
think that publishing is going to fold up tomor-
row, or to stop taking in new blood. As they
urge us to tell job applicants, "Have the hope
that you may be able to get in, but not a *blind*
hope."

CHAPTER 11

Writing and Research
in the Business Community

. . . The New York financial community
has hundreds of BA's in English and
history. If people can think, speak,
and write clearly and analytically they
are equipped to do a great variety of
things.--Letter from William Bliss,
Director, Yale Alumni Placement Service, to author

Since they [English majors and graduate degree holders] have already had
substantial training in how to commu-
nicate--both on paper, from years of
writing class papers, and orally,
assuming that many of them have had
to pass graduate oral exams and have
held teaching assistantships--they
are ten steps ahead of the average
business major who never learns how
to put pen to paper. . . . Remember
that the communications skills are
already proven by success in school,
and only need to be translated into
business areas. The translation to
a specific position or company or
skill is not too hard to obtain: it
says to a business employer that one
understands the business orientation,

that one is not an unemployed teacher,
but a skilled and prepared communications expert.--Member of management at
Pacific Northwest Bell

Kenneth Haas, whose dissertation at Ohio University was a textual and bibliographical study of
Tennyson's *Gareth and Lynette* idyll, is now in
charge of the on-the-job training of over ten
thousand employees of Korvette, Inc., in New
York City. Blanche Adams, a Ph.D. candidate
writing a dissertation on Elizabethan drama,
spends two days a week as a well-paid consultant
in the offices of a large accounting firm where
she works with its executives, both singly and
in small classes, on their writing. Meg
Wingard, a B.A. in English from the University
of Washington, is in charge of publications for
a medical instrument company. Vicki Hill, who
though not an English major took many English
courses at Washington State University, recently
left a position as information specialist for
Group Health Cooperative of Puget Sound, where
she wrote consumer bulletins which sometimes
reached one hundred thousand readers. Earl
Grout, a recent Ph.D. whose dissertation dealt
with James Boswell, now works for the New York
Life Insurance Company.

All five of these people say that they enjoy
their jobs and that they feel competent in them.
But are such positions rarities? Or is there a
widespread need in business today for people
with backgrounds like theirs? A number of business men and women are beginning to say that
there *is* such a need. "Communications is
[G.E.'s] most important problem," says Paul
Gorman of General Electric.[1] The Chase Manhattan Bank has Ph.D.'s in English among its

management.[2] John Harper of Alcoa wrote last
year in *The New York Times*: "I spend more time
than I used to with people outside the company,
explaining what we're doing. And I try to do a
better job, too, of internal communication."[3]

Prof. Daniel Marder, head of the Department
of English at the University of Tulsa, looking
around to see what kind of businesses hire English majors, writes that

> seldom if ever does a career opportunity
> [in business] exist specifically for the
> English major. But it is surprising and
> gratifying to find so many [of them] who
> rise to the top of business, industry,
> and government. I have found them
> everywhere . . . [e.g., as] President
> of Blue Cross–Blue Shield in Western
> Pennsylvania, . . . project director
> of an intelligence systems analysis
> team working on government contracts
> at HRB–Singer in State College, Penn-
> sylvania, . . . marketing supervisor
> of Phillips Petroleum, the vice presi-
> dent of a food chain in Oklahoma, an
> IBM systems executive in St. Louis,
> . . . an agent of the CIA, a manager
> of the land-leasing division of a major
> oil company, numerous public relations
> and personnel directors and sales
> managers. . . . A bank president, who
> was not an English major, wished that
> some English majors would apply for the
> juicier jobs at his institution. He
> was disappointed with M.B.A.'s. "I
> want people who can think beyond their
> tracks."[4]

Linwood Orange, an English professor at the
University of Southern Mississippi who has done

considerable searching out of alternative
careers for English majors, in his 1973 survey
asked over four hundred business firms the question, "Do you hire college graduates who have a
liberal arts education with a major in English
even though they lack special training in your
area?" He reports that "eighty five percent of
over four hundred organizations answered re-
soundingly 'yes.'" Among these firms were "companies such as Allis-Chalmers, American Airlines, American Broadcasting Company, Bank of
America, Bethlehem Steel, Blue Cross-Blue
Shield, Boeing, Borden, General Electric, General Mills, General Motors, IBM, Litton Industries, Lockheed, Minnesota Mining and Manufacturing, Sears Roebuck, Standard Oil, Procter and
Gamble, Westinghouse, and Xerox."[5]
    In analyzing the various ways in which busi-
nesses currently make use of the talents and
training of people with B.A.'s or advanced degrees in English, one finds six very broad categories of positions: editing and writing (including technical writing); training; sales and
marketing; personnel relations; management; and
research and development.

EDITING AND WRITING

    Seemingly the most logical slot for an Eng-
lish major in business, this area has many sub-
divisions: internal and external communications
(both general and technical editing and writing), public relations, advertising, and the
upgrading of writing for company executives and
employees.
    Editors and writers of internal communica-
tions for businesses may have such assignments
as putting together a company newsletter or
writing reports to keep the various departments
abreast of what the others are doing. Or these

editors may have more specialized assignments,
ones which involve the ability to do technical
writing. One woman who has worked for the past
year for a medical instrument company does some
of both kinds. In addition to supervising and
copy-editing all the firm's publications, she
writes for the monthly in-house newsletter.
"Once you get over your surprise at not being
in a job connected with the Humanities," she
says, "you find a certain excitement in solving
the problems of how to organize the technical
material you work with. Sometimes you have the
challenge of interpreting material from specialists in one part of the company to specialists
in other parts of it. And there's a pleasure
that comes from learning more and more in order
to make new ideas and information clear to other
people."

Her preparation included a B.A. in English,
a quarter in the graphics program at Bellevue
Community College, an internship in public relations at the Seattle Visitors' and Convention
Bureau, an editing internship at Battelle
Seattle Research Center, and a position at
Honeywell, Inc., plus free-lance editing as a
member of Editorial Consultants, Inc. She had
had no academic work leading directly into her
present field. "But just because you start out
not knowing a great deal about the area in which
you find yourself working," she says, "don't
think you're doomed to stay uninformed. Get
books from the Public Library, beginning with
the most general ones. Then work up to the more
technical ones in the university library. Don't
be afraid to ask questions, and don't begrudge
using some of your own free time to fill in your
background."[6]

Other "internal communications" positions
involve working on or producing not only employees' newsletters but magazines, annual and

quarterly reports, house organs (there are fifty
thousand of these currently issued[7]), interde-
partmental memoranda, program evaluations, handbooks, instruction manuals, and policy manuals.
Stephanie Campbell, personnel officer of the
Rainier National Bank of Seattle, said that they
had three or four full-time people in such writing jobs. This bank also has "staff coordinators" who write speeches for senior officers, do
research for these and other speeches, and
travel around to branches, gathering news for
the bank newspaper.[8] Two other large Seattle
banks have within the past year hired women
with backgrounds in English--Angela Hollis and
Blanche Adams--full time for several months to
work with them on complete revisions of their
manuals of policies and procedures. Another
major West Coast bank has recently hired a woman
for a full-time position. As "Internal Communications Editor" her job as she outlines it involves having

> complete responsibility for writing,
> editing, and producing two newsletters
> per month (for employees) and one 20
> page magazine every two months. [It]
> includes making all arrangements for
> artwork, photography, and printing,
> conducting interviews for the articles,
> and originating ideas for both publi-
> cations. [I] coordinate 95 corres-
> pondents throughout the banking system
> and visit banking centers across the
> state [and have] additional responsi-
> bility for consulting on PR releases
> and planning for bank openings and such
> events.[9]

To uncover other positions writing or editing in-house publications, look up large com-

panies in your area and find out, through someone you may know who works at one of them,
through their personnel offices, or through the
business department of a public or university
library, what newsletters, handbooks, or other
material these firms publish for their employees.
Look at as many issues as you can find, so as to
get the feeling of what is being done.   Then,
whether you apply for an advertised position or
talk with a company officer "cold," you'll have
a chance to develop some ideas of your own about
what you might contribute to such projects.

Still other internal communications, aimed
for a less general audience within an industry,
often come under the heading of technical writing.   As a bulletin for the Society of Technical
Communication explains, "there is a need for
technical writing wherever scientific or engineering work is done—a research laboratory, a
university, a chemical manufacturing company,
an assembly plant."[10]

According to Prof. James Souther of the University of Washington's technical communications
program, "people often speak of technical writing when they really mean technical editing."
For technical writing, much of which is equip-
ment-oriented, you are substantially better off
if you have had, if not a college minor in science or math, at least some courses in and some
working familiarity with these fields.   Technical writing, according to Prof. John Walter of
the University of Texas, is a species differing
from other types of exposition in four ways.
First, the writer-reader relationship is a close
one.   The technical writer "usually knows who
will be reading this document, and why."   Second, there is a clear function and purpose for
most technical writing, in that "it must inform
the reader and provide a basis for immediate
action."   Third, the style and form must be

"clear, simple, and unambiguous." Finally, in
the organization of technical writing, Walter
believes that "a logical pattern must often give
way to a psychological pattern," that is, the
writer recognizes "the importance of giving the
reader (often a boss or potential customer)
what he wants *when* he wants it."

In case any readers with literary backgrounds dismiss technical writing as unchalleng-
ing, Walter reminds them that the Shakespearean
scholar, G. B. Harrison, said:

> It is far easier to discuss Hamlet's
> complexes than to write orders which
> ensure that five working parties from
> five different units arrive at the
> right place at the right time equipped
> with proper tools for the job. One
> soon learns that the most seemingly
> simple statement can bear two mean-
> ings and that when instructions are
> misunderstood the fault usually lies
> with the wording of the original
> order.[11]

Currently a great deal of technical writing
is directed toward purchasers and users of heavy
equipment. Manufacturers are finding that they
"can't sell a piece of machinery without selling
a document to go with it," Souther points out.
These documents--such publications as the handbooks and operations manuals for the DC-10 or
the Boeing 747--are "consumer publications," yet
certainly not for the general public. Souther
cites the *Volkswagen Repair Manual* as an outstanding example of the clarity and logical organization that such writing should have. The
writing of handbooks--only one small part of the
increasingly important field of technical writ-
ing--Souther says is particularly important in

relation to military systems and equipment, as
well as to industrial consumers.

Other technical writing jobs may involve
both writing and editing. Technical editors
often take draft material from others and put
it through publication; jet propulsion labs have
hired English editors to do this, as have
applied physics labs at large universities.
Writer/editors are also being hired by industrial and institutional libraries to abstract
works to put in their newsletters so as to update the knowledge of their staffs, says Souther.
"There's often a lot more writing involved in
editing than people realize," says Souther.

There are also many chances to do free-lance
technical writing, on contract, by the job, for
which you can set your own hours and, within
limits, your hourly fees. The Society for Technical Communication offers information on how to
start your own free-lance technical writing
service.[12]

Whether you are applying for an advertised
position or looking for work as a free-lancer,
Souther suggests five steps which will help prepare you. First, your B.A. or advanced degree
in English should have given you the interest
and competency in writing which is basic
(Souther himself was an English and drama major
and graduate student, and his colleague Myron
White wrote a dissertation on D. H. Lawrence).

Second, employers will have more confidence
in you if you have had one or more courses in a
technical communications program such as the
ones at Boston University, at the Montana College of Mineral Science and Technology, or at
one of the several dozen others around the country.[13] Third, if through taking one of these
courses you can arrange for an internship in
which you actually work for two or three months
doing editing or writing for a company, a re-

search institute, or a periodical, this experience will be extremely helpful both in what it
teaches you and in what it conveys to an employer.[14] Fourth, before you look for a job you
should "poke around a library"--i.e., the business section of a public or university library,
or any company library to which you can get
access--and find out what kind of articles and
reports are currently being published, looking
at not only the ones issued by the various companies but also the articles in the journal
Technical Communication. Finally, Souther
urges, you should "develop a portfolio to show
what you have done and can do. Get together a
few articles you have edited, articles that you
have written, brochures that you may have de-
signed--perhaps half a dozen examples, showing
both variety and quality." These suggestions
apply, Souther believes, to any specialized
field of writing, whether in engineering and
the physical sciences (with which his own work
is most closely connected currently) or with
the biological sciences (where there is also an
expanding field in writing and editing on medical, nursing, and environmental subjects).

  There are also positions as writers, editors, or researchers for consumer publications
of the less specialized kind. In these fields,
business firms and nonprofit organizations alike
make use of information specialists and writers
in many ways. One of the commonest is putting
together catalogues and handbooks for the general public. Another is in issuing brochures or
articles designed to increase public good will.
Most utility companies and investment houses,
as well as nonprofit foundations from art museums to zoos, regularly send out newsletters or
magazines. In addition they use fliers, bulletins, letters, and brochures to raise funds or
publicize special events. Today it is accepted

that any agency or firm whose products are in-
tangible will use the printed word to alert the
public either to how well it is doing or how
much it needs and deserves financial support.
As we glance at these mailings, we tend to take
them for granted; it is not until we try to produce something like this ourselves that we realize how much research, imagination, and sheer
writing skill goes into the ones which stand out
from the mass and achieve their purpose. Although writing such material is often done by
professional advertising copy-writers, occasionally there are openings for those of you
with backgrounds in English--provided that you
have some acquaintance with the aims and the
accomplishments of the institution where you
are applying, and can provide examples of your
own previous work when you are interviewed.

There are several hundred business firms and
nonprofit agencies in every metropolitan area
who make use of writers for their consumer publications. Typical among them are local and
state arts groups, the American Cancer Society,
the American Red Cross, the United Way and other
community social agencies, fund drives, major
cultural institutions (theaters, musical foundations, art schools, opera companies, and museums). Other institutions employing writers and
information specialists include four-year and
community colleges, all major hospitals and
health plans, all large banks and insurance companies, and industry-oriented magazines.

If you succeed in obtaining a writing or
editing job with one of these, you may be classified as a publicist, an information specialist, a public relations person, or simply a
writer. Although some of these positions are
part-time or seasonal, many are full-time professional positions. And some of the companies
or agencies, such as large communications firms,

municipal agencies such as city ports, and the
largest health plans and banks, often have
three, four, or half a dozen such persons on
their staffs at once.

The training in analysis and research acquired through getting a degree in English is
a definite asset in any of these positions,
Rainier Bank's Stephanie Campbell believes.
"Important as a basic qualification is the . . .
organized writing ability which most English
majors have acquired during their academic
careers," says Mark Loftin of the Chase Manhattan Bank.[15] In the banking world you can
either move into writing and PR jobs through
management training (as did probably three-
fourths of the people now holding them), or be
hired directly for the writing job. When you
apply, says Campbell, take with you not only
your résumé but samples of your writing and of
any speeches you have prepared. Most banks try
to match an applicant's educational level with
the appropriate job. Personnel departments
often take résumés and keep them on file for a
year. Since there are frequent job changes in
this field, even if your inquiry meets with the
reply "I'm sorry, but we have no vacancies at
this time, and we do not anticipate any," you
need not feel that the door will never open.

You will find still more potential positions
editing or writing for consumer publications and
house organs if you are free to relocate geo-
graphically. Look in *The Writer's Market '77*,
under the headings "Company Publications," "Consumer Publications," and "Trade, Technical, and
Professional Journals." You will find there
are over six hundred pages of companies issuing
such magazines, among the best known of which
are the ones published by the airlines and the
automobile manufacturers. Every major airline
has a magazine for its customers similar to

Aside from Teaching English

United's *Mainliner*, and each of the main auto
manufacturers has a magazine, such as *Ford
Times*, sent to new owners of its cars. Editing
one of these is usually a full-time position,
for which you could eventually be qualified
after working on smaller local publications.

Among other kinds of consumer publications
you should not overlook those in health care,
according to Vicki Hill, who has just moved from
a PR position at Group Health Cooperative in
Seattle to a post as information specialist for
the Satellite Project at the University of Washington School of Nursing. "There is a tremen-
dous need on the part of the consumer for health
information," she believes. She found her work
at Group Health rewarding because it gave her
more of a chance to feel useful than any other
job she had held. As an example she cited her
pamphlet, *Group Health Cooperative: Using Its
Services*, which was sent to over one hundred
thousand subscribers of the organization. Her
challenge in this booklet was to put herself in
the place of a newcomer who knew nothing at all
about such a health plan, to explain its workings in a way that readers of all educational
levels would understand and remember, and in so
doing to avoid the "legalese" in which most
medical coverage agreements are written. Since
the essence of Hill's job with Group Health and
her present one with the Satellite Project of
the School of Nursing is conveying information
to a wide general public, what she does is not
considered technical writing. Hill's general
communications background has served her well;
in fact she says that in these positions, "it
actually helps not to have a Health Sciences
background. Without one, you have to ask yourself and others enough questions about the material so as to be absolutely sure that you understand it, and then you have to be careful to

restate it in terms so that a wide range of
people, none of whom probably do much reading outside their own fields, can absorb it
easily."[16]

Still another way that people with backgrounds in English can increasingly fill a need
of business is to teach in-service courses in
writing. As Fred Pneuman of Weyerhaeuser says,
such courses can often help upgrade the writing
of company executives, most of whom had no writing courses in college and who over the years
have followed more and more closely a set format in their business writing. Pneuman is considering hiring a Ph.D. in English to design
and teach a course in report writing which will
fit the particular professional needs of his
staff.[17] Other companies, ranging from small
ones such as the Human Resources Development
Corporation to giants such as Boeing, have
established or are establishing courses for
their staffs.

What actually goes on in these courses?
Does an English Ph.D. who teaches them simply
preach adherence to the principles of what used
to be called "business English?" According to
Blanche Adams, her job teaching the executives
of a major accounting firm is broader in scope
than that. One of her typical assignments last
month was to help a department head recast
letters so that they would have a conciliatory
rather than an adversary tone toward a client
who was causing problems. Another was to rewrite the firm's reports in terms that stock-
holders and officers of client companies not
specializing in accounting could understand.
Still another was to redo several kinds of internal communications so that the staff members
to whom they were sent would be interested
enough to read them before having them filed.

When asked what she did with the executives'

writing to help bring about greater readability,
Adams replied that she tried to do

> just about what anyone would do in
> teaching an English composition
> class. Get the students to bring
> in first drafts of what they are
> writing; get them to read them over,
> aloud if possible, so as to see
> whether their meaning came through,
> and in the tone they'd intended.
> Next, to get them to cut out all
> the words that they recognize as
> not absolutely needed, and then to
> cut out still more; to be sure that
> there are clear transitions; and
> most of all to try to be specific
> and direct instead of abstract and
> pompous. These executives have
> graduated from college, and some
> of them have M.B.A.'s; they don't
> make the big obvious mistakes in
> grammar and punctuation that many
> freshmen do; but they've been
> writing for so long in a stereo-
> typed financial-page jargon that
> they forget to think of their readers.

Somewhat to her surprise at first, Adams'
clients have respected her expertise; they take
her word for changes that she suggests. Meanwhile she is trying not only to deal with their
writing piece by piece but to establish guidelines for the future. Recently she received a
vote of confidence; after the company went
through a drastic reshuffle of personnel and
programs, her project of upgrading company writing remained unchanged. In fact, it won the
comment, "This program is one of the best
things we've started in a long time."[18]

On the West Coast, the accounting firm which
hired Blanche Adams is, along with another accounting firm, making somewhat of a pioneering
effort. On the East Coast, however, it was over
twenty years ago that Dr. Henrietta J. Tichy
began to help accountants, engineers, and other
business executives to write better. A Ph.D.
and an associate professor of English at Hunter
College, Tichy also enjoys a career as consultant and lecturer for firms in management,
science, and technology. She has been invited
to advise and teach specialists in advertising
and promotion, financial analysis, library
science, manufacturing, marketing, medical
writing, personnel and training, production,
public relations, research and development, and
other branches of business and industry. If
after reading the comments on technical writing
in this and earlier chapters you still wonder
what exactly it is, what it does, to what extent
it differs from the kind of writing you have
been trying to achieve or to teach as an English
major or instructor, Tichy's text, *Effective
Writing*, will give you an excellent survey of
the field and its problems, and one which reveals how familiar many of them are.[19]

PERSONNEL

The wording of job descriptions and the
writing and interpreting of personnel evaluations has come in large firms to be a specialty
in itself. There are also manuals and programmed learning guides to be written and
edited, questionnaires, tests, and application
forms to be designed and updated, and a great
deal of correspondence to be dealt with. Although many people doing this kind of writing
in personnel departments have come up from
entry-level personnel jobs, occasionally a

"communications expert" is taken on for that
purpose. If you are interested, watch the job
descriptions for personnel vacancies in large
companies. Alice Dickie of Weyerhaeuser is one
of several business persons interviewed who suggested "personnel job descriptions writing" as
a job for which an English major would be well
qualified.[20]

MANAGEMENT AND RESEARCH AND DEVELOPMENT

These terms can of course cover vastly different positions in different firms, and usually
the best way into management is still through
learning the business at various levels on the
way up. Fred Pneuman of Weyerhaeuser suggests
that a good way for a person with writing competence to get started is to "assist with or
produce top management productions," including
reports, speeches, and audiovisual aids. Eventually, perhaps, "with supplemental business
training, an English major could work his/her
way into company management by making use of
communications skills to further company objectives."[21] John Harwood, after being extensively
interviewed by business employers when looking
for an alternative position, came away with the
conviction that college teachers were "superbly
equipped to assume managerial responsibilities
in many sectors of American business"--provided
only that they could translate the skills gained
while studying and teaching into language that
would make the business employer realize that
these were the capabilities that he was looking
for.[22] In a similar vein, a personnel manager
of one of the 400 blue-chip companies surveyed
by Linwood Orange told Professor Orange that
"if these [English majors] have the imagination
and are willing to accept the challenge, there
is no job in management . . . which could not

be theirs and in which they could not be of definite service."[23]

   As a member of management, you might become
involved in planning or performing some of the
activities covered by that all-purpose magical
phrase of our time, "research and development."
The more experience you have had in writing reports, helping design and interpret marketing
surveys, and making long-range plans and projections of any kind, the more likely you are
to move into "research and development." To
find such positions in a company where you have
not already had experience, probably your best
move is to present yourself as someone already
involved in the "problem-solving" approach.
This general phrase, however, is becoming rather
well worn; you will have to have something in
your experience with which to back it up--
courses in business theory or, better, achieve-
ments in another business where you actually
were successful in problem-solving.

TRAINING

   Positions for teaching writing to business
executives and staff members are sometimes part
of in-service training programs which teach en-
trants to a company job-related skills or update the knowledge of long-time employees. The
Boeing, Safeco, and Korvette companies offer
examples of such programs; Pacific Northwest
Bell often takes experienced teachers and
trains them to teach others.

   One woman who has made such an application
of the techniques of investigation, planning,
and organization which she developed in graduate school is Ellen Messer-Davidow, a Ph.D.
candidate in English at the University of Cincinnati. Working on a committee set up by the
Office of University Commitment for Human Re-

sources, she helped design and set up an "admin-
istrative/management training program" for women and minority faculty members already hired
by the university. This program in its recent
sessions began with a three-week seminar that
was followed by a two-quarter practicum period.
These sessions were staffed by a pool of faculty, administrators, and business executives from
both within and without the university. In the
curriculum they dealt with such topics as "Col-
lective Bargaining," "Organizational Planning,
Motivation, and Evaluation," "Techniques of Management as Viewed by Major Decision-Makers,"
"Affirmative Action Impact on Higher Education,"
and a dozen others. Such seminars suggest various potential offshoots, both in educational
and business settings, as well as offering, in
themselves, interesting examples to other institutions.[24]

Another enthusiastic proponent of the role
of the English Ph.D. in administering training
programs is Kenneth Haas, who left an assistant
professorship in 1973 for a position in charge
of executive training at the Lazarus Company in
Columbus, Ohio. (Two years later, when he re-
signed from that position to take charge of
Korvette's Management Training Program, his re-
placement was another Ph.D.) His overall responsibility at Korvette is program building
and curriculum development. What Haas actually
does, he told me recently, is to set up training courses "both for the rank and file and the
people at the top of the house." Some are writing workshops, some are speaking workshops, some
are "sales support training," and some are
"human relations skills training." He designs,
monitors, and sometimes teaches these courses;
he picks out the staff who teach them in the
field (Korvette has over ten thousand employees
in its New York City, its southern, and its mid-

western branches); he updates the curriculum and
plans new courses as needed.

In urging me to tell readers that there *is*
job availability in such fields, he talked about
his own preparation. With a B.A. from Duquesne
University (major: English, minor: Philosophy)
and a Ph.D. from Ohio University, he said that
his own preparation for the position he now held
seemed to have been just about right. His education has been a traditional one, with no
business courses, no internships (he has designed and monitored internship programs, but
has a few reservations about their practicality).[25] He did, however, after getting his
doctor's degree, take several continuing education courses in management theory and in the
behavorial sciences. He also attended seminars
on business-related subjects. He thinks that
his education in English has taught him several
skills that are applicable to his present
duties: how to work with broad general concepts; how to pay attention to minute details;
how, when he needs answers to a problem, "to
get in there and dig it all out"; and especially how to put together seemingly unrelated
pieces of evidence into a coherent whole.

> "On my dissertation I was working
> with 27 different manuscripts of
> *Gareth and Lynette*. At first it
> seemed pretty hopeless: very few
> of them were dated; there was
> very little evidence as to the
> relation between one document and
> another. Gradually I pieced things
> together and finally emerged with
> some conclusions about what Tennyson
> had been doing as he wrote. Now
> although there was certainly no
> *direct* connection between coping

with evidence like this and doing my
present job, you do develop a kind
of confidence in your ability to deal
with details and still to work toward some sort of big picture too."[26]

For those of you hoping to find or develop
positions like Messer-Davidow's or Haas's,
their comments on how they got their jobs may
offer a few clues. Messer-Davidow says that
she got her assignment as special assistant to
the president on the basis of having done a
lot of writing (both journalism and fiction),
having experience with various organizations
that were working for social change and having
made personal contact with the university administration. Haas says that running training
programs for business is initially a tough
field to crack, not because of employers' objections to academics but because of the stiff
competition from other academics with degrees
in the behavioral sciences. But "look into any
businesses which are labor-intensive, especially
banking and retailing," he suggests. "If you
see an ad for someone with a behavioral science
degree, apply anyway." When being interviewed
by employers looking for behavioral scientists,
he would tell them, as he reports, something
like this: "I've been teaching and studying
literature. But authors write novels about
only two things: one is people and the other
is ideas. What I've been dealing with for the
last six years is how people act and what makes
them act that way." This approach of finding a
common denominator between his education and a
business job has been successful for him both
times he has depended upon it.
    Projecting his ideas about jobs for English
doctorates into the future, Haas sees another
possibility opening up: merchandising infor-

mation systems. He considers that a person who
has intensively studied English makes the ideal
interface between the computers and the industrial and business users, translating the data
generated by the computer for the people who
have to use it. Such jobs are *not* matters of
computer programming, he says, but instead are
communications functions.

One last point that Haas makes offers at
least a partial answer to the many graduate students who, as William Irmscher of the University
of Washington says, "hesitate to take these alternative jobs because it means that if they
do, they'll have to give up their preoccupation
with literature." Do they actually have to
turn their backs on literature? Has Haas made
a sharp break between his present executive life
and his old scholarly one? He says not.

> Teaching in a college or univer-
> sity is a most unusual situation.
> While you're doing it, you may think
> it's the norm, but it's not. You
> have to realize the fact that a uni-
> versity succeeds in totally integrating
> vocation and avocation for its faculty.
> When you go into business, there may
> be nothing in your job *directly* con-
> nected with literature. But you have
> a good chance to keep abreast of
> your field as an avocation. You
> can do it more easily than you think
> if you realize it's absolutely up to
> you.

So in his previous business job in Columbus,
Haas worked actively on the board of an organization to preserve Appalachian song and dance;
now that he works for a firm in New York City
he teaches extension courses in literature near

his Long Island home, does research in the Victorian period, and reads papers before various
societies of scholars and of book collectors.[27]

To sum up, the experience of Haas, Messer-
Davidow, and several other successful job
candidates I interviewed validates in one way
or another the remarks of Mark Loftin of the
Chase Manhattan Bank:

> It is important [to dispense with]
> the old notion that if one looks to
> business, he must prostitute his
> long fought-for credentials as a
> humanist and give himself up to the
> establishment as a banker, a stock-
> broker, or an operations manager.
> In the past five years, business has
> undergone a major change in attitude
> . . . especially with the advent of
> the human resources philosophy. This
> means . . . a marked increase in the
> need to provide ways to train and
> develop manpower. . . . This area
> of training and education in busi-
> ness and industry . . . provides one
> meaningful alternative to students
> making career decisions about col-
> lege teaching. . . . The field of
> training is rapidly growing into a
> recognized profession, staffed, and
> in many ways defined by those who
> ventured into it from academic
> careers.[28]

Even though you realize that there are many
ways in which business firms might be able to
make use of your skills--as a writer or editor,
in personnel, in training, management, or possibly in research and development--you may
think you have a problem in bridging the *appar-*

ent gap between your English degree or degrees
and the segment of the "real world" you are trying to enter. You are probably aware that not
all business executives are as enthusiastic
about people with liberal arts degrees, particularly graduate ones in English, as are Haas's
employers or the people quoted at the beginning
of this chapter. Categorically dismissing
Ph.D.'s, Mary McMahon, an assistant vice-
president for Equitable Life, recently declared
that her company "need[s] creative thinking, not
their specialized knowledge."[29] So it is up to
you to demonstrate that these two qualities are
not mutually exclusive, that you have brought
with you from the campus not only information
but mental elasticity and an ability to solve
problems.

There are various ways of making these qualities visible to a business employer. Here are
some of the methods that are currently working
for many people.

• To John T. Harwood of The College of
William and Mary, the problem is "ultimately a
matter of rhetoric; it is a matter of translating academic experience . . . into the categories by which businessmen perceive themselves
and their work." Accordingly, he steeped himself in job advertisements and their business
terminology, repeated a good deal of the language of the advertisement in the cover letter
with which he answered each ad, and found himself receiving offers from various businesses.[30]

• Kenneth Haas reports that, without going
to such elaborate lengths, he had no trouble
convincing business employers that his graduate
education and college teaching were germane to
the jobs that they needed to get done. One
probable reason for Haas's credibility is that,
having had six years of active duty in the army,
he could point to the fact that he had already

directed large numbers of personnel and had been
able to deal with a wide variety of people. He
suggests that if you are an academician applying
for a position in business, you emphasize whatever successful "real world" experience you have
had; it will usually have some relevance to the
job for which you are applying.

    • A person in management at Pacific North-
west Bell emphasizes the importance of doing
research on the company before the interview.
Take several days or longer to find out all you
can through the business departments of public
and university libraries as well as through
trade papers and the *Wall Street Journal*. The
more you know about what the company is trying
to do, the more chance you ordinarily have to
be hired in at a status and rate of pay above
that of entry level. Or, taking the opposite
tack from the above, stress your interest in
the general business environment, the administrative end rather than a specialty. (Do this
only if you have had some successful previous
experience which could be broadly interpreted
as "administrative.")

    • Acquire an ancillary skill such as com-
puter programming, or take at least a few general business courses such as labor relations,
advertising, accounting, or marketing, in order
to have a bridge between your English degree
and the position you're seeking. (As examples
of classes which he would recommend, depending
upon the field which most interests you, one
executive suggested taking one or more of the
following: technical writing or editing; advertising layout or copy; marketing theory;
public relations techniques; journalism—news
reporting or copy-writing; anything in the computer field; or the making of documentary films
(the writing or the actual production end).)

• In conclusion, says the same Pacific
Northwest Bell executive,

> having an advanced degree in English
> doesn't mean that you are an egg-
> head; English education strengthens
> the ability to organize, synthesize,
> analyze, and work comfortably with
> abstractions. Certainly the ability
> to research around an abstract thesis
> and pull it together into a working
> statement is directly translatable
> from your undergraduate or graduate
> work in English.
>   A writing and literature back-
> ground is a huge creative well, some-
> thing no marketing theory class will
> ever match. Picking up a technical
> orientation later is far from impos-
> sible. Read books, sit in on or en-
> roll in a class--just use a little
> of the same determination that kept
> you in school for up to twenty years.[31]

CHAPTER 12

The Need of Government To Be Understood: Working for Local and Federal Agencies

If you are looking for a job, consider
giving the Federal Government a try.
The U.S. Government is the largest
single employer in the country, and
one of the largest employers in the
world. It offers the usual job benefits enjoyed in private industry, and
even more job security. Its ranks include every known occupation (and some
which are generally unknown) outside
of the government. No matter what
your background and special interest: professional, technical secretarial and clerical, or blue-collar,
there is a place for you.--Susan
Lukowski and Marget Piton, *Strategy
and Tactics for Getting a Government
Job*

There simply can't be a "freeze" on
Government employment. Too many
civil servants are retiring from
government service, job hopping from
one agency to another, dropping out
from the job scene altogether, returning to school, being reassigned--
all of which means open slots for

job seekers.--Richard K. Irish, *Go
Hire Yourself an Employer*

Looking for a job with any branch of the government, whether city, county, state, or federal,
may call upon even more of your patience, persistence, and initiative than is needed for the
other positions mentioned in this handbook. Yet
I have talked with a number of people who, at
the end of their search, claim to have found
their ideal job.

Before you begin to look for any government
job at all, it would be a good idea to define
your goals and resources. As Charles Ruemelin
suggests in his *Guide to Government and Public
Service Employment,* you should think through
carefully such questions as, for example, the
region where you want to work, at what level
(federal, state, or local), in what branch (legislative, executive, or judicial), how closely
directed you like to be, how research-oriented
you are, how directly you hope to make use of
your academic background, how willing you are
to travel in your job, and whether you hope to
start upwards on a career ladder or are merely
looking for an interim position.[1]

Ruemelin advises that you assess your resources realistically in terms of five types
of expertise or experience: (1) specific
skills, "which may include computer programming,
interviewing, polling, statistics, questionnaire
design, writing and editing abilities, typing
(which can serve as entree to an excellent
opportunity but can also stigmatize you as a
clerical assistant), and coordination of volunteer programs"; (2) "generalist skills," including "analytical abilities, problem-solving

capabilities, the capacity to express yourself,
and the ability to work with others [toward] a
common objective"; (3) any campaign or other
political experience you have had; (4) any
"working knowledge of a particular field (transportation, economics, welfare policy, energy
planning, etc.)"; and (5) possible residual
value of other experience you have had. "Remember that almost any paid or volunteer work
experience or avocational pursuit can at least
indirectly enhance your employability. If you
have participated fully in any job, you have
learned a great deal more about the organization and its concerns than the actual performance of that job may have demanded."[2]

Having decided what you want and what you
have to offer, you are ready to identify the
particular job or range of jobs you want and
to begin the process of submitting forms, taking tests, and waiting to hear the results.
With unusual luck, you may find that your job
hunt takes under three months, as did Ana
Zambrano, a Ph.D. in English and specialist in
Victorian literature who until recently taught
English at the University of Southern California. She took an M.A. in public administration
in night school, set her sights on an administrative job in the Long Beach and Los Angeles
area, sent out a large number of applications,
and after three months was offered and accepted
a position that seemed to meet all her requirements, that of an administrative analyst working for the City of Long Beach.[3]

Lacking such clear ideas of what they want
at the beginning of their search, other job-
seekers have conducted a longer hunt with results that were equally satisfying to them in
the end. Sometimes you can make your own way,
if you are determined enough, to the post you
want through starting at an entry-level job and

gradually getting yourself reclassified upwards,
shaping your responsibilities and your job
titles yourself as you get farther and farther
into the work of a government agency. The experience of one woman with a nearly completed
Ph.D. in English literature who started back to
work after her children were in high school is
a case in point. With no recent job experience,
and no credentials in government or budgetary
work, she has in two and a half years pro-
gressed to exactly the job she wants, that of
systems analyst for a City of Seattle department. Her account shows what part individual
initiative can play:

>   Aside from my work in English--an
> undergraduate major and an M.A., plus
> having finished everything for a Ph.D.
> in English at the University of Illi-
> nois except my dissertation--I had no
> formal background at all--certainly
> nothing that would fit me for a manage-
> ment position, helping to deal with a
> budget. Yet that was the kind of thing
> I wanted. So I started in with a city
> department as a secretary. Very soon
> I was being asked to edit, and then to
> write, a departmental newsletter that
> my boss was getting out. Then, after
> other people in the office started to
> give me reports to edit or write, my
> boss got my job reclassified, and I
> got the title of "Research and Evalu-
> ation Assistant," with a higher
> salary and more responsibilities.
>   But I still wanted something even
> more interesting, something that
> would give me a chance to use my
> head more and to do more writing.
> So, after looking around, I found that

being a Systems Analyst would most
nearly fill my specifications of anything likely to come up within the
next few years. To help qualify myself for that, I took three evening
courses, one after another: Basic
Principles of Accounting, Introduction
to Computer Language, and College Alge-
bra. I took two of them at the UW, one
at a community college. And I bought
half a dozen accounting books and half
a dozen books about systems analysis,
and I read each one through. Gradually budgets became more understandable and everything began to fit
together.

I also went on Saturdays whenever
I could to the Business Administration
Library of the university and read
every journal there that I could understand. *But of all the kinds of preparation probably the most useful was
the one I already had--the ability to
analyze a problem into its parts, to
do research, and to write about what
I found out--which I had gotten long
ago as an English major.* Now that
I'm in the job I want, and have proved
that I can understand the mathematical
part, I find that what I draw upon most
are my writing abilities. I use them
all the time. Tell the people who
read your handbook that the best
thing their English backgrounds may
have given them is that, as graduate
students, they know, or can find out,
where to go in any library. If they
don't know something, at least they
know how to find it out. Lots of
the people I work with have M.B.A.'s;

I don't, but I can talk on an equal
basis with them in analyzing most problems. If once in a while I'm not up
with them at the beginning, I'm only
a week or two behind them, and I've
learned to catch up pretty quickly.[4]

She recommends, therefore, that you look
through the range of municipal jobs, talk un-
officially with anyone you know or can make
contact with to find out what the job really
involves, then set your sights on a particular
area and prepare yourself, in as much of your
spare time as you can manage, to work in it--
whether in budgets, social services, community
development, minority affairs, or whatever sub-
division of the municipal structure most interests you. An information specialist for
Seattle City Light agrees with her. This
woman, who has an M.A. in English and communications, taught freshman composition at the
University of Montana and the University of
Oklahoma before coming to City Light, where
she makes surveys, arranges meetings, super-
vises and edits publications on safety and on
energy conservation.[5]
    Despite occasional local differences, the
process of hunting for a governmental position
is similar in most cities. From time to time,
positions with city offices are advertised in
newspaper classified sections and at campus
placement centers, but certainly not all of
them will be publicized this way. To find out
what other municipal jobs exist, it is usually
best to go down to your city hall or municipal
building to scan the bulletin boards and make
inquiries. Usually a receptionist will be
helpful about answering your questions and
will, if asked, direct you to sets of loose-
leaf notebooks containing descriptions of hun-

dreds of jobs and their requirements. Be sure
to remember, however, that usually only a few
of these jobs are open at any one time and that
you must find the tentative calendars of exams
that will be given in the near future for specific jobs. Often there will be a list in the
daily newspapers of upcoming examinations and
the filing period (sometimes only ten days)
within which application will be accepted.

These examinations of course vary with the
job; they "may include written tests, physical
ability tests, tests of performance and work
skills, and a personal qualifications test (interview)." Final passing grades determine
whether you are put on the "register" (a list
of successful candidates by grade). Departments
fill vacancies, as they occur, from this register. In many cities your name remains on an
open competitive register for one year, or on
a promotional register for two years.[6]

As you look through the job descriptions,
do not be put off by the fact that few of the
government jobs involving writing are classified
under the headings "Writers" or "Researchers."
In the City of Seattle, for example, at least
twenty departments employ writers as public relations people, but under a dozen are so
labeled. A few of these jobs are titled "Information Officers," but most will be called
something like "Administrative Assistant,"
"Administrative Trainee," or "Urban Affairs
Intern." Nonetheless, any writing or research
expertise may be called upon in even the least
impressive-sounding of these jobs, and you may
be on your way to a position in which writing
becomes one of your main responsibilities.[7]

Among the municipal departments employing
writers in one way or another in most large
cities are the department of human resources,
the office of community relations, the office

of government relations, the planning services,
the arts commission, the board of public works,
the human rights commission, the department of
community development, the communications division of the general services department, the
environmental management program, the office of
urban conservation, the office of women's
rights, the human resources' division of aging,
and various cultural and historical
commissions.[8]

Before being called for the tests, you
should be finding out all you can about the
activities, programs, and problems of the kind
of agency you would like to work for. Consult
your campus placement center for sources also;
collect and read critically any bulletins which
the agency distributes to the public; and don't
forget that the business and government departments of most public libraries, as well as most
colleges and universities, have clipping files
on various government departments.

An example of one city department using
writers is the Department of Human Resources of
Seattle, a widely diversified department with
about 120 employees. A personnel officer gave
the following information about kinds of positions of possible interest to readers of this
book.

Positions:

> Administrative Assistant: would make use
> of research, writing, and editing
> skills.
> Planner: does report writing, monitoring
> of programs, systems development, and
> research.
> Administrator: writes reports and propo-
> sals, reviews those of others, prepares
> grant proposals and other written
> material.

Qualifications: An English liberal arts background which includes research and writing
expertise would be extremely useful. To
be competitive, the applicant should also
have some experience, paid or volunteer,
in committee organization or in interviewing people. Although a degree in public
administration or public affairs would be
an ideal addition to a writing background,
the Department now gives on-the-job training; there are also City-sponsored in-
service courses in management training.
How to apply: Although some of this department's positions go through the city civil
service, the department is so new that many
of the positions are still termed "provisional." For these, the department sends
job descriptions to college and university
placement centers, requesting résumés and
applications. After these are screened,
interviews are held, and the job is awarded
directly. For someone with research and
writing skills, the chances seem reasonably
good.
Comments: The personnel officer points out
that one's chances of promotion from a relatively routine job to one involving
writing and research are much better in a
new department such as hers than in an old
established one with rigid job descriptions. (She herself is an English B.A.
who, after a year of substitute teaching,
went to work for the city.)[9]

One of the things to check carefully in
municipal jobs, says an employee of Seattle's
Department of Human Resources, is whether you
are applying to a new and flexible program or
a long-established one. The new ones, she
found, having no long-hallowed job descrip-

tions, allowed great flexibility when she accepted a position there three years ago. Gradually she has turned her job more and more into one that is about 50 percent writing and 50 percent dealing with people.[10]

Other positions listed that call upon writing and research abilities include such titles as human relations representative, community relations specialist, community relations coordinator, community service specialist, and program coordinator. Most of them included in the job description something like the following: "Duties: writes, reviews, edits, and submits press and other related releases pertinent to department planning, projects, programs, and policy"; or "must have ability to prepare analytic reports"; or "should have the ability to write clearly, concisely, and accurately, and to evaluate, approve, and prepare materials for news, radio, television, and other media release."

It is true, however, that most of the positions call for something in addition, such as "from one to three years' experience, paid or volunteer," working with community relations, minority groups, recreational activities, or something else. You have two ways of meeting this test. Some of these positions allow substitution of additional education, such as graduate work, for some of the years of experience.[11] For other positions, you may have a chance to present volunteer work, or jobs you may have held while working your way through college or graduate school, as evidence that you meet the qualifications.

Municipal officials at nearly all levels agree emphatically that their agencies need people who can find and organize material, write reports and speeches, draft summaries, plans, and proposals, as well as evaluate the

proposals of others. In particular every office
and agency needs people who can transmit ideas
clearly and concisely. As Walter Hundley of
Seattle complained not long ago, "Half of the
reports that come to any office are so care-
lessly written that nobody can be sure what they
mean." When asked what was being done to improve communication, he replied that there were
simply not enough qualified people available to
afford much hope for change. Here then is an
opportunity for some of you, if you have the
drive to get past some of the apparent hurdles
looming up during the first part of your search
for such positions.

APPLYING TO COUNTY GOVERNMENTS

Most county departments are separate from
the city and state ones which, to a great extent, they parallel. To apply for jobs, the
method is similar to that of applying for municipal positions: you must familiarize yourself
with the range of job descriptions, find out
which jobs will soon have open filing periods
for applications, apply, and then, if found to
be eligible, take an exam. If you pass with a
sufficiently high rating you are put on a register, and then as a vacancy needs to be filled,
you may be interviewed.

Many counties, like many cities, having
suffered recent budget cuts, have had to stop
accepting applicants' "interest cards" and no-
tifying job-seekers of upcoming application
filing periods or exams. But in most areas
such filing periods are listed in the newspapers
and on bulletin boards in the county courthouse;
complete information is usually available in the
various county personnel offices.

Among the typical county departments and
commissions in which readers of these guidelines

might find positions involving public relations, writing, gathering information, or teaching in-service courses are the arts commissions,
community and environmental development departments, community relations, housing and community development planning, human services, long-
range planning, personnel, public employment
programs, and youth affairs bureaus.

Here, as with municipal positions, you will
find that other experience or capabilities in
addition to your writing, editing, and research
skills will be called for in the job description. It is up to you either to make the most
of experience that you have had or else to make
your entry as a secretary and ultimately get
your position reclassified as an information
specialist, special writer, public relations
specialist, or whatever it is that you and your
employer find will both describe what you are
doing and give you a chance for advancement.

WORKING FOR YOUR STATE GOVERNMENT

Probably the state government offers an
even greater number and variety of possibilities to readers of this handbook than does city
or county government.

One Ph.D. in English who had taught successfully in a university for six years found,
upon deciding to make a job change, that she
could do very well in a public relations position at the museum of a southwestern state.
She is now in charge of its publicity for all
media and enjoys making budgetary decisions as
well as supervising every detail of the releases about the museum in newspapers and
posters, on radio, and on TV. "If you get into the milieu of the museums," she says, "this
is one place besides the world of teaching
where your academic background is really appre-

ciated and a Ph.D. is definitely valued. So,
though the starting salary isn't high, there is
a very good chcnce of advancement."
    Her experience in getting the position was
typical of the way most state jobs at the higher
levels are filled.

> First you have to get to know the insti-
> tution where you want to work, so as to
> find out definitely that there will be
> a job. Then you have to present your
> qualifications to the person who can
> hire you in such a way that he or she
> does decide to hire you. Then you
> have to find out what the job will be
> called, what kind of state civil serv-
> ice exam to take and when to take it
> so that you can get on the Register
> and be interviewed for that job. With
> me, the whole process took about six
> months, from when I first heard that
> there might be such a position created
> until I started work.[12]

    Other state positions cover a wide spectrum.
For the current listing--not of actual jobs but
of the various state and interstate agencies,
offices, and commissions across the country and
in your own state--consult the latest edition
of *The Book of the States,* issued biennally,
Selected State Officials and the Legislatures,
and *State Administrative Officials Classified
by Functions,* all published by the Council of
State Governments, Lexington, Kentucky.
    A sampling of actual positions--not spelled
out in the three above reference works but dis-
coverable through information provided by each
State Civil Service Commission--yields many

that might interest people with backgrounds in
research and writing:

> *Editor:* writes and edits newsletters, as
> for instance for the state education
> association.
>
> *Education specialist:* plans programs at
> all levels for institutionalized stu-
> dents and sometimes teaches these
> courses, for example at McNeill Island
> in Washington, or at other prisons in
> other states.
>
> *Human rights commission*: at times there
> are positions involving public rela-
> tions, writing, and research here.
>
> *Staff development center*: teaching and
> evaluation goes on here. Some back-
> ground in education courses as well
> as in research techniques is required
> of job applicants.
>
> *Office of community development*: involves
> research, writing, public relations.
>
> *Office of citizen participation*: involves
> research, writing, speaking, public
> relations skills, along with experience
> in working with groups of all kinds of
> people.
>
> *Personnel department:* positions require
> ability to write clearly and to evalu-
> ate written material from others.
>
> *Publicist and editor of newsletter* (note
> also other PR positions for other com-
> missions): experienced and versatile
> writers are needed to work with indi-
> vidual legislators in their communica-
> tions caucuses and to write press
> releases.
>
> *Research analysts*: such positions, which
> may occur in connection with almost any

state commission or department, are well
worth looking into. One advertised
through a university placement center
recently was with marine land management. The requirement was a B.A. with
"one year's experience in research helpful, not mandatory."
Research positions in the legislature:
these are sometimes available and involve serving on a back-up committee to
provide information to a legislator.
Although it helps to have a specialty,
such as education or environmental
studies, you may soon find that you
have branched out into other fields.
*Research and writing positions on state
board for community colleges*
*Research and writing positions on your
state's council for higher education*
(see above)
Secretary to a legislator: acts as researcher, as speech writer, and may
help get out periodic reports to
constituents.

Although most of these jobs are carried on
in the state capitol, some jobs for which you
might be qualified (i.e., community affairs
analyst, community affairs consultant or
planner, community service specialist, or information officer) are performed in other
areas throughout most states.
The qualifications listed usually include
a B.A. plus relevant experience; only in some
specialized technical fields is a graduate degree specified. Nonetheless, having advanced
degrees in any of the humanities will not brand
you as "overqualified" if you can show the connection between research abilities you have

developed and the kind of work you are seeking.
When applying you should, however, stress any
unacademic work, paid or volunteer, that you
have done, and present graduate degrees as
merely an added qualification. In the eyes of
many legislators moreover, these degrees will
seem desirable. Says Representative Jeff
Douthwaite of Washington: "Legislators need
bright, able, well-trained people to help them,
both as researchers and as speech-writers."[13]
David Strohnmeyer, a member of the Oregon
legislature, agrees with him. "Government
is a good field for people with writing and
researching abilities," he says. "Working as
a legislative assistant or as secretary to a
legislator will give you a chance to make use
of a great many of the capabilities you
developed in graduate school."[14]

It is important to remember that there are
two types of state jobs. Some are under the
state civil service rules and others, including
many legislative jobs, are exempt from them.
To obtain one of the latter posts, in which you
might do back-up research and eventually writing for a legislator, the best plan according
to Strohnmeyer and others is to get started
before a campaign begins, so that you can "pick
a winner and latch on to him or her." Demonstrate your usefulness in information-gathering
to a candidate; help write his campaign material, on a volunteer basis if necessary, until
the time comes when he may be in a position to
add you to his paid staff. As Jeff Douthwaite
points out, "Patronage jobs follow people who
show willingness to work at the grass roots
level."

According to Douthwaite, the time to get
started working for a legislator is one or two
months before the beginning of his campaign,
or at least as early as possible during his

campaign. Tell a candidate whose qualifications
appeal to you that you are interested in government service, and show evidence on paper that
you can find material, organize presentations,
marshall facts, and write. Ask how you could
be useful to him or, if he is elected, to any
member of his committees. Alternatively, if you
have not gotten started working for a candidate
early in his campaign, it is a good idea, if you
have the time, to do volunteer information-
gathering and other work, as needed, for legislators during a session. Such help will usually increase the chances of your being hired
later.[15]

    If you are looking for a civil service job,
it will be necessary, as Strohnmeyer puts it,
"to work both ends of the system at once."
That is, you have to line up a particular kind
of opening with a particular agency or commission, but you cannot actually be appointed to
that job unless you are on the state's central
register.

    To get on the civil service register in your
state, you should go to the civil service office
of state personnel and look at the job descriptions and the dates of upcoming tests. You cannot take a test until one for a specific job
category comes up, and this does not happen until a vacancy has been announced. Having taken
the tests, and passed with a high score, you
are then listed in the register, and any state
office or agency which has a vacancy in that
job category may then request your services.

    Should you succeed in getting on the regis-
ter before you have lined up an agency which
wants your services, it helps to visit Olympia
once every three weeks with your portfolio of
recent work and with copies of your résumé.
Make rounds of department heads, chairmen of
commissions, and offices of any group which

could conceivably need someone with research, interviewing, or writing ability.

You should be advised that even after you have gotten on the register and have been requested as a department's choice to fill a vacancy or a newly created job, it may take from three to six months for the paper work to be handled so that you are officially on the payroll. "Everybody who hires you will regard Personnel as a stumbling block," said one person who works in a state capitol, "but it's a narrow gate you have to go through."

Despite the long time it takes to get hired, most people who work for a state government find it interesting in itself and valuable in what it can lead to. If you are hoping eventually to get into journalism, your work for a legislator or a committee will have given you a background in state politics, and probably in one or two special areas such as education, the environment, transportation, labor, or civil rights. If on the other hand you would like to stay in government work, there are career positions for writers in most state capitals. Successful experience in working for a state government can also help you if you hope eventually to work for the federal government.

WORKING FOR THE FEDERAL GOVERNMENT

The national capital is another place where, according to several people interviewed, advanced degrees do carry a certain prestige. "So many people working there have law degrees or Ph.D.'s in economics or in planning that it has come to be expected that people involved in the higher levels of the various government agencies will have impressive academic qualifications," says Diane Bolay of HEW.

You can get lists of open federal positions

at your nearest civil service commission job information center. This list is fuller and more
recent than the information likely to be available at your campus placement center. There are
also some federal positions available from time
to time at local branches of federal agencies,
such as the ten regional offices of the U.S.
Office of Education.[16]

Application procedures for federal and state
positions are, in general, parallel: you have
to obtain a "rating" before you can be hired for
a specific job. If you are seeking a mid-level
rating (GS-5 through GS-7), where currently the
jobs are more plentiful, you should get the
brochure for the new Professional and Administrative Career Examination (PACE) and plan to
take the test the next time it is given. If,
however, you wish to apply for the rating of
GS-9 or above, for which your Ph.D. qualifies
you, you need not take the examination; simply
file a Mid-Level Positions Qualifications Brief.

In either case, receiving your rating, as
the authors of the MLA's *Guide for Job Candidates* point out, is only the beginning. "Do
not wait to be contacted about a job. Since
your GS rating is little more than a 'hunting
license,' you must *actively* seek employment by
contacting as many agencies as you can."[17] If
you are interested in the specific details of
tracking down and applying for federal jobs,
read the concise summary in the MLA *Guide* and
the full treatment in the handbook by Susan
Lukowski and Margaret Piton, *Strategy and Tactics for Getting a Government Job.*[18]

You should also read the realistic analysis
of the federal job application process made by
Ann Pincus in a June 1976 article appearing in
The Washington Monthly. She discusses the PACE
level (Professional and Administrative Career
Examination) jobs (GS-5 and GS-7), with base

annual salaries of $8,925 and $11,046, pointing out that every year between 1,600 and 2,000
of them are listed on the Civil Service register, that "others are not listed because of
being filled from within the agency, in-house
promotions, transfers from other agencies or
persons coming back into government." She
shows, too, the complexities of the system,
whereby "high marks on the [PACE] exam alone
do not get you into the civil service. There
is something called the quota system, which
means that every state has a certain number of
jobs--based on population--it can fill in
Washington."

Proceeding to the mid-level jobs (GS-9
through GS-12, base pay approximately $13,500
to $19,500), Pincus explains that "you do not
take an examination for mid-level jobs in Washington, but you still must compete with about
15,000 on the register." She also describes
the senior-level jobs, GS-13 through 15 (base
pay approximately $23,000 to $31,500) on the
register, but points out that 95 percent of
these jobs are filled from within the government. ("This leaves 480 senior-level jobs, 80
percent of which are going to be filled by name
requests.") The final category is super grade:
GS-16, 17, and 18 (base pay, approximately
$36,500). Of the career super-grade appoint-
ments, 92 percent were filled from within the
government.

According to Pincus, therefore, you have
about one chance in sixty-five to get one of
these positions at any grade unless you become
a "name request." To achieve such a status,
you should visit your senator or congressman,
remind him of your qualifications and of any
work you might have done on his campaign. Tell
him the department or agency in which you want
to work; he then may or may not be able to put

pressure on someone there who is in charge of
hiring. Subsequently your application may be
circulated with "must hire" written on it, and
someone writes up a job description and a name
request and sends it over to the Civil Service
Commission.

Although Pincus' account is written in a
cynical tone, she does concede that outsiders
do sometimes succeed in getting Washington
federal jobs. Perhaps to academics, accustomed
as we have lately become to hearing of 300 to
600 qualified applicants for every available
college teaching job in English, her estimate
of one chance in sixty-five doesn't seem as
unexpected as it does to others.[19]

Another useful (and less discouraging)
source of information about the federal job hunt
is Zambrano and Entine's *Career Alternatives for
Academics*, which points out that "it is easier
to get an entry-level position with a newly
opening agency or commission that is still re-
cruiting and still sensitive to new ideas" than
with a more established one. "Moreover, turn-
over is likely to be high in new agencies, thus
increasing the chances of promotions." These
authors also remind you that your academic de-
gree(s) can add points to your rating (up to
three years' experience credit) "both at entry
level and when you're being considered for
advancement."

In view of the "job security and generous
fringe benefits" of federal employment, they
seem to consider it worth looking into. If you
do, you should be sure to consult for reference the latest issues of the following four
volumes: the *Congressional Directory*, the *Congressional Staff Directory*, the *Federal Career
Directory*, and the *Guide to Federal Career
Literature*.[20]

You should also realize that there are certain federal positions which are not filled
through civil service procedures. Among these
are the U.S. Information Agency, the C.I.A.,
the F.B.I., the Energy Research and Development
Administration, the National Security Agency,
and the Postal Service. Some of these agencies
advertise and recruit for positions at university and college placement centers.

There is also to be found, particularly
around universities and research institutes,
still another type of federally funded position
exempt from civil service procedures. Such
positions, advertised through campus placement
centers, involve writing and editing for HEW or
other projects operating through federal grants
or contracts. In most cases, the monthly
salaries are paid through the university system.
The fact that such positions, operating on
"soft money," may terminate after ten months
or a year or two is compensated for, in the
minds of a number of English M.A.'s and Ph.D.'s
who have held them, by several considerations.
The work is interesting; moreover, those who
do it think, in their more optimistic moments,
that it could have an impact on public policy
on such matters as nursing homes, health main-
tenance organizations, ways of keeping patients'
records, and other urgent problems. If you obtain such work, the writing and editing you do
will involve practical application of much that
you have learned as a student or instructor of
English. The salaries in such positions, moreover, tend to be higher than those for comparable editing and writing jobs in education or
in industry.

There is also an expanding field of quasi-
governmental jobs involving the arts. If you
have communication skills, some background in

the arts, and some administrative experience,
you might investigate positions opening up at
all four levels--city, county, state, and
federal--involving editing newsletters, doing
public relations, or administering grants for
the visual and performing arts. Consult the
monthly newsletter, *Arts, inc.*, as well as your
state Council on the Humanities for current
opportunities.[21] People filling this kind of
position are more apt to have a writing background than to be themselves practicing artists.

Government, then, is a field you should not
overlook. Work in any one sector of it gives
you a chance for mobility; once you have gotten
your first government position, it is often not
too difficult to transfer to other regions or
other government agencies.[22] Furthermore, the
variety of government positions is enormous.
You can be a researcher or writer in a "working
with people" program such as HEW, personnel, or
consumer affairs, or an environmental program
such as conservation, or an administrative field
such as management analysis. In the words of
Dr. Ruth Von Behren, who made a long leap from
her graduate work in German medieval history to
her current GS-11 position as management analyst
for the State of California, "When you decide
to work for the Government, take your intellectual curiosity with you; working in an unfamiliar area can be intellectually stimulating."[23]

CHAPTER 13

In Conclusion

The journals and bulletins in which members of
the English teaching profession talk to one
another are full of articles suggesting improvements in the English curriculum and in the
liaison between graduates of English programs
and the world of employment. Broaden the English curriculum, some writers propose: make
contacts with business and government; develop
internships, traineeships, and double majors.
Keep the curriculum the way it is, other writers
urge: concentrate on doing better what traditional English curricula already do well, but
be more selective about which students are admitted, especially to graduate school. These
improvements and many more are described so
persuasively that as one reads one feels that
they are on the verge of being implemented.
     Yet all academic reforms take time, funding,
and the approval of administrators. Meanwhile,
you as a job-seeker cannot wait nor can you
undertake your education all over again according to a more rational plan. What do the pre-
ceding twelve chapters give you to start
applying now? In looking back, I find that,
in addition to the specific points made chapter
by chapter, several general conclusions emerge.
     • Many job-holders and their employers are
convinced that the B.A. in English *is* a viable

degree. With it you can make your way into
journalism, editing, publishing, personnel work,
or do writing and research for business or government; you can enter almost any of the professions discussed in this book except teach-
ing--provided that while working toward this
B.A. and afterward you consciously develop "the
kind of skills you need to get to the place you
need to be."

• The fact must be faced that an advanced
degree in English probably will not carry the
weight outside academia that, if you hold a
doctorate, you may expect it to carry. Nobody
is advertising "Editor/writer needed immediately; recent Ph.D. with college teaching experience preferred." Few employers outside of
colleges and universities think in terms of
advanced degrees; employers ordinarily are concerned instead with demonstrable skills. Among
the places where the mere fact of having an
advanced degree *is* an asset, however, would be
administrative positions in a foundation, on
the staff of a museum, in the middle and higher
ranks of federal government jobs, in overseas
teaching, or in administering management training for a business firm. But, more important,
the skills and techniques that you developed
while earning your advanced degree can stand
you in good stead in almost any career--provided
that you remember to extrapolate from your
graduate school experience and apply what you
have learned (how to dig out information, for
example, how to organize it, how to take account of the smallest detail yet come up eventually with conclusions).

• Although the various fields and professions discussed here all call upon one or more
of the skills learned and interests developed
by English majors, the way one approaches and
holds a position in each of them differs. Talk

to people who are doing what you want to do;
ask them how they heard about and got their
jobs, as well as what they would advise someone
to do who is just starting out. It is important to notice what is possible, what is usual,
and what is simply unthinkable as a way to enter
or advance in each field. For example, try to
find where you can and where you can't expect,
given hard work and luck, to receive a promotion from volunteer work to paid work, from
part-time to full-time, from hourly to salaried,
or from clerical to professional status. In
publishing, for example, as you saw in Chapter
10, there can be a gradual progression from
entry-level secretarial or traveling sales positions up finally to editorships; in radio,
public relations, or writing for local or state
government officials it is not unusual to have
a volunteer position finally turned into a paid
one. In other fields such as college teaching,
upward mobility after a clerical or volunteer
start is almost unheard of. If you don't observe and deduce where the entrances and exits
lie for the kind of position that is your particular goal, you can waste years of your life in
a state of chronic frustration. If you *do*
notice the rites of entry and advancement
peculiar to different fields, you can make use
of your varied experience to add to your employability rather than, like the compulsive
diggers mentioned earlier by James Adams,
digging "the same post hole deeper in the wrong
place."

    • Finally, a point of view implicit through-
out this book may be worth spelling out. If you
are still one of those who really does not want
an alternative job, who believes that your education in the world's great literature somehow
entitles you to spend the rest of your life doing something more rarefied than writing for a

newspaper, sending out newsletters for an organization, cranking out grant proposals, or
writing political speeches, stop and consider.
Before you decide that it's just too rude a
shock to your expectations to "put aside your
preoccupation with literature," take a moment
to recall what you know about the lives of a
great many of those who wrote it. Think of
Henry Fielding spending his time on the magis-
trate's bench, Herman Melville working at the
customs' house, Matthew Arnold inspecting British schools, Anton Chekov and William Carlos
Williams each visiting his patients, T. S.
Eliot working in a bank and then in a publishing house, and Virginia Woolf teaching evening
courses in composition and literature at an
obscure London evening school. If working in
"the real world" didn't noticeably hamper such
writers as these, who are you and I to think
that we must keep our distance from such occupations? Rather than adopting such a stance,
I hope that you will find it challenging to
follow the lead of a Ph.D. in English now writing for a public utility company whose advice
is to "find out where your strengths and talents
truly lie, and then learn how best to sell
them."

If, without giving in to feelings of rancor
or desperation, you can follow or adapt some
of the suggestions in this book, you will have
done two important things. Even though you
will not have changed an educational system
that badly needs rethinking, you will have re-
gained your own feeling of autonomy and personal worth. And, if you and others like you
refuse to see yourselves as victims of a narrow
and rigid system, if more and more of you begin
to realize that you can take the methods and insights of the humanities into new territories,
the system itself may grow flexible and humane.

Some Useful Courses and Programs

Courses Dealing with Publishing, Editing, and Graphics

These courses are examples of the kind that often usefully supplement academic preparation in English. For others, consult *The Literary Market Place*, then check with the schools and addresses listed for their current bulletins. For courses dealing specifically with education at the professional level for all aspects of the publishing industry, see Ann Heidbreder Eastman and Grant Lee, "Directory of Courses in Book Publishing," in *Education for Publishing*, a survey report compiled for the Association of American Publishers, 1976. Don't overlook the fact that excellent new courses may appear at any time in any locality, in response to popular demand. Inquire of your nearest university extension program (credit or noncredit) and of the continuing education programs of nearby community colleges. Remember that what you should be looking for in most of these courses is added competence rather than more credentials.

Cambridge Center for Adult Education
42 Brattle Street
Cambridge, MA 02138
    Noncredit courses such as communication
    workshop, books, printing and typography
    layout and design, introduction to printing,
    the news and print media, getting into
    print, writing news and criticism, free-
    lance writing, many others

Columbia University
Writing Division, School of the Arts
404 Dodge
Columbia University
New York, NY 10027
    Graduate writing program; two-year course
    leading to M.F.A. degree

Graphic Arts Education Center
Graphic Arts Association of Delaware Valley,
    Inc.
1900 Cherry Street
Philadelphia, PA 19103
    Courses in proofreading, procedures, pro-
    duction planning, introduction to the
    graphic arts, typographic layout & adver-
    tising, design, etc.

Harvard Summer School
Radcliffe's Course in Publishing Procedures
10 Garden Street
Cambridge, MA 02138
    For recent college graduates. Director:
    Mrs. Diggory Venn. Intensive six-week
    summer course covering main phases of book
    and magazine publishing. Faculty is made
    up of 50 publishing executives who lecture
    on their specialties. Workshops and field
    trips. Early application necessary; group

limited to 75; serious commitment to publishing
required

Hunter College
School of General Studies (Adult Education Pro-
    gram)
659 Park Avenue
New York, NY 10021
    Book editing, copy editing, and proof-
    reading; prose writing workshop; study of
    English words; review of English grammar;
    etc.

New School for Social Research
66 West 12th Street
New York, NY 10011
    Director: Hayes B. Jacobs.
    Courses and workshops in nearly every form
    of writing, both fiction and nonfiction

New York City Community College
300 Jay Street
Brooklyn, NY 11201
    Graphic arts & advertising technology

New York University
School of Continuing Education
2 University Place
New York, NY 10003
    Courses offered at the Washington Square
    Writing Center: writing effective English;
    communication and the written word; business
    writing; structure, style, syntax; research
    techniques and fact-finding; book design;
    book production; proofreading and copy-
    editing workshop; magazine editing workshop;
    etc.

Northwestern University
Medill School of Journalism
Evening Division, Wieboldt Hall
339 East Chicago Avenue
Chicago, IL 60611
    Courses in newswriting, advertising, inter-
    viewing, and public relations

Pacific Lutheran University
122nd and Park Avenue
Tacoma, WA 98447
    Spring and summer sequence of courses in
    publishing procedures for graduates and
    undergraduates

Printing Industries of Metropolitan New York,
    Inc.
461 Eighth Avenue
New York, NY 10001
    Evening courses in printing, preparing art
    for reproduction, and graphic communica-
    tions

University of Puget Sound
Writing Institute
1500 North Warner
Tacoma, WA 98416
    Spring quarter course for juniors, seniors,
    and graduates looking forward to nonteach-
    ing careers involving writing; taught by
    Prof. Rosemary T. Van Arsdel

Simmons College
300 The Fenway
Boston, MA 02115
    Course in modern publishing and librarian-
    ship, 4 semester hours

University of Wisconsin Extension
Journalism and Mass Communications Dept.
221 Howell Hall
610 Langdon Street
Madison, WI 53706
> Courses taught by correspondence from pub-
> lished study guides: publications design
> and production; news writing; writing of
> magazine and feature articles; public rela-
> tions; etc.

The Writing Shop
16123 41st Avenue Northeast
Seattle, WA 98155
> Gordon and Mary Anne Mauerman, directors;
> courses in writing for publication, fiction
> and nonfiction

Programs and Courses in Technical Writing and Editing

(For description of course content and for admission requirements, write the director of each
program.)

Technical and Scientific Communications
Michigan Technological University
Houghton, MI 49931
Prof. Clarence A. Andrews, director

Technical Industrial Communication
Kalamazoo Valley Community College
Kalamazoo, MI 49009
Prof. Russell Briggs

Science Information Program
Illinois Institute of Technology
Chicago, IL 60616
Prof. Albert J. Brouse, director

Science Communication Program
School of Public Communication
Boston University
112 Cummington Street
Boston, MA 02215
Prof. Harold G. Buchbinder, director

Department of Technical Journalism
Colorado State University
Fort Collins, CO 80521
Prof. David G. Clark, chairman

Department of Humanities
Carnegie-Mellon University
Pittsburgh, PA 15213
Prof. Beekman Cottrell

Department of Language, Literature, and
    Communication
Rensselaer Polytechnic Institute
Troy, NY 12181
Prof. Robert W. Elmer, chairman

Technical Communications
Texas State Technical Institute
James Connally Campus
Waco, TX 76705
Prof. Robert Gentry

Technical Illustration
Los Angeles Trade: Technical College
400 West Washington Boulevard
Los Angeles, CA 90015
Prof. Laura Ann Gilchrist

Department of Journalism and Mass Communication
South Dakota State University
Brookings, SD 57006
Dr. Vernon A. Keel, head

Department of Communications
California State University
Fullerton, CA 92634
Dr. Martin Klein

School of Journalism
University of Missouri
Columbia, MO 65201
Prof. Joye Patterson, coordinator, science
    writing

Department of Rhetoric
University of Minnesota
St. Paul, MN 55101
Prof. Thomas E. Pearsall

William Rainey Harper College
Palatine, IL 60067
Prof. Philip M. Rubens, director of technical
    communications

Department of Journalism and Mass Communication
Iowa State University
Ames, IA 50010
Dr. J. W. Schwartz, head

Department of English
University of Wisconsin-Stout
Menomonie, WI 54751
Prof. Morrell Solem

Department of Humanities
The University of South Dakota
Springfield, SD 57062
Prof. Thomas L. Warren

Department of Humanistic-Social Studies
356 Loew Hall FH-40
University of Washington
Seattle, WA 98195
Prof. M. L. White

Department of English
Metropolitan State College
250 West 14th Avenue
Denver, CO 80204
Prof. Joy Unker

Survey Questionnaires

Questionnaire Sent to Editors and Information
Specialists (See Chapter 8)

Dear Editor/Writer/Information Specialist:

As the cover letter explains more fully, you can
by filling out this questionnaire help job-
hunters in your field learn a little more than
they now know about what to expect and how to
prepare themselves. Please answer as frankly
as you feel inclined to, using the other side
of the paper or adding another sheet if you
wish. You will not be quoted by name unless you
check the box giving permission. If you have
friends or colleagues who could also provide
helpful information, please Xerox this blank and
have them return theirs with yours in the enclosed stamped, addressed envelope. Thank you
very much.

1. What is your job title?
   How long have you held this position?
   What are your current duties?

2. How much editing/writing or related experience (teaching English or Communications,
   doing research, other) had you had before

taking your present job? What were your
previous positions?

3. What was your academic background (degrees
    or kinds of courses taken, institutions
    where you studied, additional [non-degree]
    course work)?

4. How did you find out about your current job
    opening?

5. In view of the tight job market right now,
    have you any advice or suggestions for
    people with backgrounds in Humanities sub-
    jects, especially English, as they search
    for non-teaching jobs? Or, to put it an-
    other way, have you any advice to people
    trying to get a start in your field now?

6. What do you consider the main value of your
    college degree(s) to be?

7. What do you consider the pluses and mi-
    nuses, in terms of satisfaction and oppor-
    tunity, of your present job to be? (How
    well does your present position meet the
    expectations you had as you got started?)

8. Name and address (optional)

9. In my forthcoming book, *Aside from Teaching
    English* . . . may I

    a. quote any of your comments, attributing
        them to you by name and position

                    yes ___ no ___

b. quote your comments, assigning them only
to a spokesman for your job category,
general type of position, and possibly
your geographical region

yes ___ no ___

Or would you prefer that I simply lump your
opinion in with others, in an inclusive
paraphrase?

Again, thanks very much.

Sincerely yours,

Dorothy K. Bestor
356 Loew Hall
University of Washington

Questionnaire Sent to Book Publishers (See
Chapter 10)

These questions are intended merely as suggestions; feel free to comment in any form that you
wish.

I. Which of the following kinds of preparation do you see as especially valuable
for people hoping to enter your firm or
other publishing houses? (Obviously
different kinds of publishing positions
draw upon different areas of preparation;
please circle any background that would
seem helpful, and indicate, where possible, for what kind of job it would be an
important qualification.)

A. Undergraduate major in: English?
Communications? Modern Languages?
Business? Other? (Please spec-
ify)

B. Graduate work in: English?
Communications? Modern Languages?
Business? Other? (Please spec-
ify)

C. Professional writing experience?

D. Newspaper or magazine experience--
in editing, copy-editing, other?

E. Completion of one of the currently
offered courses in Publishing Procedures, as given by Radcliffe
College, Hunter College, University of Wisconsin, University of
North Dakota, and elsewhere?

F. Work with other publishing houses?

G. Teaching experience in writing or
other liberal arts areas--at the
college level? In Continuing
Education programs? Other?

H. Business experience in: Marketing? Advertising? Book store
sales? Public opinion surveying?
Other?

II. Is there a possibility that your firm will
be hiring any new staff members during
this year or the next? For what kind of
position(s): Editorial? Business?
Production?

III. If so, to whom should applicants write?

 IV. Would you be willing to put us on your
      mailing list for notices/job descriptions
      of any vacancies that may be coming up in
      your firm?

  V. If not your firm, do you know of any
      possible hiring in other publishing firms?

 VI. In any case, may we tell qualified job
      candidates that you are interested in
      receiving résumés and/or letters of appli-
      cation which you will file in the event
      of possible vacancies?

Thank you very much indeed for answering any or
all of these questions. Please return in the
enclosed envelope to the Placement Center, 301
Loew Hall, University of Washington, Seattle,
WA 98195.

APPENDIX C

Two Responses from Publishers

This appendix contains two of the seventy replies received in answer to the publishers'
questionnaire reproduced in Appendix B.
(Approximately one-quarter of the respondents
sent letters rather than filling out the form.)
These two seem interesting in themselves and
representative of the concerns of, respectively,
a commercial publishing house and a university
press.)

HARCOURT BRACE JOVANOVICH, INC.
757 Third Avenue, New York, N.Y. 10017

February 14, 1975

Dorothy K. Bestor
Placement Counselor
University of Washington
Seattle, Washington 98195

Dear Dorothy K. Bestor:

Rather than respond directly to your questionnaire, I will--as you suggested--comment in the
form which is not only the most time-saving,
but perhaps the most useful. And that is to
first make some general remarks about the best

preparation for entering the field of book publishing, and then make some specific suggestion
for making application for work at HBJ.

From our point of view, the most useful type of
preparation for work in the publishing industry
is--unfortunately--prior experience in the industry. This of course brings up the dilemma
all students seeking their first job normally
face, which is--how can you get the experience
required to get a job when nobody will give you
a job in the first place? It is a conundrum--
but luckily, one which most job-seekers solve
sooner or later, and for better or for worse.

To our way of thinking, the best course is as
follows: the first thing to decide is--just
what aspect of book publishing are you interested in? Most people usually think of editing
when they think of working in book publishing,
but there are many other areas in a trade book
publishing house that offer interest, challenge
and reward. . . .

The point, of course, is that although book
publishing is not really a large industry by
American business standards, it is a highly
evolved and complex one, and therefore perhaps
the first thing a student interested in the
industry should do is try to find out more
about it. One of the things you suggested in
your letter is that the job-seeker should read
Publishers Weekly. This is not only a good way
to find out what jobs are available; it is the
main publication of the American book publishing trade, and provides a great deal of information about what is happening in the industry.
A student genuinely interested in working in
book publishing should familiarize him or herself as quickly as possible with this weekly

publication, which is doubtless available in
your university library and in your city
libraries. . . .

Once the potential applicant has determined the
area of most interest, he or she should try to
gain as much practical experience as possible.
A solid background in literature--with perhaps
a special emphasis on modern American and English literature--is of course a given. But
the candidate should also try to acquire the
special skills he or she might effectively use
in the work area of greatest interest. If
editing has the strongest appeal, and there is
some sort of book publishing enterprise on or
near the campus, the student might try for
part-time work there as a proofreader or copy
editor--or for that matter, in any other area
where they will have the chance to observe
what's going on and ask questions. (Magazine
publishing is quite a different enterprise, and
although it might provide valuable experience
for the student, it will probably not translate
very easily into a book publishing environment.) If they have an interest in the business or data processing areas, then these of
course should be included in course planning.
Part-time work in the college bookstore or in
the bookstore in the area could provide good
insight into the kind of market to which publishers are selling. And of course typing is
always useful. Most editors and other professionals use the typewriter from time to time
in their work--and it is often a requirement
for entry-level jobs for women and men alike.

. . . Many of the leaders in the industry--
including Mr. Jovanovich--started as "college
travelers," or trade book salesmen. In terms
of further training, the Radcliffe College

summer program in book publishing has an excellent reputation. New York University also
has a Center for Publishing and Graphic Design
which offers both night and day classes which
are taught by people presently working in the
book industry, and I understand that Hunter
College also has a good program. . . .

Unfortunately, all of my work experience in
book publishing has been in New York, which may
be biasing my advice somewhat. The situation
may be somewhat different in such areas as the
West Coast. But I shouldn't be surprised if
most of the same principles are at work there--
and that the more experience you have in book
publishing and/or related fields, the more
likely you are to find the kind of job that you
want. Extended graduate work is probably only
valuable if you are interested in working in
higher level educational publishing.

Harcourt Brace Jovanovich will doubtless have
many openings in various areas of its book
publishing and trade magazine publishing enterprise in the coming year. Interested applicants should forward résumés to the Personnel
Dept., Harcourt Brace Jovanovich, Inc., 757
Third Avenue, New York, N.Y. 10022--or even
better, should pay a visit to the building to
inspect notices of job openings posted on the
7th floor.

We hope this gives you some guidelines for advising and helping place those students interested in the field of book publishing. We do
think it is useful for them to keep in mind
that it is a business--and that while creativity and imagination are vital ingredients for
the man or woman who wishes to make good in
the field, a realistic understanding of all of

the parts of the business will make them a much
more promising candidate and very likely a much
more successful part of the book publishing
industry.

Cordially,

Carol Meyer
Assistant to the Director
Trade Department

UNIVERSITY OF TEXAS PRESS
P.O. Box 7819, Austin, Texas 78712

20 January 1977

Ms. Dorothy Bestor
Placement Counselor
University of Washington
Seattle, Washington 98195

Dear Ms. Bestor:

As in other businesses which are broadly gauged
and that attempt to deal with varied audiences
or services, the book industry is as concerned
with the individual qualities of its job candidates as it is with the individual's formal
training. That is, a person who is resourceful
enough to find the kind of publishing he/she
wants to do and where (locale) he wants to do it
is well ahead of the game. A prospective employer is apt to be more impressed by a candidate who knows the job he wants to do than by
someone with only a vague notion. Skill at
applying for a job—the proper job—can be as
convincing to a prospective employer as a high
grade average. There are many kinds of publishing within just the book industry and equally

varied opportunities within the field of
periodical publishing.

One of the problems that young people have is
that they take a narrowly conceived view of
what publishing is and try to fit themselves
into that tiny space. For example, it is my
experience that 95% of the people who have come
to my office for advice on publishing respond
"editorial" when asked what sort of work they
want to do in book publishing. When one in-
quires what sort of editing they would want,
virtually none is aware that there are various
kinds such as copyediting, project editing,
acquisition editing and variations on those
themes. To continue that and the earlier line
of thought, I have never had an advisee asking
about chances to become a "rights and permissions" professional. All of this points to the
fact that either these young people are unaware
of the occupational variety in publishing (which
may mean they haven't done their homework) or
they are not getting the counseling they require to open their eyes to opportunity.

Harvard University's summer program notwith-
standing, I still believe that the best place
to learn this business is from within a company. A small company is preferable to a large
house simply because one does more kinds of
jobs than would be the case in large companies
with an abundance of specialists. But don't
let your people think only in terms of book
publishing because there are great opportunities to be found in the field of periodicals
(journals, magazines, annual reports, public
relations handouts, medical bulletins, etc.).
In fact, book publishing is an idiosyncratic
business as businesses go with very little
transference out of the book trade. This is

not the case with periodicals since a person
working for a journal who learns editorial,
production and marketing functions pretty well
would find that information more readily trans-
ferrable to a variety of places whether in an
academic or a commercial setting.

Is it enough to advise your people that they
should study the methods and performance of a
company which is located within a geographical
region where they choose to live and then "just
get in the door" to look around for greater opportunity? That may help but they should also
know that, like Broadway, book publishing is a
competitive industry which requires persever-
ance and a willingness to do lowly jobs until
something better comes to their attention.
Some caution should be exercised in accepting
a job in, say, editorial only to find that a
change to marketing or production a few years
later results in a downward salary adjustment
as the employer contemplates the cost involved
in making you competent in another specialty.
It helps to get started on the right track or
to make the change as soon as possible after
your error comes to light.

In composing this letter I am painfully aware
of how difficult it is to fully describe or
adequately prescribe those circumstances and
strategies which will be most helpful to those
interested in publishing. Fortunately this
difficulty is compensated for in that this is,
after all, a human business where common sense
still has a great deal of meaning. Most who
survive the rigors are those who have an ample
amount of sense. Those who succeed tend to be
walking advertisements for the Puritan Ethic of
work hard at getting work and work harder at
making it worthwhile.

Much more can be said but, perhaps, I have already said enough to begin controversy among my peers who, as in most things, see things differently.

                            Sincerely yours,

                            Philip D. Jones
                            Director

APPENDIX D

A Note on Internships

The idea of supplementing liberal arts education with some sort of applied experience or
field work has been gradually increasing in
popularity during the half-century since
Antioch College began its program of alter-
nating periods of classroom study and off-
campus paid work in a student's chosen field.
Within the past five years, several institutions in various parts of the country have
developed "internships," among them some for
English majors and other aspirants to careers
in writing or communications.

Such internships as now flourish have
arisen mainly for undergraduates. To my knowledge, at least five college and universities
have them currently; there may be others.

At Fiorello LaGuardia Community College,
New York, freshmen spend three out of their
four quarters in classroom study, and then in
either their third or fourth quarter they work
on off-campus internships sponsored by the
college's Cooperative Education Division.
Sophomores alternate two quarters of classroom
study with two of internships (some of them
abroad). Some of these students have been
secretary-translators in Madrid, teachers in
Puerto Rico, teacher's aides on a Navaho reser-
vation; others have worked with publications at

a Planned Parenthood affiliate or learned editing in the publications office of FLCC. (See
"Work Opportunities for the English Major: A
New Look at Career Possibilities," *ADE Bulletin*
36 [March 1973]: 22-24.)

At the University of Puget Sound and at
Pacific Lutheran University, both in Tacoma,
Washington, students who complete their newly
developed professional programs (The Writing
Institute at UPS and the publications procedures course at PLU) can look forward to gaining experience for two to three months in the
offices of local businesses, publishers, or
private agencies where writing and editing is
carried on. At North Carolina State University
the English Department has set up a whole writ-
ing-editing curriculum involving many options
for course work and for writing experience
gained from employment in local offices, agencies, and printing and publishing firms. A
similar but more elaborate curriculum has been
in force for the past several years at the University of Redlands in California. Reports
from students and faculty in all these programs
are enthusiastic.

A somewhat different kind of internship, designed not for undergraduates but for women who
have been out of college and out of the job market for some time, is a part of the "Career
Explorations" noncredit course given at the University of Washington through the Office of
Women's Programs. Here women take a quarter-
long course during which they try to clarify
their career goals as they listen to representatives of various fields and do intensive reading
in areas of their own special interests. Following completion of one quarter, they often
receive placement for a quarter in a job where,
under supervision, they gain firsthand experience. Although these internships are not

limited to the fields of writing, editing, and
publishing, I know of several women who have
gotten very good starts in these fields through
one of the "Career Explorations" internships.
   Other internships have been developed recently at research centers such as the Pacific
Northwest Science Center, where interns help
edit the magazine *Pacific Search,* and at
Battelle Seattle Research Center, where interns
who have taken the technical writing/editing
sequence at the University of Washington have
recently been given considerable responsibility
for editing monographs in the natural and social sciences.
   Probably among the best known and most
flourishing internships are those sponsored
annually by newspapers who select promising
college students (whether majors in communications, English, or other subjects) for summer
work. Interested students should ordinarily
apply in November and December of their junior
years for work the following summer. The best
source of information about these newspaper
internships is Ronald H. Claxton and Biddie
Lorenzen, *The Student Guide to Mass Media Internships* (Boulder, Colo.: The School of Journalism, 1975). Several editors I talked to
suggested that students might also "try to make
their own internships--ask in February or March
for work the following summer, when vacation
replacements for reporters and desk people are
needed."
   A few university presses here and there are
beginning to develop traineeships or internships. One such arrangement, sponsored by the
University of Washington Press since 1970, has
been designed as "a student training program
aimed at bringing members of minority groups
into scholarly publishing." In the ten weeks
the first student took part in the program, she

apparently received a very good introduction to
the process of editing books.

Among one group of people not ordinarily
recipients of writing/editing internships
(graduate students in English), there is an
increasing number who wish that some such arrangement were available, particularly something whereby they could learn the theory and
practice of editing. At the 1976 meeting of
the MLA there were reports on several programs
newly designed to broaden the competence of the
Ph.D. and to include practical experience
through some form of internship. Among them
were an optional "professional skills minor" at
Penn State University and combined programs
involving other departments at the University
of Virginia and at Wayne State University.
Some graduate students, moreover, are able to
get internships of a different kind: one or
two quarters of supervised teaching in a community college are part of the English M.A.
program at the University of Western Washington, at Bellingham. Probably other state universities have similar arrangements with nearby
community colleges. Actually, that well-known
institution, the university teaching assistantship, could be said to have some of the char-
acteristics of an internship.

The few dissenting views of internships
heard come not from the student beneficiaries
but from those with responsibility for making
the arrangements. There are occasionally problems in setting up the internships: as
Rosemary VanArsdel of the University of Puget
Sound remarks, it is sometimes hard in a small
city to find enough business or professional
people who are willing to take the time to
supervise new trainees. There are also several
questions involving payment for the intern's

services. This payment is sometimes in academic credit, sometimes a token wage, and sometimes a "real" wage, at the going rate. The
first and third arrangements present fewer
problems than the second. Kenneth Haas of
Korvette is one who has expressed concern about
paying trainees or interns less than regular,
newly hired job applicants. There is the danger that doing so could involve a college both
in legal difficulties and in problems with
unions.

Most people involved with internships, however, hail them as a way to counteract the
narrowness of a liberal arts major's college
experience, as well as to help students begin
to make bridges between their classroom learning and their business or professional life
ahead. Both students and faculty members reading this note are urged to write the institutions mentioned for further information.

Resource Organizations

Although there are an almost endless number of
organizations, associations, and resources of
various kinds which might be helpful in your
job search, the list below will serve as a
starting point from which you can branch out on
your own. Many of these associations publish
career information and sponsor conferences,
workshops, and journals. For other associations
see *A Career Guide to Professional Associations*
(Cranston, R.I.: The Carroll Press, 1976),
with its annotated list of organizations by
field.

General Information (All Fields)

CATALYST
14 East 60th Street
New York, NY 10022

Educational Career Services
12 Nassau Street, Box 672
Princeton, NJ 08540

Federal Employment & Guidance Service
215 Park Avenue South
New York, NY 10003

National Alliance of Businessmen
1730 K Street, NW, Suite 558
Washington, DC 20006

National Federation of Business &
    Professional Women's Clubs, Inc.
2012 Massachusetts Avenue, NW
Washington, DC 20036

Women's Educational and Industrial Union
264 Boylston Street
Boston, MA 02116

Careers Related to the Media

American Business Press
205 East 42nd Street
New York, NY 10017

American Newspaper Women's Club
1607 22nd Street, NW
Washington, DC 20008

American Society of Indexers
c/o Xerox / University Microfilms
300 North Zeeb Road
Ann Arbor, MI 48106

American Society of Business Press Editors
2550 Green Bay Road
Evanston, IL 60201

American Society of Magazine Editors
575 Lexington Avenue
New York, NY 10022

American Society of Newspaper Editors
1350 Sullivan Trail, Box 551
Easton, PA 18042

Associated Business Writers of America
Box 135
Monmouth Junction, NY 08852

International Association of Business
    Communicators
2108 Braewick Circle
Akron, OH 44313

International Society of Weekly Newspaper
    Editors
School of Journalism
Southern Illinois University
Carbondale, IL 62901

International Labor Press Association
815 16th Street, NW
Washington, DC 20006

National Association of Science Writers
Box H
Sea Cliff, NY 11579

National Federation of Press Women
1105 Main Street
Blue Springs, MO 64015

National Society of Film Critics
562 West End Avenue
New York, NY 10024

Newspaper Fund
P.O. Box 300
Princeton, NJ 08540

New York Business Communicators
P.O. Box 2025
Grand Central Station
New York, NY 10017

New York Financial Writers' Association
41 Park Avenue
New York, NY 10017

American Society of Indexers
c/o Mr. Peter Rooney, Executive Secretary
30 Charles Street, #64
New York, NY 10014

Society of Technical Communications
1010 Vermont Avenue, NW
Washington, DC 20005

Women in Communications, Inc.
8305-A Shoal Creek Boulevard
Austin, TX 78758

Sources of Information about Other Careers
Which Were Mentioned in the Text

American Academy of Advertising
c/o Prof. Kenward Atkins, President
Department of Communications
California State University
Fullerton, CA 92634

American Bar Association
1155 East 60th Street
Chicago, IL 60637

American College Public Relations
      Association
One Dupont Circle
Washington, DC 20036

American Library Association
50 East Huron Street
Chicago, IL 60611

American Society for Public Administration
1225 Connecticut Avenue, NW
Washington, DC 20036

College and University Personnel
    Association
One Dupont Circle, Suite 525
Washington, DC 20005

Council on Social Work Education
345 East 46th Street
New York, NY 10017

National Association of Social Workers
1425 H Street, NW
Washington, DC 20005

Society of Public Health Education
655 Sutter Street
San Francisco, CA 94102

Public Relations Society of America
845 Third Avenue
New York, NY 10022

Careers in Local, State, County, and Federal Government

For the address of the nearest city, county,
or state government employment information center, and for intergovernmental agency information, consult your local phone book and that of
your state capital. For federal employment,
start with the following list.

Civil Service Commission Information Centers

Central Office
    Civil Service Commission
    Washington, DC

Atlanta Region
      Atlanta Merchandise Mart
      240 Peachtree Street, NE
      Atlanta, GA 30303

Boston Region
      Post Office & Court House Building
      Boston, MA 02019

Chicago Region
      Post Office Building
      433 West Van Buren Street
      Chicago, IL 60607

Dallas Region
      1114 Commerce Street
      Dallas, TX 75202

Denver Region
      Denver Federal Center
      Denver, CO 80225

New York Region
      News Building
      220 East 42nd Street
      New York, NY 10017

Philadelphia Region
      Chestnut House
      Chestnut Street
      Philadelphia, PA 19106

St. Louis Region
      Federal Building
      1520 Market Street
      St. Louis, MO 63103

San Francisco Region
      Box 36010, 450 Golden Gate Avenue
      San Francisco, CA 94102

Seattle Region
    Federal Building
    First Avenue
    Seattle, WA 98104

Notes

Chapter 1

1. "Slim Pickings for the Class of '76," *Time*, March 1976, pp. 46–49; "Who Needs College?" *Newsweek*, April 26, 1976, pp. 60–69. See also "Jobs Available for NW College Graduates with Right Specialty," *Seattle Post-Intelligencer*, May 23, 1976, p. A-11.

2. Dael Wolfle and Charles V. Kidd, "The Future Market for Ph.D.'s," *AAUP Bulletin* 58 (March 1972): 5. The article first appeared in *Science* 173 (Aug. 27, 1971): 784–93.

3. George W. Bonham, introduction to Ana L. Zambrano and Alan D. Entine, *A Guide to Career Alternatives for Academics* (New Rochelle, N.Y.: Change Magazine Press, 1976), p. 5.

4. Gloria Steinem, conversation with author, May 25, 1976.

5. Personal interview, Jan. 3 and 4, 1977.

6. See Edwin Newman, *Strictly Speaking: Will America Be the Death of English?* (Indianapolis and New York: Bobbs-Merrill, 1974); and *A Civil Tongue* (Indianapolis and New York: Bobbs-Merrill, 1976); Gene Lyons, "The Higher Illiteracy," *Harper's Magazine*, no. 253 (Sept. 1976), pp. 33–40, and in the same issue, James P. Degnan, "Masters of Babble," pp. 37–39; Jean Stafford, "Plight of the American Language,"

Saturday Review World, Dec. 4, 1973, pp. 14-18;
Ralph H. Lewis, "A Rose Is a Flowerization,"
Seattle Post-Intelligencer, June 11, 1976, p.
A-11 (reprinted from the *Harvard Business Re-
view);* and A. B. Giametti et al. in a symposium,
"The Writing Gap," in the *Yale Alumni Magazine*
28, no. 1 (Jan. 1976): 30-35.

7. As quoted in "Students Still Can't
Write," *Bulletin,* Council for Basic Education,
Washington, D.C., 20 (Feb. 1976): 1-4. This
brief article gives a good summary of efforts
nationwide to improve writing, as does the
National Assessment of Writing Survey, available
for $1.30 from the U.S. Superintendent of Docu-
ments (Stock No. 017-080-01854-3, *Writing
Mechanics,* 1969-74.)

8. "Why Johnny Can't Write," *Newsweek,* Feb.
16, 1976, pp. 30-36.

9. Bliss to author, Jan. 26, 1977.

10. Personal interview, Jan. 3, 1977.

11. Eric Berne, *Games People Play* (New York:
Grove Press, 1967), "Why Don't You?--'Yes,
But . . . ,'" pp. 115-22.

12. James L. Adams, *Conceptual Blockbusting:
A Guide to Better Ideas* (San Francisco: W. H.
Freeman, 1974), p. 23.

13. For details, see Chapter 12.

14. For details, see Chapter 7.

15. Wolfle and Kidd, "The Future Market for
Ph.D.'s," p. 5.

16. Steinem, speech at meeting of the Seattle
Advertising Federation, May 25, 1976.

Chapter 2

1. As Richard Bolles points out, there is
confusion in the current usage of several words
such as "tasks, aptitudes, abilities, and
skills." Some speakers differentiate them
rigidly and others make them almost synonymous

(*What Color Is Your Parachute?* [rev. ed.; Berkeley, Calif.: The Ten Speed Press, 1976], p. 97). In many academic circles, the word "skill" means something limited and fairly mechanical, as in the second definition of the word in *The American Heritage Dictionary of the English Language* (1969): "An art, trade, or technique, particularly one requiring use of the hands or body." In my discussion, however, I am using "skill" as Bolles does ("Skills are things you do well and enjoy") and thus in the sense of the first meaning in *American Heritage:* "Proficiency, ability." According to this definition, the ability to organize ideas clearly for written presentation would be a skill, as would the ability to revise a manuscript, write a summary, compile a bibliography, or convey ideas in a lecture.

2. Sylvia Plath, *The Bell Jar* (New York: Bantam Books, Harper and Row, 1971), p. 62.

3. Richard K. Irish, *Go Hire Yourself an Employer* (New York: Doubleday Anchor Books, 1973); see also John Harwood, "Nonacademic Job Hunting," *AAUP Bulletin* 60 (Autumn 1974): 313-16.

4. For examples of student work demonstrating these and other skills, see the two sample papers in Sheridan Baker, *The Complete Stylist* (2d ed.; New York: Thomas Crowell, 1972), pp. 283-314; and S. L. Rubinstein and Robert G. Weaver, *The Plain Rhetoric* (2d ed.; Boston: Allyn and Bacon, 1968), pp. 224-43.

5. Hollis to author, Oct. 20, 1976.

6. Telephone conversation with author, Oct. 22, 1976.

7. For details, see Chapter 12.

8. For details, see Chapters 6 and 8.

9. For details, see Chapter 12.

10. For further discussion, see Chapter 10.

11. For kinds of courses useful by way of

supplementing an English major, see Chapter 4
and Appendix A.

12. Conversations with author, in Seattle,
Oct. 5 and 19, 1976.

13. See Chapters 11 and 12.

14. Ellen Messer-Davidow, "The Unwise 'No,'"
paper presented on Dec. 29, 1976, at the Modern
Language Association of America annual meeting,
New York City, at an ADE/ADFL Workshop: "Preparing and Advising Graduate Students for Nonacademic Work."

15. The attempt to identify skills learned
as an English major has been made several times,
beginning with Elizabeth Berry, *The Careers of
English Majors* (Champaign, Ill.: National Council of Teachers of English, 1966), and Linwood
T. Orange, *English: The Pre-Professional Major*
(New York: MLA, 1972), p. 2. Both of these
guidebooks were compiled, however, before the
current job crunch and, moreover, they concentrate upon the uses of an undergraduate rather
than a graduate degree in English. By far the
most helpful discussion to date for graduate
degree holders is the revised *MLA Guide for Job
Candidates and Department Chairmen in English
and Foreign Languages* (New York: MLA, 1975).
Yet since it does not attempt to go into detail
about regional opportunities or about publishing, editing, and working on the staff of educational institutions, its users may, I hope,
find that it and the selection of advice from
employers and job-seekers in the present handbook form a useful complement to one another.

16. Orange, *English,* p. 2.

17. Ruth Von Behren, "Clio's Children: Out
of the Ivory Tower and into the Marketplace:
Alternative Employment," paper presented at
meeting of the Pacific Coast Branch, American
Historical Association, Aug. 27, 1974, University of Washington.

Chapter 3

1. Richard Nelson Bolles, *What Color Is Your Parachute?* (rev. ed.; Berkeley, Calif.: The Ten Speed Press, 1976), pp. 41-42.
2. Mrs. Lucille Borrow, former placement counselor at the University of Washington, to author, Oct. 28, 1976.
3. Bolles, *Parachute*, pp. 125-31.

Chapter 4

1. See Richard Nelson Bolles, *What Color Is Your Parachute?* (rev. ed.; Berkeley, Calif.: The Ten Speed Press, 1976), pp. 61-62. See also the growing body of books and articles on career switching, as, for example, "Starting Afresh: The Art of Changing Your Life," *Harper's Magazine* 246 (Feb. 1973): 3-10, 107-14; Warren Boroson, "New Careers for Old," *Money* 3, no. 4 (April 1974): 22-26; John N. Coleman, *Blue-Collar Journal* (New York: Harper and Row, 1975).
2. According to Constance Remo, staff assistant in Harvard's Office of Placement Services, when interviewed on Jan. 4, 1977.
3. Noyes, telephone interview, March 3, 1977.
4. Herbert B. Livesey and Harold Doughty, *Guide to American Graduate Schools* (3d ed.; New York: Viking Press, 1976).
5. The comments included here from representatives of seven professional programs at the University of Washington originated in interviews by the author during the summer and fall of 1975 and the spring of 1976.
6. Adrianne Richmond, *New Careers for Social Workers* (Chicago: Henry Regnery, 1974).
7. For details, see Chapters 11 and 12.
8. Bliss to author, Jan. 26, 1977.
9. Theodore Grieder, "Professional Librari-

anship as a Career for the Ph.D.," *ADE Bulletin*
40 (March 1974): 45-50.

10. Personal interview, Jan. 4, 1977. One
might, however, make an exception to the warning
expressed in this chapter. In general, taking
a second master's degree is more practical than
going into a second doctoral or professional
program. Some community college teachers of
English have found taking another M.A. in a related field such as communications, drama, comparative literature, or speech to be helpful; a
few college English teachers have found that an
M.B.A. or a master's in public administration
gave them a quicker entry into administrative
jobs than they might otherwise have had.

11. Roger Rosenblatt, "The Uses of a Literary
Education," paper presented on Dec. 28, 1976, at
the MLA annual meeting, New York City, at a
forum on "The Uses of the Humanities."

Chapter 5

1. Myron White and James Souther, *Scientific
and Technical Communication* (Seattle: University of Washington College of Engineering, n.d.).
Interested students should write for a copy of
this leaflet to the Department of Humanistic-
Social Studies, 356 Loew Hall, FH-40, University
of Washington, Seattle, WA 98195; you should
also browse in such periodicals as *The Journal
of Technical Writing and Communication* and write
to the Society for Technical Communication, 1010
Vermont Avenue NW, Washington, DC 20005, for
its brochures on career opportunities (e.g.,
Facts and *Is Technical Writing Your Career?*).

2. Paul V. Anderson, "Background and Resources for New Teachers of Technical Writing,"
introductory remarks to a special session,
"Teaching Technical Writing: A Unique Chal-

lenge," Dec. 28, 1976, annual MLA meeting, New York City.

3. See Merrill Whitburn, "Technical Communication: An Unexplored Area for English," *ADE Bulletin* 45 (May 1975): 11-14. (Readers unfamiliar with this journal should note that it is subtitled *A Journal for Administrators of Departments of English in American Colleges and Universities* and, as such, it is not widely circulated; in fact, it does not usually find its way to college and university libraries. But since the last few years' issues contain excellent articles on alternatives to teaching, it is worthwhile asking to consult them at the office of the college or university English department nearest you.)

4. See Carol Gay, "The Onus of Teaching Children's Literature," *ADE Bulletin* 47 (Nov. 1975): 15-20.

5. For places to write for information, see Pat Kern McIntyre, *American Students and Teachers Abroad: Sources of Information about Overseas Study, Teaching, Work, and Travel* (Washington, D.C.: G.P.O., 1976).

6. For information about courses in ESL, write Prof. Louis Trimble, Department of Humanistic-Social Studies, 356 Loew Hall, FH-40, University of Washington, Seattle, WA 98195, or inquire of one of the institutions listed in this chapter on pp. 67-68.

7. For courses in popular culture, see the catalogues of Hofstra, Bowling Green, and Long Island universities. An informative article by Thomas Meehan, "Pop-Eyed Professors" (*New York Times* Magazine, June 1, 1975, pp. 33-37), describes the growth of interest in this area to the point where Hofstra now gives both B.A.'s and M.A.'s in it.

8. For a general overview of teaching opportunities abroad, see Curtis W. Casewit, *Overseas*

Jobs: The Ten Best Countries (New York: Warner
Paperback Library, 1972), and Robert Hopkins,
I've Had It: A Practical Guide to Moving Abroad
(New York: Holt, Rinehart & Winston, 1972).
Both of them deal with a wide range of jobs, in-
cluding teaching. Also inquire at any campus
where ESL is taught; such offices tend to re-
ceive frequent notices of actual vacancies in
Africa, Asia, islands of the South Pacific, and
the Middle East.

9. If you are interested, most campus placement centers can direct you to sources of
further information. Bear in mind that the
Australian and New Zealand academic calendars
are almost the reverse of ours, and that the
Japanese school year begins in March. Don't
forget such details as the need for visas and
work permits for overseas teaching. Note too
that in Australia and New Zealand you may find
few, if any, writing courses in university catalogues; students there, like those in the British universities, are supposed to have learned
in secondary school how to write well. So no
matter how strong your background is in teaching
writing, you will need other specialties for
university-level English instruction wherever
the British educational tradition dominates.

10. If you write to apply for some of these
positions, don't be discouraged by a negative
reply; several job candidates, having been told
that an overseas job was filled, were invited six
months later to apply for other positions.
Apparently overseas employers tend to keep
applications on file and go back to them more
often than many employers do here.

11. See Selden Menefee, "Community Colleges:
Finding New Directions," *Change: The Magazine
of Higher Learning*, Summer 1974, pp. 54-63.

12. See, as one example of the ascendancy of
the community college, Elizabeth Cowan, "Turn-

about in the Job Market: The University Goes
to the Community College," *ADE/ADFL Bulletin*
(Special Joint Issue, English and Foreign Languages: Employment and the Profession [Sept.
1976]), pp. 53-56.

13. Although most appointments to community
college English departments represent a long
process of carefully sifting more than a hundred
applications, often last-minute changes in registration necessitate the hiring of one or two
extra part-time instructors.

14. Mort Young, "When One Can't Read or
Write," *Seattle Post-Intelligencer*, Dec. 7,
1976.

15. See the bulletin, "Seeking a Job in a
Two-Year College," available from the American
Association of Junior Colleges, One Dupont
Circle, NW, Washington, DC 20036. See also Ely
Stock, "From Ivy League to Community College,
ADE Bulletin 39 (Dec. 1973): 13-15.

16. Although there has been some improvement
in the status of part-time community college
instructors during the past four years, wages
and morale among part-timers are still generally
low. See three articles on the exploitation of
part-timers, whether at two-year or four-year
colleges: Jane Flanders, "The Use and Abuse of
Part-time Faculty," *ADE/ADFL Bulletin* (Special
Joint Issue [Sept. 1976]), pp. 49-52; Lawrence
Berlow and Alana L. Collos, "Part-time Employment: We Teach; Therefore, We Are," and
Cortland P. Auser, "Part-time Employment:
' . . . Nothing So Desperate . . . ,'" both in
ADE Bulletin 43 (Nov. 1974): 9-12.

17. Personal interview, May 20, 1975.

18. Gary K. Wolfe and Carol Traynor Williams,
"All Education Is 'Adult Education,'" *AAUP
Bulletin*, Sept. 1974, pp. 291-95.

19. For information about some of these
alternatives, see your nearest campus placement

center. One of these options, CETA jobs (Comprehensive Educational Training Act is the
funding source), can be interpreted in many
different innovative ways by resourceful job
candidates. Margaret Hodge, a poet and an M.A.
in English, made a proposal to use poetry "in
any way that would enhance the quality of life"
for whatever group (whether in a prison, a hospital, or a nursing home) might want to explore
poetry writing with her. She was assigned to
work with several senior citizens' clubs, which
she did for six months, and she reports having
had a satisfying teaching experience as well as
editing a volume of poems some of her class
members wrote. Others with degrees in English
have held CETA posts recently, although they
used them as fellowships on which to live while
writing their own poetry.

20. Such opportunities to design and teach
writing classes to meet the specialized needs of
professional people are seldom advertised because there is usually no specific "vacancy";
involvement in such teaching tends to be a spin-
off from teaching regularly scheduled continuing
education courses through an institution.

21. Francis Keppel, keynote address at a conference on "Changing Perspectives in Education,"
Dec. 6-7, 1973, Seattle, sponsored by the League
of Women Voters of Washington. Dr. Keppel is
now chairman of the board, General Learning Corporation, New York City.

22. See *The New York Times* Book Review Section, March 15, 1974.

23. For an informative and enthusiastic discussion of what such centers can accomplish,
see William W. Bernhardt, "Working in a College
Skills Center," *ADE Bulletin* 44 (Feb. 1975):
10-13.

24. *Seattle Times,* Sept. 14, 1975.

25. To cite only one example, during the four

academic years 1969-73 there were each year from
200 to 220 part-time instructors teaching each
year at Bellevue Community College. During that
time, exactly six of them were promoted to full-
time positions at the same college. In some
parts of the country there is apparently more
chance for qualified part-timers to receive
full-time status, according to Russell Mauch of
Columbia-Greene Community College, Hudson, New
York; yet Bellevue's situation is far from
unusual.

26. See the comments of Kenneth Haas, below,
Chapter 11.

27. Richard Nelson Bolles, *What Color Is Your
Parachute?* (rev. ed.; Berkeley, Calif.: The Ten
Speed Press, 1976), p. 67.

28. This axiom, which seemed astonishing when
first proposed four years ago by Dr. Hilde
Birnbaum of Bellevue Community College, has
since been borne out by the experience of a
number of job candidates. One young woman with
a M.A.T. in English turned her one quarter of
part-time community college teaching and one
quarter of part-time internship at the Battelle
Seattle Research Center into qualifications for
a full-time instructorship at Oregon State University. Another woman, with a Ph.D. in English, after one quarter of part-time teaching
at one Puget Sound area community college and
two quarters teaching part-time in another one,
now holds an assistant professorship at a southwestern state university. Still another woman,
with a B.A. and an M.A. in English, was chosen
over many other applicants for one of the few
new full-time community college positions in
English in her area, largely because of her
successful teaching of a single course, "Women
in Literature," in the University of Washington's informal, unacademic Experimental College.

29. See Daniel Fedo, "The Promise of Academic

Exile," *The Chronicle of Higher Education*, Oct.
21, 1975.
    30. For example, a Joyce scholar has just
found some of Joyce's early and hitherto unknown
essays in Padua. Again, in the National Library
at Wellington, New Zealand, there are thick
folders of Katherine Mansfield's early unpub-
lished letters and diaries, as well as one of
the six best collections of early editions of
Milton's poems in the world. Comparable opportunities for research could turn up almost anywhere you go overseas to teach, provided that
you make the time to explore libraries and special collections.
    31. For information about writing schools in
the Pacific Northwest see Eileen Kernaghan,
Edith Surridge, and Patrick Kernaghan, *The Upper
Left-Hand Corner: A Writer's Guide for the
Northwest* (Vancouver, B.C.: J. J. Douglas;
Seattle: Madrona Publishers, 1975), pp. 10, 23.
For examples of helpful writing courses and programs around the country, see below, Appendix A.
    32. Constance Wells, personal interviews,
April 30, 1975, and Jan. 15, 1976.
    33. According to a report that Constance
Wells brought back from a November 1976 continu-
ing education conference in Coeur d'Alene,
Idaho, it is predicted that accrediting bodies
will soon begin to urge, more strongly than they
have in the past, that continuing education
courses be taught by faculty members with advanced degrees in the subject disciplines they
teach.

Chapter 6

    1. *Staff Employment at the University of
Washington* (Seattle, n.d.), [p. 2]; *Wheaton
College Directory* (Norton, Mass., 1975); *The*

Lindex (McMinnville, Ore.: Linfield College, 1975).

2. For example, the University of Washington classified staff position of director of scholarly journals, or the "exempt" position of director of the Placement Center, each in its different way calls for so much professional expertise that there are very few English Ph.D's who would not feel challenged by either position. Dividing lines between "staff and "administration," as well as those between "staff" and "faculty," are differently drawn from one institution to another. For example, are heads of library divisions considered faculty or staff? Are special assistants to a president considered staff or administration? Are research editors attached to departments of a medical school listed as staff or faculty? Since the answers to these questions vary widely from campus to campus, I do not want to get into such controversies but simply in this chapter to point out the viability of many *nonteaching* positions, however designated, to be found at almost every educational institution.

3. For the difference between "classified" and "exempt" positions, see *Staff Employment at the University of Washington* or the corresponding bulletin at your state university or college. In general, when you apply for a classified position, you are applying to be on an eligibility list, from which three people are sent to be interviewed for a particular position. Since an "exempt" position is one which calls for higher specialized qualifications, it presumably cannot be filled from an eligibility list, and all the applications received for it are turned over to the department having the vacancy. Both kinds of position are subject to statewide rules and policies. Private insti-

tutions of course set their own policies in such
matters.

4. Personal interview, Jan. 4. 1977.

5. Woodruff, conversation with author at MLA
meeting, Dec. 29, 1976; Bliss to author, Jan.
26, 1977.

6. Mary Lou Baker, personal interview, May
5, 1975.

7. An information specialist working for the
English Department of the University of Washington has one of the most varied of these campus
positions, in that she makes arrangements for
visiting lecturers and poets, edits the university's *Arts and Sciences Newsletter*, handles the
department's curriculum announcements or changes
in the course schedule, writes departmental releases for publication in the student newspaper,
and is business manager for the department's
creative writing quarterly. One reason for the
diversity of her work is that it evolved before
rigid job specifications were put into effect
campus-wide.

8. Recently there have been at least five
members of the counseling staff of the University of Washington Placement Center with a
background in English, ranging from a B.A.
(English major) through M.A.'s, doctoral candidates, and a Ph.D.

9. Messer-Davidow to author, Oct. 21, 1976.

Chapter 7

1. William Bridgwater, "Copy Editing," in
Editors on Editing, ed. Gerald Gross (New York:
Grosset & Dunlap, 1962), p. 52.

2. For further details on such courses, see
Appendix A.

3. Barbara G. Cox, "The Author's Editor,"
Mayo Clinic Proceedings 49 (May 1974): 316.

4. See, for example, Kenneth W. Houp and

Thomas E. Pearsall, *Reporting Technical Information* (Beverly Hills, Calif.: The Glencoe Press, 1968); Council of Biology Editors, *CBE Style Manual* (Washington, D.C.: American Institute of Biological Sciences, 1972); Charles G. Roland, M.D., *Good Scientific Writing: An Anthology* (Chicago: The American Medical Association, 1971); and Henrietta J. Tichy, *Effective Writing* (New York: John Wiley & Sons, 1966).

5. Edwin Newman, *Strictly Speaking: Will America Be the Death of English?* (Indianapolis and New York: Bobbs-Merrill, 1974), p. 145.

6. If as the editor you point out one or two broad, underlying principles at a time to an author, starting out perhaps with an emphasis upon substituting short, concrete words for polysyllabic abstractions, you may be surprised at how quickly some writers put such ideas into practice. Probably the ideal editor, like the ideal psychiatrist, should work himself out of a job as far as each client is concerned. (He will, however, be in no danger of working himself out of a livelihood as well, because there are always other writers who need him.)

7. "What Is an Editor?" in *Editors on Editing*, pp. 3-4. It is true that Taylor is primarily talking here about the editor of a publishing house, yet the process she is referring to is one often asked of an experienced editor working for an inexperienced author.

8. (New York: Dodd, Mead, 1974); see especially Chapters 1 and 2.

9. "The Editorial Function," in *Editors on Editing*, p. 97.

10. Talk given before a meeting of the Editorial Consultants, Inc., Seattle, Wash., June 4, 1975.

11. Cox, "The Author's Editor," p. 316.

12. Ibid., p. 317.

13. See *The Literary Market Place* (New York:

R. R. Bowker, 1976), pp. 279-87. The Palo Alto
and the Seattle groups mentioned, being between
one and two years old, are not yet listed in
LMP.

14. See O'Neill and Ruder, *The Complete Guide
to Editorial Freelancing*, Chapter 2.

15. M. B. Carus of the Open Court Publishing
Co., Chicago, to author, Dec. 20, 1974.

16. (Madison: University of Wisconsin Press,
1953). See also *A Manual of Style* (12th ed.,
rev.; Chicago: University of Chicago Press,
1969).

17. Although O'Neill and Ruder report four
and five dollars an hour as the standard rate
paid by East Coast publishers in 1973, the going
rate in 1977 in many parts of the country, for
editors working for authors, is ten to fifteen
dollars an hour, depending upon the experience
of the editor and the difficulty of the
material.

Chapter 8

1. The questionnaire (reproduced in Appendix
B) was first circulated in March 1975 among
members of the University of Washington's Association of Professional Writers and Editors, who
sent in 23 responses. When I began to extend
my inquiries for the revision of this book, I
sent this questionnaire to various other editors
and information specialists around the country
(fellow members of Women in Communications and
members of the various Sea Grant research projects in particular), from whom I received 27
more responses. Contrary to the practice in
public opinion surveys, where the *number* of
respondents replying in various ways is more
important than the comments that they make, I
sent these questions to an "intentional sample."
Quoted material used in this chapter, unless

otherwise identified, comes from the fifty responses to the questionnaire.

2. For a discussion of internships, see
Appendix D.

3. See Naomi Pascal, "To Open Publishing
Doors," *Scholarly Publishing* 2 (Jan. 1971):
195-201.

4. For a selected list of some of the
national organizations that may be useful to
readers, see Appendix E.

5. Talk by Vice-president Margaret Chisholm
at a meeting of the Association of Professional
Writers and Editors, University of Washington,
Oct. 21, 1975.

Chapter 9

1. Leonard Corwin, *Your Future in Publishing*
(New York: Richard Rosen Press, 1973), p. 16.

2. Wilbur Schramm, *Men, Messages, and Media:
A Look at Human Communication* (New York: Harper
and Row, 1973).   See also Peter M. Sandman,
David M. Rubin, and David B. Sachsman, *Media:
An Introductory Analysis of American Mass Commu-
nications* (2d ed.; Englewood Cliffs, N.J.:
Prentice-Hall, 1976).

3. *A Newspaper Career and You* (Princeton,
N.J.:   The Newspaper Fund, 1974), p. 3.

4. *Press Woman,* Nov. 1976, editorial page.

5. Tom Bryan and Gerald Hedman, personal
interviews, July 20, 1974.

6. John Schacht, Champaign, Ill., to author,
Aug. 9, 1976.

7. Linda Daniel, assistant city editor,
Seattle Times, personal interview, May 10, 1975.

8. William Johnston, former newspaper editor, now professor of communications, University
of Washington, personal interview, July 16,
1976.

9. Brandt Morgan of the *Seattle Sun,* per-

sonal interview, July 17, 1976; Alan Fiskien of the *Sun*, talk given at meeting of Yale Alumni Association, Seattle, Oct. 20, 1976.

10. Panel discussion on KCTS, Channel 9, Seattle, Jan. 20, 1976.

11. See Bibliography, below.

12. "How to Apply for a Job in Media," *The Quill*, Nov. 1974, pp. 40-42.

13. *A Newspaper Career and You*, pp. 6, 8, 9.

14. Sanders of Bellevue Community College, personal interview, Jan. 20, 1976.

15. Schacht to author, Aug. 9, 1976.

16. Personal interview, May 10, 1975.

17. William Johnston, personal interview, July 16, 1976.

18. Elizabeth R. Turpin, "Alternatives to Teaching for English Professors in Journalism, Public Relations, and Editing," *ADE Bulletin* 40 (March 1974): 40-44.

19. Elbow, *Writing without Teachers* (New York: Oxford, 1973).

20. Betty Woolley, personal interview, June 10, 1976.

21. Eileen Kernaghan, Edith Surridge, and Patrick Kernaghan, *The Upper Left-Hand Corner: A Writer's Guide for the Northwest* (Vancouver, B.C.: J. J. Douglas; Seattle: Madrona Publishers, 1975), pp. 52-54, 70-71.

22. Dean Woolley, talk given at a program on careers in media, sponsored by Women in Communications and FOCUS., Seattle Public Library, May 24, 1976.

23. Jan Bridgman, Seattle, personal interview, Oct. 15, 1976.

24. Talk by Dean Woolley, May 24, 1976.

25. Brewster, personal interview, June 8, 1976.

26. Keynote speech at Public Relations Society seminar, Seattle, Sept. 23, 1976.

27. Joanne Beamer, talk given at meeting of

Pacific Northwest Writers' Conference, July 25, 1975.

28. Talks by Fern Olsen, Norma Russell, and others at a Women in Communications meeting, May 24, 1976.

29. Ibid.

30. Ibid.

31. Ibid.

32. Interview with a Seattle public relations account executive.

33. Jerry della Femina, personal interview, Seattle, Sept. 23, 1976.

34. L. Roy Blumenthal, *The Practice of Public Relations* (New York: Macmillan, 1972), p. 3.

35. Steve Seiter, personal interview, July 15, 1974.

36. Gittings, conversation with author, Aug. 10, 1974.

Chapter 10

1. Unless otherwise attributed, quotations from publishers are from the 70 responses to a questionnaire sent by the author to 125 publishers, asking for advice on entry into publishing (see Appendix B).

2. For fuller information on these volumes as well as additional ones on publishing, see the Bibliography.

3. This course, taught by T. Leslie Elliott, West Coast regional representative of Harper and Row, was initiated at Pacific Lutheran University, Tacoma, Wash., in February 1976.

4. See Appendix D.

5. Nicholls, personal interview, at the Pacific Northwest Writers Conference, Seattle University, July 25, 1975.

6. Johnston, interview, Sept. 10, 1974.

7. Thomas Weyr, "Getting into Publishing," *Publishers Weekly*, March 10, 1975, pp. 22-25.

8. Nicholls, speech at the Pacific Northwest Writers Conference, July 25, 1975.

9. In view of the differences between the way jobs are filled in publishing and the way they are in teaching, it is unrealistic to put too much faith in sending letters and résumés to publishing firms *unless* you will be able to follow up shortly afterward with a visit in person.

10. Targ, letter to *Publishers Weekly*, Dec. 2, 1974.

11. For example, Lise Blessing of Seattle has recently been appointed regional representative of the textbook division of Holt, Rinehart, and Winston.

12. Rita E. Weathersby, Patricia R. Allen, and Alan R. Blackmer, Jr., *New Roles for Educators* (Cambridge, Mass.: Harvard Graduate School of Education Publication Office, 1970). The following half dozen firms are typical of those worth your while to explore, particularly if you are interested in companies which not only publish texts but act as consultants for educational programs, experiment with "self-paced instruction," and, in the jargon of the trade, design "educational soft-ware." A number of them say that they use many writers, some of them with M.A.'s and Ph.D.'s, on their staffs.

Croft Educational Services, Inc.
100 Garfield Ave.
New London, CT 06320

Encyclopedia Britannica Education
     Corporation
425 N. Michigan Ave.
Chicago, IL 60611

General Learning Corporation
3 E. 54th St.
New York, NY 10022

Information Resources, Inc.
96 Mt. Auburn St.
Cambridge, MA 02138

Pinck and Leodas Associates, Inc.
2000 Massachusetts Ave.
Cambridge, MA 04120

Society for Visual Education
1345 Diversey Parkway
Chicago, IL 60614

13. Levant, personal interview, Feb. 8, 1976.

Chapter 11

1. See Linwood E. Orange, "Nonteaching
Careers for English Majors," *ADE Bulletin* 36
(March 1973): 18-21.

2. Mark Loftin, author of "A Portrait of the
English Major as a Young Businessman," *ADE
Bulletin* 31 (Nov. 1971), is an English Ph.D. who
was at that time second vice-president, Training
Division, Human Resources Department, Chase
Manhattan Bank.

3. *The New York Times,* March 21, 1975.

4. Daniel Marder, "The Major in the Market:
The View from the Southwest," *ADE Bulletin* 40
(1974): 30-33.

5. Linwood E. Orange, *English: The Pre-
Professional Major* (New York: MLA, 1972), p. 6.

6. Meg Wingard, personal interview, Oct.
10, 1976.

7. *Gebbie House Magazine Directory* (Burling-
ton, Iowa; Gebbie Press, 1974), *passim.*

8. Stephanie Campbell, personal interview,
July 20, 1974.

9. Wendy Dore to author, Jan. 28, 1977.

10. *Is Technical Writing Your Career?* (Washington, D.C.: Society for Technical Communication, 1975), p. 3.

11. John A. Walter, "Technical Writing:
Species or Genus?" (paper delivered at the
annual MLA meeting, 1976, New York City).
    12. For a list of available pamphlets, write
the Society for Technical Communication, 1010
Vermont Ave., NW, Washington, DC 20005.
    13. See Appendix A.
    14. See Appendix D.
    15. Mark Loftin, "A Portrait of the English
Major as a Young Businessman," *ADE Bulletin*,
pp. 14-15.
    16. Hill, personal interview, May 4, 1976.
    17. Pneuman, who believes strongly in such
courses, suggests that those who aspire to teach
them should be advised that in-service courses
such as these are often among the first expenses
to be sacrificed when budget cuts are in order.
    18. Adams, personal interviews, May 10, 1975,
and Feb. 15, 1976. Adams points out that she
does not use a "business English" text, but depends largely upon Strunk and White's *Elements
of Style*, which her company now has each executive get and refer to.
    19. Henrietta J. Tichy, *Effective Writing*
(New York: Wiley, 1964).
    20. Dickie, personal interview, Oct. 5, 1976.
    21. Pneuman to author, Oct. 20, 1976.
    22. Harwood, "From Genre Theory to the Want
Ads," *ADE Bulletin* 44 (Feb. 1975): 21-24.
    23. Orange, *English*, p. 6; see also his "Non-
teaching Careers for English Majors."
    24. Ellen Messer-Davidow to author, Oct. 20,
1976.
    25. See Appendix D.
    26. Haas, telephone interview, Oct. 21, 1976.
    27. Haas, "The Value of a Professional Eng-
lish Education," *ADE/ADFL Bulletin* (Special
Joint Issue [Sept. 1976]), pp. 61-62. Note his
comments: "In addition [to doing part-time
teaching in my field and seeking out community

service projects] I have attempted to seek out
projects among my daily job tasks that would require research and/or application of the knowledge acquired in professional study. For
example, I have participated in organizational
projects that involved synthesizing the major
cultural value shifts that took place between
the nineteenth and twentieth centuries; that included applying the black literary experience to
affirmative action programs; that required
teaching writing, ranging from a presentation
of the fundamentals of grammar to the preparation of speeches for sophisticated audiences;
and that demanded researching the creative process in an effort to develop methods of creative
thinking" (p. 62).

28. Mark Loftin, "A Portrait of the English
Major as a Young Businessman," p. 15.

29. McMahon, as quoted in "Slim Pickings for
the Class of '76," *Time,* March 29, 1976, p. 47.

30. Harwood, "Nonacademic Job Hunting," *AAUP
Bulletin* 60 (1974): 313-16.

31. Interview with a member of management at
Pacific Northwest Bell, Aug. 25, 1975.

Chapter 12

1. Ruemelin, *A Guide to Government and Public Service Employment* (Cambridge, Mass.: Harvard University, 1975), pp. 3-5.

2. Ibid., pp. 5-7.

3. Ana L. Zambrano and Alan D. Entine, *A
Guide to Career Alternatives for Academics* (New
Rochelle, N.Y.: Change Magazine Press, 1976),
p. 35.

4. Betty Blair of Seattle, personal interview, Feb. 10, 1976. Blair first looked for
work more obviously connected with her nearly
completed Ph.D. in English. Not finding what
she wanted, she arbitrarily picked a career with
a city as something challenging which would

eventually utilize her writing and research
abilities.
    5. Betty Haskell, personal interview, Feb.
12, 1976.
    6. From the *Official Bulletin* (Seattle,
Wash.: Seattle Civil Service Commission, Feb.
3, 1975). Material on application procedures is
found throughout.
    7. Lou Ann Kirby of the City of Seattle's
Department of Parks and Recreation, personal
interview, Nov. 15, 1975.
    8. Material derived from loose-leaf note-
books containing job descriptions in the City
of Seattle's Personnel Office, as of Feb. 9,
1976. Most other cities keep similar loose-leaf
listings, but be sure to check on how recently
any file has been up-dated.
    9. Linda Gorton, personal interview, Sept.
10, 1975.
    10. Glenda Spade, personal interview, Aug.
15, 1974.
    11. Job notebooks in the City of Seattle's
Personnel Office, *passim*.
    12. Susan De Witt, personal interview, Jan.
2, 1975.
    13. Jeff Douthwaite, personal interview, Feb.
25, 1976.
    14. David Strohnmeyer, personal interview,
May 4, 1975.
    15. Interview with Douthwaite, supplemented
by a report from Earl Grout, a recent Ph.D. in
English who made several trips to Olympia to see
how the system works in practice.
    16. Diane Bolay, project officer of the
Health Services Criteria Project, HEW, personal
interview, June 10, 1975. According to a leaflet distributed in May 1976 by the Seattle
office of HEW ("Career Opportunities within the
Department of Health, Education and Welfare"),
the six agencies within HEW all have offices in

the ten regional centers around the country.
These six include the Office of the Secretary
(OS), the Office of Education (OE), the Social
and Rehabilitation Services (SRS), the Social
Security Administration (SSA), the Food and Drug
Administration (FDA), and the Public Health
Service (PHS). Of these, readers of this handbook might be interested in becoming public information specialists (OS), management analysts
(OS), personnel specialists (OS), educational
program specialists (OE), grants management
specialists (OE, PHS), information and systems
specialists (SRS), or systems analysts (SSA).
Needless to say, these positions require other
skills in addition to the ones you have acquired
through being an English major or graduate student. Nonetheless your research and writing
skills would help you and you could, following
Betty Blair's example, fill in gaps in your
preparation on your own.

In the opinion of George Swift, executive
officer, HEW Regional Office, Seattle, openings
in professional positions in the near future
will be fewer than usual because of budget cuts.
During the coming year, he said, "the two divisions in our office with the most opportunities
are Adult Education and Vocational Education."

At the same time Terry Duffin, representative, Region VIII, Regional Program on Aging,
said that his division, although it had at present no positions formally described as information specialist, writer, PR person, or researcher, could from time to time use people
with backgrounds in English in such positions as
program administrator or training officer. One
former English teacher, he pointed out, is the
training officer for Oregon. In general, people
come into his office with a background in public
administration, planning, or social work.

17. *MLA Guide for Job Candidates and Depart-*

ment Chairmen in English and Foreign Languages
(New York: MLA, 1975), pp. 35-36.

18. Susan Lukowski and Margaret Piton, *Strategy and Tactics for Getting a Government Job*
(Washington, D.C.: Potomac Books, 1973),
passim.

19. Ann Pincus, "How to Get a Government
Job," *The Washington Monthly* (June 1976), pp.
22-27.

20. *The Congressional Directory* is compiled
by the U.S. Government Printing Office for each
session of Congress; *The Congressional Staff
Directory*, ed. Charles B. Brownson, is published
annually by the Congressional Staff Directory,
Mt. Vernon, Va.; the *Federal Career Directory*
is published biannually by the U.S. Civil Service Commission, Washington, D.C.; and the
Guide to Federal Career Literature is published
by the Government Printing Office.

21. *ARTS, Inc.: Newsletter for Job Referral
in the Visual and Performing Arts*, Box 32382,
Washington, DC 20007.

22. Diane Bolay, personal interview, June 10,
1975.

23. "Clio's Children: Out of the Ivory
Tower and into the Marketplace: Alternative
Employment," paper presented at Pacific Coast
Branch, American Historical Association, Aug.
27, 1974, University of Washington.

Bibliography

Most of the following titles should be generally available in university and public libraries
or in campus placement offices. Asterisks indicate the publications that are most useful in
themselves and that, in most cases, serve to
direct the reader to still other sources.

I. The Strategies of Job-seeking

*Bolles, Richard Nelson. *What Color Is Your
    Parachute? A Practical Manual for Job-
    Hunters and Career Changers.* Rev. ed.
    Berkeley: The Ten Speed Press, 1976.
    Job candidates of all ages have discovered
    that this book is full of sound, specific
    advice on résumés, interviews, "rejection
    shock," "the numbers game," and self-assess-
    ment. The bibliography and appendix alone
    are enough to make this volume indispens-
    able.
Greco, Benedetto. *New Careers for Teachers.*
    Homewood, Ill.: Dow Jones-Irwin, Inc.,
    1976.
    Written by the director of career services,
    Graduate School of Business Administration,
    University of Southern California, this book
    charts career possibilities and ways of
    approaching them. Although heavily laden

289

with business administration jargon, the
book could be useful to humanities graduates through its suggestions for self-inventory, its discussion of sources of job
leads, and its eight valuable appendixes.
Not to be confused with a book of the same
title by Bill McKee (see below).

Harwood, John T. "From Genre Theory to the Want
Ads." *ADE Bulletin* 44 (Feb. 1975): 21-24.

------. "Nonacademic Job Hunting." *AAUP Bulletin* 60 (1974): 313-16.
These articles offer advice, mainly on job
application letters, résumés, and interviews, from a recent Ph.D. who, after teaching himself to translate his background in
English literature into the language of the
business world, received numerous job offers.

Higginson, Margaret V., and Thomas Quick. *The
Ambitious Woman's Guide to a Successful
Career.* New York: Amco, 1975.
Although slanted toward women's careers in
business, this manual offers practical ideas
about job applications, interviews, and
résumés, applicable to both sexes and a wide
variety of jobs.

*Irish, Richard K. *Go Hire Yourself an Employ-
er.* Garden City, N.Y.: Anchor Press, 1973.
This handbook is particularly helpful on
résumés, on "interviewing for information
rather than for a job," and on work with the
government. Since it is dedicated to "everyone who at one time or another is told
'You're too young, old, qualified, unquali-
fied, experienced, inexperienced, beautiful,
plain, expensive, or too damn good' for the
job," many "overqualified" graduate students
should find encouragement in what it has to
say.

------. *If Things Don't Improve Soon I May Ask You to Fire Me.* Garden City, N.Y.: Anchor Press/Doubleday, 1975.
Directed toward holders of or searchers for what Irish calls "judgment jobs," this book attempts to goad people into making the best possible use of their experience and abilities even if doing so means risking security and branching out into new fields.

Jackson, Tom, and Davidyne Mayleas. *The Hidden Job Market: A System to Beat the System.* New York: Quadrangle/The New York Times Book Co., 1976.
Since this book takes you by the hand and nudges you into filling out questionnaires and self-inventory schedules, some readers may find it what they need to get started.

Jaquish, Michael P. *Personal Résumé Preparation.* New York: John Wiley and Sons, 1968.
Jaquish takes his specialty with such seriousness that a reader soon begins to feel that the résumé is almost as much of an art form in its own right as is the sonnet, with its own conventions, types, subtypes, and variants. Nonetheless, Jaquish gives useful examples of résumés, showing how one can marshall his or her assets in different ways for an academic, business, or administrative position.

Lathrop, Richard. *Who's Hiring Who.* Reston, Va.: Reston Publishing Co., 1976.
Readable and useful discussion, with many examples, of job strategies: how to evaluate your talents, prepare résumés, do advance research on the organization you want to work for; main emphasis is on business.

McKee, Bill. *New Careers for Teachers.* Rev. ed. Chicago: Henry Regnery Co., 1976.
Addressed mainly to elementary and high

school teachers, this book hardly lives up
to its promise of describing "over 100 nonteaching occupations that require no additional training." It is, however, worth
glancing at because of the sample résumé and
certain additional information.

*MLA Guide for Job Candidates and Department
Chairmen in English and Foreign Languages.
Rev. ed. New York: MLA, 1975.
The fourteen pages on "Alteratives to Teaching" should be your starting point, after
which you will be in a position to make use
of some of the more specialized and more lo-
calized information in the present handbook.
(Be sure to use the latest, rather than the
1973, edition.)

*Zambrano, Ana L., and Alan D. Entine. A Guide
to Career Alternatives for Academics. New
Rochelle, N.Y.: Change Magazine Press,
1976.
This brief pamphlet is highly recommended as
a starting point for academically trained
people in all fields as they first consider
looking for nonacademic jobs.

II. Newspaper, Periodical, and Other Serial Listings of Job Vacancies

Academe: The Newsletter of the AAUP. Washington, D.C.: The Association of American University Professors, published four times
yearly (October, December, March, and June).
Typically, the last two or three of this
newsletter's eight pages list "Academic
Vacancies."

Affirmative Action Register. St. Louis, Missouri.
A monthly publication, devoted to providing
women and minority candidates with information about professional and managerial jobs

throughout the nation. It lists both positions available and positions wanted. Note
especially those as directors of women's
centers, Affirmative Action coordinators, as
well as a few traditional academic posts.
*Chronicle of Higher Education. Washington,
D.C. Published biweekly during the academic
year, monthly during the summer.
The last half of each twenty-four page issue
has a "Bulletin Board: Positions available," wherein academic, administrative, and
public relations positions are advertised.
The alphabetization is arbitrary; a position
may be listed either under the name of the
college or the category of job.
Editor and Publisher: The Fourth Estate. New
York City. Published every Saturday.
Contains calendar of meetings, nationwide,
of editors, publishers, specialized writers'
groups; articles on the book market; and two
pages of "Help Wanted," one page of "Positions Wanted."
*Federal Employment: Job Information for Col-
lege Graduates.*
Large loose-leaf notebook, updated constantly as new folders come in, supplements *Federal Careers in the Northwest* with detailed
current job listings.
*H.E.W. Bulletins: Employers in Education Seek-
ing Minorities or Women.*
Large loose-leaf binder containing job announcements from all over the country, updated continuously.
The Job Finder. Berkeley, Calif. Western Governmental Research Association, 109 Moses
Hall, University of California, published
quarterly.
Covers vacancies in government jobs on many
levels, in many areas.
The New York Times, the Sunday edition, section

IV, "The Week in Review."
Carries from one to three pages of advertising of educational positions, including occasional college teaching or administration,
in all parts of the country.
The Personnel Journal. Swarthmore, Pa., monthly.
Contains articles on personnel policy and
practice as well as six pages of ads from
employers and job-seekers.
Publishers Weekly. New York City.
Useful for its short articles and news items
about titles and trends, as well as its
"Weekly Exchange" of help wanted ads (acqui-
sitions editors, publishers' travelers, and
some academic posts).
Teaching Opportunities Abroad. New York City.
Directory of sources of information (*not* of
specific jobs) in field of teaching opportunities worldwide. Can be ordered from the
Institute of International Education, 809
United Nations Plaza, New York, NY 10017.
University Affairs: Affaires universitaires.
Montreal, Quebec, published monthly.
Contains articles and news stories on Canadian education and many advertisements of
teaching and administrative vacancies
throughout the Canadian provinces.

III. On Communications Fields

*Bagdikian, Ben H. "Woodstein U." *Alantic Month-
ly,* March 1977, pp. 80-92.
Subtitled "Notes on the Mass Production and
Questionable Education of Journalists," this
article should be required reading for any
academic who imagines journalism to be a
greener field.
Blumenthal, L. Roy. *The Practice of Public Relations.* New York: Macmillan, 1972.

Lengthy analysis of the various branches of public relations. Excellent bibliography.

*Hilliard, Robert L. *Writing for Television and Radio*. 3d ed., rev. New York: Communications Arts Books, Hastings House, 1976.
Specific and authoritative.

Sandman, Peter M., David Rubin, and David B. Sachsman. *Media: An Introductory Analysis of American Mass Communications*. 2d ed. Englewood Cliffs, N.J.: Prentice-Hall, 1976.
Often used as a communications textook, this thorough and well-documented volume makes a good reading and reference source for anyone considering trying to enter the field.

Schramm, Wilbur. *Men, Messages, and Media: A Look at Human Communication*. New York: Harper and Row, 1973.
Comprehensive survey.

Turpin, Elizabeth R. "Alternatives to Teaching for English Professors in Journalism, Public Relations, and Editing." *ADE Bulletin* 40 (March 1974): 40-44.

Weber, Olga S. *The Audiovisual Market Place*. 3d ed. New York: R. R. Bowker, 1976.
Contains names, addresses, and description of product lines for all producers and distributors of audiovisual learning material. Lists national, professional, and trade organizations, as well as educational radio stations and television channels.

IV. Information on Publishers and Publishing

Bailey, Herbert. *The Art and Science of Book Publishing*. New York: Harper and Row, 1970.
A very thorough description.

Corwin, Leonard. *Your Future in Publishing*. New York: Richard Rosen Press, 1973.

Although a rather elementary survey, this
short guide gives a useful description of
opportunities in both the editorial and the
production sides of book, magazine, newspaper, house organ, and underground press
publishing.

*Dessauer, John R. *Book Publishing: What It
Is, What It Does.* New York: R. R. Bowker,
1974.
One of the most recent and readable discussions in the field.

*Ellinwood, Lynne, and Jo Anne Gibbons, eds.
The Writer's Market. Cincinnati, Ohio:
Writer's Digest Publishing Co.
Issued annually, this guide lists and clas-
sifies American book and magazine publishers
according to subject matter and type of
readership. It is an authoritative source
for names and addresses of editors, as well
as information about their requirements and
rates of payment (not to be confused with
The Literary Market Place, listed below).

Grannis, Chandler B., ed. *What Happens in Book
Publishing.* 2d ed. New York: Columbia
University Press, 1976.
A readable collection of articles by various
contributors. Excellent bibliographies.

*Gross, Gerald, ed. *Editors on Editing.* New
York: Grosset and Dunlap, 1962.
A uniquely valuable collection of essays
wherein editors working in different branches of publishing (commerical, university
presses, childrens' books, textbooks, and
others) describe what they actually do and
how they feel about their jobs.

*Hawes, Gene R. *To Advance Knowledge: A Hand-
book on American University Press Publishing.* New York: Association of American
University Presses, 1976.

Excellent; the only book-length treatment of
the subject.

*Kernaghan, Eileen, Edith Surridge, and Patrick
Kernaghan. *The Upper Left-Hand Corner: A
Writer's Guide for the Northwest.* Vancouver, B.C.: J. J. Douglas; Seattle, Wash.:
Madrona Publishers, 1975.
This new directory is an invaluable source
of names of publishers, periodicals, writers' markets, writers' workshops, types of
financial assistance, and other information
often needed by writers, editors, and researchers in this area.

Literary Market Place. New York: R. R. Bowker,
1976.
The best-known source of names and addresses
of book publishers both national and regional, as well as of editors, literary agents,
printers, and others in the publishing industry (not to be confused with *The Writer's
Market,* above).

*O'Neill, Carol L., and Avima Ruder. *The Com-
plete Guide to Editorial Freelancing.* New
York: Dodd, Mead and Co., 1974.
This specialized work fully lives up to its
title, in that it explains how to get started in this field, what duties proofreading
and copy editing involve, how much publishers pay, what reference books are most de-
pendable, and how to find out about free-
lance jobs.

*Pascal, Naomi B. "To Open Publishing Doors."
Scholarly Publishing 2, no. 2 (Jan. 1971):
195-201.
Firsthand account, by a university press
editor, of what students can learn through a
well-supervised internship at a medium-sized
scholarly press.

*Weathersby, Rita E., Patricia R. Allen, and

Alan R. Blackmer, Jr. *New Roles for Educators.* Cambridge, Mass.: Harvard Graduate School of Education Publications Office, 1970.
Since the focus is on publishers who are bringing out innovative course materials, programmed instruction, and the like, this small volume is strongly recommended for those interested in educational publishing.

Weyr, Thomas. "Getting into Publishing." *Publishers Weekly,* March 24, 1975, pp. 22-25.
Deals with a random sample of people working in publishing and how they found their jobs. Main conclusions: it helps to be young, and success often stems from "saying the right words on the right day."

V. On Government Employment

*The Book of the States, 1975-76. Lexington, Ky.; revised annually.
This series gives official information on the methods, structures, financing, and ongoing activities of the state governments and with intergovernmental relations. Invaluable source to consult *before* you write to or visit your state capital in search of a job.

*Lukowski, Susan, and Margaret Piton. *Strategy and Tactics for Getting a Government Job.* Washington, D.C.: Potomac Books, 1973.
This breezily written book is crammed with information about federal Civil Service exams, job sources, internships, overseas jobs, the foreign language job market, private industry in Washington, and how to get in touch with all the executive departments and independent agencies. Although it

focuses on jobs in the Washington, D.C.,
area, it gives advice about doing groundwork
locally and offers leads on a few regional
positions.

Pincus, Ann. "How to Get a Government Job."
The Washington Monthly, June 1976, pp. 22-
27.
Informative, although less encouraging than
Lukowski and Piton.

*Ruemelin, Charles. *A Guide to Government and
Public Service Employment*. Cambridge,
Mass.: Harvard University, 1975.
Although designed mainly for Harvard undergraduates, this pamphlet would be extremely
helpful to anyone considering looking for
work in any branch of the government.

The Washington Information Directory. New York:
Quadrangle/New York Times Book Co., published annually.
Resource for information, organized by subject, on current governmental issues. Indicates which people and agencies are concerned with which problem.

VI. Directories and General Reference Works

A Career Guide to Professional Associations.
Cranston, R.I.: The Carroll Press, 1976.
Lists organizations by professional field,
indicating which ones offer career information or funding.

Dictionary of Occupational Titles. 3d ed. 2
vols., 1 supplement. Washington, D.C.:
U.S. Government Printing Office, 1965-66.
Although regrettably these volumes have not
been brought up to date since 1966, they
contain a vast amount of useful information.
Their function is to describe the duties,
the qualifications, the preparation, and the

normal requirements of several thousands of
jobs, alphabetically listed, ranging from
unskilled to managerial and professional.
*Education Directory: Education Associations,
1974.* Washington, D.C.: U.S. Government
Printing Office, 1974. Stock no. 1780-
01279.
A listing of nonacademic agencies using people with teaching skills, e.g., corporate
training and education departments, local
and state councils of higher education,
foundations, private research firms, and
others.
*Livesey, Herbert B., and Harold Doughty. *Guide
to American Graduate Schools.* 3d ed., rev.
New York: Viking, 1975.
If you are considering adding to your professional credentials, this is the authoritative source for information on programs,
admission requirements, specialities, and
funding at more than 650 accredited institutions.
*McIntyre, Pat Kern. *American Students and
Teachers Abroad: Sources of Information
about Overseas Study, Teaching, Work, and
Travel.* Rev. ed. Washington, D.C.: U.S.
Government Printing Office, 1974.
Official HEW pamphlet, packed full of specific information, addresses, application
dates, and scholarship information. Much
the best starting-point for any overseas
professional planning.
*Try Us, '76: National Minority Business Direc-
tory.* Minneapolis, Minn.
Among the wide range of minority-run businesses is a section on publishing houses
specializing in books, learning kits, and
audiovisual materials on education.

VII. Background

Dugger, Ronnie. "The Community College Comes of
Age." *Change: The Magazine of Higher
Learning* 8, no. 1 (Feb. 1976): 32-37.
Appraising the strengths and weaknesses of
the community college, Dugger concludes that
its emphasis upon good teaching may enable
it soon to become "a restorative base for a
national community of enlightenment."

Fisher, Francis D. "Educating for Underemployment." *Change: The Magazine of Higher
Learning* 8, no. 1 (Feb. 1976): 16, 69.
Fisher, director of Harvard's Office of Career Services and Off-Campus Learning, hails
widespread "underemployment" as a symptom of
a healthy down-playing of education as the
key to a job, high wages, and material
goods. Although "the national question is,
What do you do?" Fisher sees hope in the way
the young increasingly look to "the world
outside of work for answers to the question,
Who am I?"

Gleiser, Molly. "An Obsolescent Life." *Harper's Magazine,* Sept. 1974, pp. 68-70.
People with seemingly unmarketable doctorates in languages and literature may benefit
from learning that their fields are not the
only overcrowded ones. In this brief, sar-
donic autobiographical sketch, a chemistry
Ph.D., author of four texts and ten published articles in her field, tells of her
job search after her position at Berkeley
was phased out for lack of funds.

Harrison, Dorothy G. "Aristotle and the Corporate Structure." *Change: The Magazine of
Higher Learning* 8, no. 8 (Sept. 1976): 9,
64.

The author, co-director of a national project funded by the Mellon Foundation to
study careers for humanists, finds "much
more congruence between graduate training in
the humanities and a variety of nonacademic
jobs than most people would imagine."
Harvey, James. "Effects of the Ph.D. Glut."
Change: The Magazine of Higher Learning 4
(April 1972): 13, 71.
Giving an overview of the ratio of Ph.D.'s
to jobs throughout academia, Harvey explores
long-range solutions. For example, "leaders
in higher education must suggest alternate
uses for Ph.D.-trained talent. . . . These
could begin with the federal funding of
multi-disciplinary research institutes, separate from university campuses, to attack
pressing social problems."
Howe, Harold, II. "Report to the President of
the United States from the Chairman of the
White House Conference on Education, August
1, 2024." *Saturday Review World* 24 (Aug.
1974): 73-76, 130-31.
Speculating on what may happen to education
in the next fifty years, Howe suggests that
B.A.'s and even Ph.D.'s may be worth obtaining just to "help us develop . . . our interests and abilities to their full potential," regardless of how we earn our living.
Huther, John W. "Small Market for Ph.D's: The
Public Two-Year College." *AAUP Bulletin* 58
(March 1972): 17-20.
While quashing the too-common idea that the
community colleges can currently absorb the
surplus of Ph.D.'s, Huther makes several
constructive suggestions. One of them involves ways in which two-year colleges could
extend their support to those of their faculty members wishing to take leaves and to
finish doctorates as "mid-career training."

*Jessup, Claudia, and Genie Chipps. *The Woman's Guide to Starting a Business*. New York: Holt, Rinehart, and Winston, 1976.
For anyone of either sex interested in starting an editorial or proofreading consulting service, or any other paying enterprise, the information and case histories in this small book are essential reading.

London, Herbert I. "The Case for Nontraditional Learning." *Change: The Magazine of Higher Learning* 8, no. 5 (June 1976): 25-29.
Examines the claims and implications of nonacademic programs such as "universities without walls."

*Orange, Linwood E. *English: The Pre-Professional Major*. New York: MLA, 1972.
Dealing with the uses of an undergraduate major in English and the positions to which it has led and can lead, Orange's study is particularly valuable for its analysis of transferable skills which a student majoring in English should have acquired.

*O'Toole, James. "The Reserve Army of the Underemployed: I--The World of Work." *Change: The Magazine of Higher Learning* 7, no. 4 (May 1975): 26-33, 63.

------. "The Reserve Army of the Underemployed: II--The Role of Education." *Change: The Magazine of Higher Learning* 7, no. 5 (June 1975): 26-33, 60-63.
A member of the Center for Future Research at UCLA explores the implications of the fact that in today's industrial societies "levels of educational attainment have tended to grow in almost geometric progression, while the number of jobs that require higher levels of education has tended to grow at a much slower pace." Part II suggests sweeping changes in attitudes to education, particularly that we "stop implic-

itly and explicitly selling it as an eco-
nomic investment."

*Terkel, Studs. *Working.* New York: Pantheon
Books, Random House, 1974.
   Subtitled *People Talk about What They Do
   All Day and How They Feel about What They
   Do,* this gigantic volume of taped interviews
   offers disgruntled academics a survey of
   how people "out there in the real world"
   feel about their occupations and professions.

Wolfe, Gary K., and Carol Traynor Williams.
   "All Education Is 'Adult Education': Some
   Observations on Curriculum and Profession
   in the Seventies." *AAUP Bulletin* 60 (Sept.
   1974).

*Wolfle, Dael, and Charles V. Kidd. "The Future
   Market for Ph.D.s." *AAUP Bulletin* 58 (March
   1972): 5-16.
   Documenting both the volume and the rate of
   the Ph.D. explosion of recent years, Wolfle
   and Kidd make a nationwide survey of the
   whole overcrowded academic field. Probably
   every graduate student should ponder one of
   this article's main conclusions, i.e., that
   "many new doctorates will enter non-traditional jobs and will do work that has not
   attracted many of their predecessors. . . .
   Few of them will be unemployed, but few will
   be employed in college and university
   teaching and research."

Index